D1267530

JAMES DOUGLAS:
Servant of Two Empires

JAMES DOUGLAS:
Servant of Two Empires

Derek Pethick

Université d'Ottawa
BIBLIOTHÈQUES
LIBRARIES
University of Ottawa

Mitchell Press Limited, Vancouver

By the same author
VICTORIA: THE FORT

Copyright © 1969
by Mitchell Press Limited
Vancouver

FC
3822.1
.D65
P45
1969

Printed in Canada

FOR TED, CAREN AND TIMOTHY

No history of the province can be written without Sir James Douglas forming the central figure around which will cluster the stirring events that have marked the advance of the province from a fur-hunting preserve for nomadic tribes to a progressive country of civilized beings, under the protection of the British flag and enjoying a stable and settled form of government.

VICTORIA COLONIST,
August 4, 1877

I ask for no prouder monument, and for no other memorial, when I die and go hence, than the testimony here offered, that I have done my duty.

SIR JAMES DOUGLAS,
April, 1864

Contents

Foreword

AN AUTHOR SHOULD always be willing to give his reasons or excuses for adding yet another to the world's already plentiful supply of books. In this case, he finds, he can offer two. It is nearly forty years since the publication of Dr. Walter Sage's valuable *Sir James Douglas and British Columbia*. In the meanwhile, new material has come to light and new perspectives opened. It seems appropriate, therefore, to recount anew the story of Douglas' life and to relate it to both his time and our own.

Moreover, we are now in the brief period between two centenaries: that of the Dominion of Canada and that of the entry into it of British Columbia. It is surely fitting that, with these major events so frequently recalled to our attention, we should reconsider what place should be assigned to Douglas in making possible the creation and the continued existence of these two entities.

My thanks are due to the staff of the Provincial Archives for help in the preparation of this account, and also to the Governor and Committee of the Hudson's Bay Company for courteously answering my enquiries.

DEREK PETHICK

CHAPTER ONE

A Century
of Revolutions

WHAT MANNER of man was James Douglas? It is nearly a century now since that day in 1877 when his bones were laid to rest in Ross Bay Cemetery. His children, too, have all followed him to the grave, and there is likely no one left who remembers "the old Governor". Moreover not only the man but his age is no longer with us. The palisaded fort from which he directed the affairs of the infant colonies on the Pacific coast has long since been dismantled; where his house once stood, imposing new buildings have arisen where the records of the region are preserved and its artifacts displayed. Even deeper differences than these, however, divide his age from ours. Where once the traveller through life took his bearings from the rock of faith, now the moral certainties have been eroded by the acids of modernity, and he seeks in vain for landmarks while his feet sink ever deeper in the shifting sands of relativism. We are inclined, then, perhaps, to dismiss Sir James Douglas, K.C.B. as one more of those Victorian worthies who stare at us so sternly from their over-ornate picture-frames, but whose ways are thankfully not our ways.

Yet if we do this, I think we make a mistake. If, as has been said, the unexamined life is not worth living, then surely the unexamined country is not worth living in; and we cannot examine at least the farthest west of our country without realizing how much of it is what it is because of James Douglas. The government and economic life of British Columbia still bear the imprint of his vision; he presided over the creation of the naval base at Esquimalt, and personally explored some of the trails which have since widened into the highway network of the Interior. The provision of schools and churches for the earliest settlers engaged his constant attention; and, deeply read and fluently bilingual himself, he encouraged the various manifestations of culture in others.

Moreover, as is hoped will become apparent in the course of this narrative, he was more than merely an important figure in the history of British Columbia. His work has affected the lives of all Canadians, for it seems certain that had he been found wanting in his fateful hours of decision, the whole subsequent course of Canadian history would have been profoundly and disastrously altered. This is not perhaps an opinion as yet in very wide circulation, but it is one which, as Douglas' achievements become better known, seems sure to gain an ever wider acceptance.

Nor does he merit our attention merely because of his public career, so far-reaching in its manifold influence. As a human being he is also of absorbing interest. If the unbending dignity which he seems never to have laid aside prevents us to some extent from perceiving the man behind the mask, at least we can find much to engage us in the mysterious workings of chance or destiny which brought him from beginnings so humble to successive positions of increasing eminence and power. His origins were obscure, his advantages few; yet he lived to become Governor of the colonies of Vancouver Island and British Columbia, and Knight Commander of the Bath; while the companion at his side, once but a fur-trapper's half-breed daughter, was to become First Lady of all the vast region between the Rockies' snow-clad crest and the western ocean's rim. Surely this is on any reckoning a fascinating story, and "dull would he be of soul" who could find no interest in it.

Before telling the story of James Douglas, we should perhaps say something of the times in which he lived. Only then will we fully understand the problems that confronted him and the choices he had to make. The nineteenth century, so turbulent and chaotic to those who moved through it, falls now into perspective; below its surface froth and commotion, we can now discern the deeper forces which carried it along.

These were in many ways like tidal waves: too strong to be reversed by even the strongest will. Bearing all before them in their headlong rush, they repeatedly forced those caught up on them to make fundamental and far-reaching choices. Some vainly spent their energies essaying to combat these surging torrents; others were content to bewail them; the wisest, at least among the children of this world, instead strove to come to terms with them and make them if possible subserve some larger good. Eventually, they had faith, the flood would recede, and in the meantime it was their duty to ensure that when that day came, the ark of civilization would be found still riding triumphant on the subsiding waters. This is the standard, surely, by which the men of the nineteenth century should be judged; it is the one which will be applied in these pages to Douglas; and it will be seen, I think, by the time we have finished this account, how high a place must be accorded to the man whose bones now rest beneath the granite monument in Ross Bay Cemetery.

We have spoken of tidal waves; we have alluded to the great flood. These metaphors are far from overblown. Living as we do in the most turbulent of all centuries, we are apt to see all previous ones as backwaters of tranquillity; yet such is far from the case. The nineteenth century, it might well be claimed, saw changes at least as all-encompassing as those of the twentieth, and those who lived through them must often have felt themselves in a world where all that had been substantial was collapsing.

Let us consider in broad outline the main features of this age, taking especial note of those which were to present major challenges to the central figure of our story.

First, perhaps, we might place the continuing process sometimes known as "filling in the map". By this was meant the bringing under the sway of the culture of Western Europe the remaining areas of the globe. This had, of course, been a feature of world history for some centuries, in fact since the successful return of Columbus. Year by year, armed with the compass, the cannon and the Bible, the tribes of Europe had subdued those of the other continents, and against this relentless onrush of power it soon appeared no force could stand. By the opening of the nineteenth century, the greater part of the globe had been parcelled out, and unsatisfied eyes were cast upon the rest. Among the areas whose future was still undecided was much of the northwest part of North America, a fact destined to be central to our story.

Several of the colonial powers had already shown an interest in this distant part of the world. For this, the discovery in the latter part of the eighteenth century that it was rich in fur-bearing animals was mainly responsible. Russia soon established itself in Alaska, while on what is now Vancouver Island and in its surrounding waters it was the Spanish and British who contended for possession.

The Spanish were in some respects in the more favorable position, since they already had well-developed colonies in South and Central America from which to mount expeditions. It was from Mexico that the first explorations of the more northerly parts of the Pacific coast were sent. First among these was that of the *Santiago* under Juan Josef Perez Hernandez, who in 1774 cast anchor in the vicinity of Nootka Sound. Other expeditions followed, notably that of the following year in which Juan Francisco de la Bodega y Quadra in the *Sonora* reached the vicinity of Alaska. Finally, in the summer of 1789 Esteban Jose Martinez formally took possession of Nootka Sound and a vaguely defined surrounding area. Spain did not, however, remain in continuous possession of the site, temporarily abandoning the settlement late in the same year— a decision that was to have a bearing on its final disposition.

Meanwhile, a new race of explorers and colonizers had made their appearance in the area. Spain, though still owning the world's largest empire, was now in the late afternoon of its glory, and more vigorous hands were reaching for the trident of the seas. Captain Cook had visited Nootka in 1778 and drawn up a meticulous report on the flora and fauna of the area; his references to the valuable furs to be found in the region had stimulated the interest of both private adventurers and the British Government. Of the former, one who was to affect by his actions the course of history was John Meares. He had arrived at Nootka in May 1788, and soon afterwards bought—or so he claimed— a piece of land from the famous chief Maquinna, on which he erected a house, or possibly a small fort. This, it was later maintained, gave the

British the legitimate title to the area—especially once the Spanish settlement had been abandoned.

For a time in this period it seemed as if a major international conflict
might erupt over rival claims to the region. However, the firmness of the
British government, the inherent weakness of Spain, and the gathering
clouds of the French Revolution, compelled the Spanish to reduce
their claims; British rights in the area were recognized, with the final
disposition of the Island still unsettled.

In the next few years both British and Spanish explorers were in the
area; on one occasion Captains Vancouver and Quadra were at anchor
together at Nootka, and dined amicably in some state with each other and
with Maquinna. Eventually their governments decided on a solution of
their rival claims; in 1795 the British flag was raised in this remote spot,
not again to be lowered; the sovereignty of at least one small part of the
Pacific Northwest had been decided.

The status of the adjoining areas of the mainland, however, as well as
large parts of the interior of the continent, remained obscure. Yet
already, as the nineteenth century opened, the outlines of the final contest
for these prizes were becoming clear. Spain, it was evident, no longer
had serious hopes of adding to her dominions; events, indeed, were
soon to show that she was unable even to retain those which she had.
This was signalled most clearly, perhaps, in 1819, when John Quincy
Adams, the American Secretary of State, persuaded her to relinquish all
rights west of the Arkansas River and north of the forty-second parallel.

Russia meanwhile was also withdrawing from the arena. Although
for a time it had contemplated a southward expansion, establishing a post
in 1812 at Bodega Bay, 65 miles north of San Francisco, in 1824 a
Russian-American agreement stipulated that the Russian sphere of
influence should not extend farther south than 54° 40'. France, having
lost its possessions in northeastern America a generation before, had no
wish to engage in adventures on the other side of the continent. The
final contestants for control of the Pacific northwest were, therefore,
reduced to two.

One of these, of course, was Great Britain, and already by the early
years of the new century her penetration of these vast areas was well

advanced. Each of the two great fur companies, the North West Company and the Hudson's Bay Company, was anxious to extend its chain of posts into the interior, so as to gain a commercial advantage over its rival. It was in the service of the former that Alexander Mackenzie made his great voyage to the western ocean, arriving there on July 22, 1793, and that Simon Fraser descended to its mouth the river that now bears his name.[1] In the same period, David Thompson explored the Kootenays and the upper basin of the Columbia, and claimed parts of the area for Britain.

In 1813, when America and Britain were at war, the North West Company was able to take over an outpost of the Pacific Fur Company (an American concern) at Astoria on the Pacific coast, while at the same time H.M.S. *Racoon* of the Royal Navy took formal possession of the area for England—a claim which of course was not recognized by the young republic.

This latter development brings to our notice Britain's great, and, as it proved, final rival for the sovereignty of this region. Ever since the first colonists had landed on the Atlantic coast of what was later to be the United States of America, there had been a steady flow of population westward. Now, hardy bands of Americans began reaching the no-man's-land of the Northwest. The explorers Lewis and Clark had made their way to the Pacific coast by land in 1805. J. J. Astor's fur company was soon attempting to establish a chain of fur-trading posts throughout the area, though at first without much success, some of the men sent out by sea being massacred by Indians, and others being forced, as we have noted, to yield their outpost at Fort Astoria to the North West Company.

The whole area, however, generally known as the "Oregon Territory", remained the possession of neither Britain nor the United States. Even though it was agreed by the two governments in 1818 that the 49th parallel should form the boundary between their possessions east of the Rocky Mountains, no such stipulation had been made regarding the area to the west of the Great Divide, and citizens of both countries remained free to come and go, to trade and settle there as they pleased.

The final outcome of their contest for possession of the region was still uncertain; but that such a contest impended was now clear. It was to stretch over most of the century, not being brought to a conclusion till the disposition of the San Juan Islands in 1872; yet its crucial period, beyond a doubt, was to be that which began in 1858 with the great rush of would-be gold miners, most of them American, to the rich diggings in the interior of what in that same year was first named British Columbia. In this decisive and turbulent time, Douglas was indisputably the key figure; it was upon his personality and actions that the whole issue would revolve, and by his will and foresight that it would be settled as it was.

This expansion, then, of the rival branches of the Anglo-Saxon race into the northwest was to be a basic feature of the background of Douglas' time and place. We may now consider two others which were also to involve him in the necessity for important decisions, and to which events were once again to show him equal.

One was the steady, silent transition of the North American economy through a rapid succession of phases. Before the arrival of the white man, hunting and fishing had been the main occupation of the natives; soon, with the advent of the fur trade, new trade goods and economic arrangements became a part of the continent's way of life. At the same time the white man had introduced agriculture, eventually to displace fur-trading as the basic occupation of the area. Finally, industry was to triumph over both; the urban way of life, with its need for roads, bridges, schools, water, gas, fire and police protection, to name but a few, would rapidly displace the rural, and the subsequent swift road to the problems of modern metropolitan existence would at least have been opened. All this was something new, and as the century wore on, the problems raised by it forced themselves ever more insistently on the attention of those in power. Inevitably, Douglas, as one of these, had to grapple with them, and once again, as we shall see, neither shrank from the conflict nor faltered in it.

Moreover, the age of monopoly, as symbolized by such great aggregations of power as the Hudson's Bay Company (or, in the other hemisphere, the East India Company), was rapidly yielding to the era of free enterprise. Every man was to buy or sell, come or go, work or starve as he pleased, yet from this multitude of individual wills and private pleasures a good society was to be shaped, largely by the silent working of what its philosophical mentor, Adam Smith, had termed the Invisible Hand.

The third great change of the nineteenth century was to be the steady movement away from oligarchy and aristocracy towards forms of government based directly on the people—or at the very least, on all adult males. This, too, was something new in history. To some, it heralded disaster; to others it was a process to be, if possible, hastened. Between these opposing viewpoints, Douglas in his term of authority was to find himself. By temperament and background a sympathizer with the older way, his intelligence, albeit reinforced by the instructions of his superiors, pointed him the true direction of the time. Thus, as he presided over the dissolution of the old order and the establishment of the new, he strove to see that it was accompanied by neither acrimony nor undue grinding of the gears.

These, then—the final division of the continent, the economic transition from trapline to factory, and the political transition from feudalism to democracy—were the tides which were to sweep across the spot of space and time where James Douglas was to find himself. How he faced the challenges they brought, what decisions he made, and how they have affected us today, will be the main subject of these pages; first, however, we must give some account of those earlier years when, though his marshal's baton was perhaps already in his knapsack, he was still but a simple soldier in the great army of humanity.

NOTE

[1] Fraser (1776-1862) reached the Gulf of Georgia on July 2, 1808; he was then 32. An account of his journey is to be found in *The Letters and Journals of Simon Fraser 1806-1808*, ed. W. K. Lamb, Macmillan, Toronto, 1960. Various mementoes connected with him are on display in the Provincial Archives, Victoria.

CHAPTER TWO

Lights and Shadows

ONE REMARKABLE feature of the life of James Douglas is that although its later portions were to be passed on the well-lit stage of history before the eyes of so many of his fellow-citizens, its earliest years are cloaked in a certain mystery. We cannot be sure of at least three facts which in the case of most major figures of recent centuries have been established beyond dispute: the place of Douglas' birth, its exact date, and the identity of his mother. In the case of the first of these, even the hemisphere is in doubt. Professor Walter Sage, who published a biography of Douglas in 1930, was informed by Douglas' daughter Agnes (Mrs. Arthur Bushby, who lived on till 1928), that he was born in Lanarkshire, Scotland;[1] the preponderance of opinion today, however, is that his birthplace was in the vicinity of Demerara, British Guiana. Certainly his superiors in the Hudson's Bay Company and some of his old acquaintances seemed in no doubt that he had first seen the light of day in the tropics, and this is the conclusion most consonant with the established facts.[2]

The year is not in doubt; it was 1803. The exact date, however, is in some dispute. In his own handwriting in an old account book, Douglas recorded it as June 5.[3] This might seem incontrovertible evidence, but against it must be set the fact that in the same list of landmarks in his life he wrote "1840. Sept. My father died", and it is certain from obituary notices in the English press of the time that this actually occurred on June 30 of that year.[4] Douglas' descendants evidently believed that his birthday was August 15, for on that date in 1872 one of his granddaughters marked the occasion by giving him a shilling, saying "Now, grandpa, that's for you to spend on yourself in any way you like".[5] Moreover, the family monument in Ross Bay Cemetery has, cut into the enduring granite, the date August 15. An examination of Douglas' birth certificate would, of course, resolve this discrepancy; this document, however, if it ever existed, has not yet been found.

Finally, the name and background of his mother remain hidden, perhaps forever. That his father was John Douglas, a prosperous Scottish merchant with interests in a sugar plantation in British Guiana, there is no question; but as to what other blood was mingled in his son, he left no record.

Nor did that son, if indeed he ever knew. His earliest recollections may well have been of her face bending above his own; perhaps seven decades later such scenes were still sometimes before him; but he was content to let death, when it came to him in 1877, efface all. Only a line remains in an old account book; there, in his own handwriting, along with notes of a few other landmarks in his life, are the words: 1839. July. My mother died.[6]

It seems certain, then, that the future governor of British Columbia and trusted servant of the Crown was illegitimate. There is also a possibility that he was partly what is known as "colored". He was remarkably dark of complexion, a matter often commented on, as, indeed, was his daughter Cecilia, later to become the wife of Dr. J. S. Helmcken.[7] A letter written while he was still in the early stages of his career by someone familiar with much personal detail about important officials of the Hudson's Bay Company speaks of him as a "mulatto".[8] But these slight scraps of evidence are not conclusive; the unknown figure who gave him birth still remains within the shadows.

We can say, though, that Douglas was the fruit of no casual episode. Three children in all were born to his parents; the others being Alexander, born in 1801 or 1802, and Cecilia, born in 1812.[9] Of the former but little is known, but, as we shall see, the subsequent story of the latter is a matter both of record and of interest.

From this point, however, we are on firmer ground. His father clearly assumed responsibility for his offspring, sending the two boys to a preparatory school in Lanark, where they received a good grounding in the elements of education. In later life, Douglas spoke French impeccably, and it has been conjectured that the basis of this accomplishment was also laid in this period.

Soon, however, distant horizons beckoned to his restless spirit. Though he was not yet sixteen, he resolved to try his luck in the New World.[10] He entered the service of the North West Company, and on May 7, 1819 sailed from Liverpool aboard the brig *Matthews*, outward bound toward his eventual high destiny. Seven weeks later the ship reached Quebec, from where, it is assumed, he proceeded to Montreal for instructions. He was assigned to the post at Fort William, and was taken there in one of the many canoes that moved continuously along the inland waterways of the continent.

Though he left no record of this journey, we can be sure from other accounts of the time that it must have been a remarkable experience for him. The canoes were usually about thirty-six feet long and six feet wide, with frames made of cedar, covered with birchbark. Spruce roots served as rope and the yellow pine provided gum, which between them held the bark on the frame; only a few nails were employed. In such canoes, paddled by sturdy voyageurs, travellers were carried through the wilderness. Elms and oaks lined the rivers; wild raspberries and gooseberries abounded; in summer, the forest flowers lit up the meadows; wild roses were in bloom. The noise of woodpeckers pierced the great silence, while eagles majestically circled far above them. From time to time they were forced to make a portage around dangerous rapids; even in what seemed safe waters, there was always the danger of striking a hidden rock and suffering disaster. Here and there along the route were crosses lining the banks, mutely testifying where others before them had drowned in the treacherous currents. To keep up their spirits and lighten the hard labor of paddling, the voyageurs sometimes burst into vigorously rhythmic songs. At night, the parties would land and quickly set up their tents, light fires, and cook a hasty meal. Fireflies danced in the night air; clouds of mosquitoes made sleep or comfort difficult; cries of unknown animals pierced the darkness; in the distance was often heard the roar of a waterfall.

Sometimes in this vast wilderness they met other human beings—native Indians, perhaps, bringing trout or maple sugar to barter for tobacco, rum or biscuits. To the European eye, they seemed as if from another planet, with their painted bodies and rings in their noses or ears. On occasion, they would perform their wild dances; as the brown bodies leapt and flashed in the light of the campfires, those watching them must have felt themselves looking back along the echoing corridors of time.

Sometimes, too, a white man would emerge from a hut on the river bank to greet them. Nearly always he was an employee of one of the two great fur companies. Nor was he often alone; usually his Indian help-meet would be seen shyly peeping from the cabin, while their children played happily outside the door.

Such were the scenes through which the traveller would be borne, and such in all likelihood were those through which young Douglas passed. Eventually on August 6 he arrived at Fort William. He was now sixteen—young indeed to begin a hard unfamiliar way of life in the rigors of this northern wilderness. When autumn gave way to winter, and the thermometer sank to unimaginable depths, he must sometimes, perhaps, have regretted his decision; if indeed he had once lived among lush tropical growth under the brass vault of an equatorial sky, he must often have compared those days with these. Yet whatever his inner feelings, he had made his choice, he had accepted the duties imposed on him, and from them he would not retreat.

This was one feature of his character that would be constant to the end. A glimpse of another—a certain quickness of temper—would be given in the following year. In 1820 young Douglas was transferred to Ile-à-la-crosse, (about two hundred miles sorthwest by north from the present site of Prince Albert, Saskatchewan), and there he fought a duel with an employee of the Hudson's Bay Company. Such outbreaks of personal violence between the two rival fur companies were far from unknown in this period; fortunately, on this occasion, there was no blood shed.[11]

Little is known about the five years that Douglas spent at this isolated post. The area was rich in furs, and there was abundance of fish and wildfowl. He no doubt performed his duties to the satisfaction of his superiors, and also found profitable employment for his spare time. The well-turned though often too ornate phraseology which in later years he used in his correspondence reflects a considerable effort made at some time or other to improve his skill in language; it seems likely that he took some books with him into this remote spot, and carefully studied the elements of composition. Confirmation of this is perhaps to be found in an essay on Indian life which seems almost certainly to have been composed in this period. Still preserved by a succession of lucky chances in the Provincial Archives at Victoria, it reflects several characteristic features both of its author and of the Victorian age which was then just dawning. Its style is formal and somewhat stilted, a feature of Douglas' mode of writing and speaking that remained with him all his days; it sees its subject completely from the outside, never betraying a suggestion that the essential difference between the "theology" of the white man and the "mythology" of the red man was not so much a contrast between light and darkness as mere variations on a common theme, the accidents of time and place; and it disregards the fact that in comparing two cultures it is hardly proper to take for comparison the ideals of one and the realities of the other. For all that, Douglas' essay is certainly not a composition that many of his fellow-employees of a comparable age could have produced. A few extracts may be of interest:

The North American Indians, like all other barbarous nations, profess a body of traditionary history, or perhaps, more properly speaking, a patched medley of absurd fables interwoven with real events; some of these traditions I have collected, as they exhibit the unaided workings of the human mind, and illustrate the moral and social feelings of man in the earliest stage of savage life, when the untutored reason, darkened by ignorance, is overcome by the fierce impulses of the passions, and the mere animal instincts given for the support and preservation of life hold absolute sway. The idea of God, that is of a Being who created the world, is familiar to all the American Tribes, with a few solitary exceptions, wherein the knowledge of God has been entirely obliterated, as among the Chinooks, who are beyond exception the most licentious and demoralized people that I have seen, as if the fearful words of St. Paul referred to them as well as to other heathen nations—"even as they did not like to retain God in their knowledge, God gave them over to a reprobate mind".

The most enlightened of the Tribes, however, are not agreed on the subject of the Divine attributes—some entertain rational ideas, while others invest the Deity with irreconcilable qualities, such as bound-less power, with an extreme simplicity, that the most stupid animals can puzzle and deceive; probably they have no clear and well defined ideas on these abstruse points, which are not of a nature to attract their attention, and they merely repeat the tradition as it was received from their fathers, without scrutiny or comment of their own.

The Indians of the northwest coast believe in the existence of a supreme benevolent Being whose name is "Yealth", and that he has a son named "Yealth Yay", i.e. "The son of God"; they also think that there is a malevolent Being called Coostahooshticacah. Yealth wears the human form; he made the earth, then man was formed, a faint light afterwards appeared, gradually growing in brightness until the stars were seen, then the moon was made, and lastly the sun shone forth in all his glory . . . When all things were finished, he commanded them to do good and to commit no wickedness, while at the same time he urged them to retaliate the hostile attacks of other nations and return injury for injury; he added "I am now going away, but my eye will always be upon you; if you live wicked lives, you cannot come to me, as the good only can live in my place"; with these words he left the earth and has not since that time returned to it, and they do not know where he is at present . ..

The knowledge of these things has no perceptible effect on their conduct; they steal and cheat and lie whenever they feel an interest in doing so, without any visible apprehension of exciting Yealth's displeasure; they however all admit that theft, falsehood and roguery are criminal, but nevertheless have recourse to them without hesitation whenever it suits their purpose . . .

So, in this lonely outpost of commerce, the years passed. During the period, a development took place which would greatly affect its obscure employee. In 1821, weary from years of unprofitable rivalry, the two great fur companies amalgamated. Henceforth the North West Company disappears from history, and the Hudson's Bay Company, with whose name Douglas' was for so long to be closely linked, survived.

By 1825, Douglas was twenty-two; then, once again, he was moved westward. He was still only one of the ranks, but he was now coming several hundred miles nearer to the stage on which he would eventually play so prominent a role. His new home—though in fact, till he retired, the fur-trader had "no continuing city"—was now in New Caledonia, as the northern interior of British Columbia was then called. Leaving Ile-à-la-crosse on April 5, 1825, and probably spending part of the summer at Fort Chipewyan on Lake Athabaska, he crossed the Rocky Mountains and arrived at Fort McLeod on Lake McLeod on November 9.

Here the officer in charge was John Tod, born in Scotland in 1794 and destined, like Douglas, after a career of distinction, to die in Victoria.[12] Tod had long been a trusted servant of the Hudson's Bay Company, entering its service about 1810. Quite a number of the letters which he wrote to friends at the coast during his time in New Caledonia have been preserved; they give us a vivid picture of the conditions which many of the Company's servants were forced to endure. Loneliness and danger, a scanty and unbalanced diet, formed their lot; while for those of cultivated tastes the absence of the amenities of culture was an added turn of the screw. Tod, for example, on one occasion referred to the area as "this land of sin & misery"[13], and declared himself "almost as unruly and restless as a ghost in an uninhabited castle".[14] He had keen musical tastes, and recalled them in a letter dated February 27, 1826:

> . . . I must not omit observing the pleasure I derived from many parts of your letter—I was transported in imagination back to that innocent period of our life we spent with so much felicity together —when we could indulge in our favourite and delightful amusement —music—and when the pleasing sound of a violin & flute used to be considered no crime . . . Let us hope times even superior to those may yet return . . .
>
> . . . I trust in God, that in compassion for the miseries I have endured in this land of savages, that he will be pleased to spare us both to live & see that day, when we may participate in the pleasure of each other's company & spend a Sunday's evening with the same sacred harmony we were wont to do.[15]

In the meantime, he availed himself of what consolations he could:

. . . my fellow labourer in the vineyard is possessed of an excellent ear for music & never fails to accompany me on the flute with her voice when I take up the instrument.[16]

Douglas did not himself remain long at Fort McLeod, but proceeded to the somewhat more important post at Fort St. James, some eighty miles to the southwest.[17] Here for the next five years he was to remain, and we begin in this period to gain slightly more knowledge of his character and actions.

It was at Fort St. James that young Douglas first met his future father-in-law, William Connolly, who had at that time attained the rank of Chief Factor. It was from here, too, that Douglas made his first journey to the Pacific coast. Once a year, the precious furs acquired during the previous season were taken down to the depot at Fort Vancouver, and in the year 1826 Douglas was one of those selected to accompany Connolly to the coast.

The journey was a lengthy and sometimes dangerous one. Boats took the party down the Fraser to Fort Alexandria. From there the furs were transferred to pack trains, and the horses carried them to Kamloops and then down the shores of Okanagan Lake to Fort Okanogan at the junction of the Okanagan and Columbia Rivers.[18] The cargo was then once more embarked on boats which carried the party down the Columbia to Fort Vancouver. Here, after a journey of over five weeks and perhaps a thousand miles, they arrived on June 12.

After resting for three weeks, the brigade began the return journey. It is interesting to note that it was accompanied on this occasion by David Douglas (no relation to James, but a well-known botanist, after whom the Douglas Fir is named). In September, the little party was once more safely back at Fort St. James.

Information regarding Douglas' activities in the year 1827 is somewhat sketchy. He apparently aided in setting up a fishery in the area, in order that the monotonous and sometimes scanty diet of the furtraders might be supplemented.

A much more important milestone in his life came in the spring of 1828. It was on April 27 of that year that Douglas went through a form of marriage usually known as "the custom of the country" with

Amelia Connolly, the half-breed daughter of the Chief Factor at Stuart Lake.[19] The bride was shy and remarkably young, being then in her sixteenth year; but the young couple were apparently well suited to each other. Little could they have foreseen that they were destined one day to hold the highest position in the gift of the Crown throughout the vast area from the Rockies to the Pacific Ocean.

As it happened, before many months had passed, an incident took place which might well have ended young Douglas' career forever. Connolly was temporarily absent from the fort, and his son-in-law was left in charge. Five years before, at Fort George, two Indians had slain two employees of the Company. One of the murderers had been caught and despatched, but the other had remained at large. In 1828 the latter had made a visit to the Stuart Lake area. Douglas was informed of the fact and with a few assistants went to the Indian camp, located the wanted man, and beat him to death on the spot. Then, according to one historian who made a careful investigation (though some fifty years later) of the affair, on Douglas' orders a rope was passed around the neck of the corpse and it was dragged back to the fort, with the intention of letting it there be eaten by the dogs.[20]

Douglas no doubt imagined that the incident was now closed, but such was not to prove the case. The Chief of the Stuart Lake Indians, Quah or Kwah,[21] learned of the affair and was highly indignant. With a considerable number of his followers, he invaded the fort one day and in effect held Douglas prisoner.

The exact details of how the young fur-trader succeeded in freeing himself from this dangerous situation are in dispute; several accounts of the affair are in existence. Father Morice declares that the Chief's nephew pointed a dagger at Douglas' heart, asking, "Shall I strike?", and that his life was only saved by two women in the fort throwing down clothing and trade goods from a balcony, which the Indians found an acceptable ransom.[22] John McLean, a long-time servant of the HBC, asserts that the interpreter's wife persuaded the Indians by a vigorous harangue to release Douglas, and that there then resulted an "amicable conference".[23]

Admiral Moresby, who as a young naval lieutenant met Douglas, by then Governor of Vancouver Island, in Victoria in 1852, has yet another version:

> Douglas (then in command), the centre of a horde of maddened Indians, was at his last struggle, when, like Pocahontas herself, an Indian girl, the daughter of a chief, tore her way to his side, held back the savages, and pleaded his cause with such passion that the red man granted his life to her entreaties. She lived to share his honours, and to become Lady Douglas, wife of the Governor and Commander-in-chief of British Columbia.[24]

The most detailed account of these events is that of John Tod, an old friend and associate of Douglas:

> Mr. Douglas was first seized, bound and carried away to the mess room of the fort. All this time Douglas kept struggling and swearing, but what could he do. They laid him flat on the table; he kicked and plunged, exhausting himself. The Chief looked at him, saying "You are tired; now I can talk to you". This only exasperated Mr. Douglas the more, and he renewed his struggle, damning and swearing, calling them big rascals, etc.
>
> The Indians replied by saying "Oh, you must lie down again", etc. At last the Indians commenced to state that Mr. Douglas killed an Indian; that it was right that he should have been killed, but that it was not right that the Indians should be killed in their camp. Had it occurred anywhere else, outside of their camp, they observed, they could do nothing. The Chief then stated that what they wanted was some food to give the friends of the dead man in return for the body.
>
> Mr. Douglas was again vehement and protested against giving anything in return.
>
> The Chief once more retorted: "Then sit down".
>
> Mr. Douglas finally asked them what they wanted. They replied that they wanted clothing, axes, tobacco, guns etc. for the father, mother, brother and sister of the deceased; that they were present and held them responsible for the deed . . .
>
> Mr. Douglas was set free, and having promised, he gave the goods to quiet the matter.[25]

A month later, the Fort received a most important and distinguished visitor: Sir George Simpson himself, the top official of the HBC in North America. He was on one of his numerous tours of inspection, during which he invariably travelled at lightning speed from post to post, and also investigated conditions at each one with a penetrating eye. In the absence of Connolly, Douglas gave him a ceremonious welcome on September 17. In the next few days Simpson met Chief Quah, and no doubt heard much from him and from others concerning the recent disturbance at the Fort. He may well have decided at this time that Douglas should be moved to a new location.

Certainly conditions in the area showed small sign of returning to normal. On November 3, Douglas was "assaulted by the Indians of Fraser Lake"; no other details are available than these, recorded by him in an old account book.[27] On the following New Year's Day, usually a time of festivity when whites and Indians mingled amicably in the trading post, there was further trouble; the whites, perhaps in revenge, having got the Indians befuddled with drink, then proceeded to beat some of them unmercifully.[28]

Tension remained high for some months, as Tod reported to a friend on February 14, 1829:

> The news of this quarter are various & interesting enough, at least to us here—we have the misfortune to have another poor man murdered by the savages last Spring, which at the moment created a good deal of agitation amongst us; but it has since, as well as the unfortunate affair of Fort George, been sufficiently revenged—the perpetrators of these atrocious acts were all cut off last summer to a man—yet notwithstanding the justness of our cause, things have come to that pitch which makes it necessary for us to be continually on the alert in order to take every precaution so as to guard ourselves against either the open attacks or insidious advances of our savage neighbours, many of whom seem considerably irritated at the late examples—but it is to be hoped that time, with good management, will at length effectually calm their present turbulent disposition, and bring things back to their former peace and tranquillity.[29]

At all events, it was now deemed best by his superiors that Douglas should make a fresh start elsewhere. For a moment, indeed, he seems to have contemplated abandoning the fur trade altogether.[30] However, these feelings soon passed, and on January 30, 1830 he left Fort St. James for the more salubrious and civilized destination of Fort Vancouver, where, a few months later, he was joined by his wife.

He was still only a clerk; he had been the cause of some difficulties for his employers; there seemed little sign that he was marked for great-ness. One thing, though, had changed decisively; he now stood infinitely closer to the seats of power. A decade was to elapse before he glimpsed the island that would be forever linked with his name; twenty years before he assumed the titles, duties and privileges of the chief servant of the Crown in the Northwest. Yet the scales of destiny had tipped silently in his favor; James Douglas had arrived on the Pacific coast.

NOTES

1 Sage, *Sir James Douglas and British Columbia*, U. of Toronto, 1930, p. 14.
2 See Douglas Mackay, *The Honourable Company*, McClelland and Stewart, Toronto, 1936, p. 200.
John Tod, an old friend and associate of Douglas, in his "History of New Caledonia and the North West Coast", (unpublished MS in Provincial Archives, Victoria), says, "He was a native of the West Indies (Jamaica) and his mother was a Creole."
3 Sage, *Douglas*, pp. 14 and 363.
4 Sage, *Op. Cit.*, p. 363; W.K. Lamb "Some notes on the Douglas family", *BCHQ*, Vol. 17, Nos. 1 and 2, January 1953, p. 45.
5 B.A. McKelvie, "Douglas: a new portrait", *BCHQ*, Vol. VII, No. 2, April 1943, p. 101. Douglas' account of the incident (letter to Martha Douglas, August 15, 1872) is: "Dear little Dolly came in with a rush, to wish me many happy returns of the day, leaving in my hand a shilling as a birthday gift, and went off like a shot, for fear I should return it to her. Nice, is it not?"
When Douglas died five years later, the shilling was found in the back of his watch-case.
6 Sage, *Douglas*, p. 363.
John Douglas married Miss Jessie Hamilton of Glasgow in 1809. (W. K. Lamb, "Some notes on the Douglas family", *BCHQ*, Vol. 17, January 1953, p. 43). As a result of this marriage, Douglas acquired three half-sisters, Cecilia, Georgiana and Jane. In later years Douglas corresponded regularly with Jane, declaring (letter of June 2, 1870), "Ours is no formal correspondence, but one founded on the affections of the heart". After his retirement from public life he visited her in Paris.
It is known that Douglas wrote to his father at least once in his life (Lamb, *Op. Cit.*, p. 46), but no correspondence has survived. Douglas' rather laconic account of his death is: "Father died in London, where he was sud-denly taken ill at the house of his solicitor, and died in a few minutes, it is supposed of disease of the heart — having been subject to such attacks for the last 10 years of his life. In the intervals he enjoyed good health, and had fine teeth to the last". (Lamb, *Op. Cit.*, p. 45; also Douglas' Travel Diary of 1864-1865 (MS in PABC).

7 J. S. Helmcken, Reminiscences, II, pp. 84-86 (MS in PABC).

8 M. A. MacLeod (ed.) *The Letters of Letitia Hargrave*, Toronto, The Champlain Society, 1947, p. 132.

9 W. K. Lamb, "Some notes on the Douglas family", *BCHQ*, Vol. 17, Nos. 1 and 2, January 1953, p. 43.
Douglas eventually had four relatives named Cecilia: his sister (later to become the wife of Chief Justice Cameron; she died in Victoria in 1859); her daughter; a half-sister (his father's daughter by his marriage to Jessie Hamilton); and a daughter (later Mrs. J. S. Helmcken; she died in 1865). His niece, Cecilia Eliza Cowan Cameron, married W. A. G. Young, Colonial Secretary of Vancouver Island and British Columbia. One of their sons became Sir William Douglas Young, Governor of the Falkland Islands (died 1943), and another became Chief Justice of the Supreme Court of Fiji (died 1942).

10 His brother Alexander had entered the service of the North West Company in 1818. He did not do well, being described by his superiors as "stupid & inactive, deficient in education, not adapted for the country", and returned to England in 1824. No details of the remainder of his life are available. See W. K. Lamb, "Some notes on the Douglas family", *BCHQ*, Vol. 17, No. 2, Jan.-Apr. 1953, p. 46.

11 Sage, *Douglas*, p. 21.

12 On August 31, 1882. See the article "John Tod: career of a Scotch boy", in the *BCHQ* for July-Oct. 1954.

13 Tod to Ermatinger, April 10, 1831. Ermatinger Papers, PABC.

14 Tod to Ermatinger, Feb. 14, 1829. Ermatinger Papers, PABC.

15 Tod to Ermatinger, Ermatinger Papers, PABC.

16 Tod to Ermatinger, Feb. 27, 1826. Ermatinger Papers, PABC. This attachment continued for a considerable time. On Feb. 14, 1829, Tod wrote: "You ask me what is become of the girl who used to sing at McLeod's Lake . . . why then in plain language she still continues the only companion of my solitude—without her, or some other substitute, life, in such a wretched place as this, would be altogether insupportable". (Ermatinger Papers, PABC).

17 Fort St. James and Fort McLeod are believed to be the two oldest continuously inhabited settlements west of the Rockies.

18 Today the form "Okanogan" is used south of the border, and "Okanagan" above it. At this period this usage had not yet become fixed.

19 Amelia was born at Norway House, in what is now Manitoba, on January 1, 1812, and died at Victoria on Jan. 8, 1890; there are still a few residents of Victoria who remember her. Her mother was a Cree woman named Suzanne (from whom numerous distinguished Victoria citizens are descended). Connolly lived with her for nearly thirty years, and then left her to marry a white woman, Julia Woolrich. The courts eventually decided that Connolly's first marriage had been valid; part of Lady Douglas' reluctance to take part in public life in her later years was probably due to sensitivity regarding the question of her legitimacy.
There is a rather startling reference to Connolly in one of John Tod's letters. Referring to a minor contretemps at the Fort, Tod wrote to a friend: "Mr.

C. has been like a bear dancing on a hot girdle about it." (Letter to Edward
Ermatinger, Feb. 14, 1829. Ermatinger Papers, PABC).

[20] Rev. A. G. Morice, *History of the Northern Interior of British Columbia,
formerly New Caledonia.* (Toronto, William Briggs, 1904, pp. 137-140).
There are other accounts of this incident and its sequel which differ from that
of Father Morice. See John McLean, *Notes of a twenty-five years' service
in the Hudson's Bay Territory,* London, 1849. Reprinted by the Cham-
plain Society, Toronto, 1932, (pp. 162-164). Also the article "John
Tod: career of a Scotch Boy" in the *BCHQ* for 1954 and J. R. Anderson,
Notes and Comments on early days and events in British Columbia, Wash-
ington and Oregon, 1925, p. 236. (unpublished manuscript in Provincial
Archives, Victoria).
I have given summaries of the various accounts in my *Victoria: The Fort*
(Mitchell Press, Vancouver, 1968) pp. 40-42.

[21] There is an article on Chief Kwah in the *Beaver* for September 1943. It
contains a picture of his grave on the banks of the Stuart River and of the
dagger that threatened Douglas' life.

[22] Morice, *Op. cit.,* pp. 137-140.

[23] McLean, *Op. cit.,* p. 164.

[24] Moresby, *Two Admirals,* London, John Murray, 1909, p. 122.

[25] John Tod, History of New Caledonia and the Northwest Coast, Victoria,
1878 (unpublished MS in Provincial Archives).

[26] The background of Simpson, for over thirty years the dominant figure in the
Company, remains obscure. Like Douglas, he was illegitimate, and the exact
date of his birth is unknown. Unlike Douglas, he had numerous illegitimate
children scattered about the continent. See J. S. Galbraith, *The Hudson's
Bay Company as an Imperial Factor, 1821-1869,* U. of Toronto Press,
1957, p. 20, and Douglas Mackay, *The Honourable Company,* McClelland
and Stewart, Toronto, 1936, p. 198. Also the *Dictionary of National
Biography.*

[27] Sage, *Douglas,* pp. 50-51 and 363.

[28] Morice, *History,* p. 147.

[29] Tod to Ermatinger, Feb. 14, 1829. Ermatinger Papers, PABC.

[30] Sage, *Douglas,* p. 51.

CHAPTER THREE

The Swelling Prologue
To The Imperial Theme

Now THE TEMPO quickens. No longer was Douglas marooned in the wilderness; he was installed at the capital of affairs. Nor was his head-quarters a pitiful collection of huts, all but isolated from the outside world; instead, it was now a flourishing community, linked by the sea with the four quarters of the globe. Here, too, three things would lie close to hand: the amenities of life, scope for his talents, and the imme-diate notice of an influential superior. The first would provide some comforts for his young family, while the other two might lead him—who knows where?

Hard work, sober habits, attention to detail—these were the qualities he had developed, and these were the stepping stones to advancement at Fort Vancouver. Such was the invariable rule of John McLoughlin, the formidable autocrat of the Columbia Department. McLoughlin was a striking figure, well over six feet tall, with large blue eyes and white hair extending down to his shoulders. He was thought by some to resemble the eagles of the district. Though unyielding in his demand for efficiency in business, he was a man of culture and personal kindliness, willing in "off-hours" to discuss the world of ideas outside the counting house.[1]

McLoughlin, like Douglas, had taken a half-breed as his mate, and the two when seen together presented a remarkable contrast:

Though his wife was a half-breed of the Ojibway nation, coarse, bent, fat, and flabby, he treated her like a princess. In public and in private he was as loyal to her as if she had been a daughter of Queen Victoria . . . He would suffer no indignity or slight to her. His fine handsome form beside the uncorseted figure of the old Indian woman presented a strange contrast, as she waddled beside him like a being of another species. His gallantry to her knew no bound. On state occasions, straight as an arrow and magnificently apparelled, he would stand like a splendid statue, while this female aboriginal rolled out before him in plain clothes and no figure whatever.[2]

Douglas was given the position of accountant at the fort, and under this stern but sympathetic taskmaster his fidelity to duty soon earned him the golden opinions that he craved.

At this period the fort was in its glory. Outside its walls, fertile fields and orchards stretched over hundreds of acres. Large crops of wheat, barley, oats, peas and potatoes were raised, while hundreds of cattle, hogs, sheep and oxen contributed to the settlement's comfort and pros-perity. No government had yet reached out to take the area irrevocably under its control; fur was still king, and the wealth that poured from the trapping grounds through the funnel near the mouth of the Columbia was comparable to that which a generation later would pour through Victoria from the goldfields of the Fraser. The historian Bancroft has given us a vivid picture of what was almost a "city-state":

> The fort was not formidable in appearance. It consisted of a strong stockade about twenty feet high, without bastions, embracing an area of two hundred and fifty by one hundred and fifty yards. Within this enclosure, around three sides, were ranged the dwellings and offices of the gentlemen in the company's service. In the centre, facing the main entrance or great gate, was the residence of Doctor John McLoughlin, the governor by courtesy of the Hudson's Bay Company in Oregon, a French Canadian structure, painted white, with piazza and flower beds in front, and grape-vines trained along a rude trellis. The steps leading to the hall of the governor's house were of horseshoe form, and between the two flights stood a twenty-four-pound cannon, mounted on a ship's carriage, and on either side of this were two mortar guns, all with shot piled orderly about them, but otherwise looking innocent enough in their peaceful resting-places. There were no galleries around the walls for sentries, nor loop-holes for small-arms, no appearances, in fact, indicating a

dangerous neighborhood. Near the centre of the enclosure rose the company's flag-staff, and everything about the place was orderly, neat, and business-like. The magazine, warehouses, store, and shops were all contained within the palisades, and during the hours appointed for labor every man attended to his duties, whether as trader, clerk, smith, baker, or tailor.

A bell large enough for a country church was supported by three stout poles about twenty feet high, covered with a little pointed roof to keep off the rain. This brazen monitor rang out at five o'clock in the morning, rousing the furriers, mechanics, and farmers to their tasks. At eight it announced breakfast; at nine, work again; at twelve, dinner; at one, work; at six, suspension of labor, and supper. Saturday's work ended at five in the afternoon, at which time the physician of the establishment served to the men their week's rations, consisting in winter of eight gallons of potatoes and eight salt salmon, and in summer of pease and tallow; no bread or meat being allowed, except occasionally. The Indian servants of the Indian wives hunted and fished for additional supplies. Nor was this unremitting industry unnecessary. The management of the Hudson's Bay Company required its posts to be self-supporting. The extent of territory they traded over was immense, and the number of their forts increased the demand for such articles as could be produced only in favorable localities. For instance, at Fort Vancouver the demand for axes and hatchets for the trappers and Indians required fifty of them to be made daily. In addition to the manufacture of these, the smiths had plenty to do in repairing farming tools and milling machinery, and making the various articles required by a community of several hundred people. The carpenter, the turner, and the tailor were equally busy; two or three men were constantly employed making bread for the fort people and sea-biscuit for the coasting vessels. The furs had to be beaten once a week to drive out moths and dust. The clerks had not only to keep accounts and copy letters, but keep a journal of every day's affairs. Among so many persons, some were sure to be in the hospital, and on these the best medical care was bestowed. Though so far from the world as to seem removed from the world's wants, Fort Vancouver was no place for the indulgence of poetic idleness.[3]

Meanwhile, silently, like a mole, Douglas burrowed through mounds of paper-work, reducing the financial affairs of the department to easily understood statements of profit and loss. McLoughlin found he could trust him, and even depend on him for advice; eventually he became thought of as indispensable.

A letter written by Douglas in this period gives us a glimpse of not only the young clerk but also of some of the uncertainties of the enterprise he served. It is interesting to note that his style had not yet acquired the marked formality of his later years:

Jno. McLeod, Esquire,   *Vancouver, 12th March, 1832.*
Dear Sir,

I have the pleasure to inform you that in compliance with your request, I now forward a box to your address, containing a variety of prickly pears, which I hope will reach your distant quarter without injury. Our Columbia news are of a varied nature, a proportion of good mixed up with evil, but on the whole I believe the good predominates; at all events I am convinced that the best news are always the most gratifying, and will on that account leave the most unpleasant to bring up the rear.

The Nass party left us in the early part of April, Mr. Ogden being the superintendent of the land operations, with Captain Simpson to command the shipping. They were greatly retarded on the passage by contrary winds, and in consequence did not reach their destination before the 11th May.

To their great surprise and not a little to their satisfaction the natives received them in the most friendly manner, nor have they as yet displayed any symptoms of a hostile or turbulent disposition. They are nevertheless keen hands at the bargain and make the most of competition among the traders. If they cannot do business with one party they make no ceremony in trying what can be done with the other. The returns of the Coast are something like 3000 skins, upon which there is a loss of £1600.

Your friend Archy has been doing wonders at Fort Langley; he has collected about 2000 Beavers, and is not a little vain of his feat. Your old post Thompsons River seems determined to remain in the background. I believe its resources are exhausted, or perhaps Langley and Colville have a share of the trade which in your time it exclusively enjoyed.

This place as well as Nez Perces show an increase of returns, but I cannot say how the campaign will end in New Caledonia, as we have had no late intelligence from that quarter. The Brigade on its return to the interior met with a serious accident between the Portage Neuf and Cascades, by which two men and nearly forty pieces of property were lost. Another poor man was drowned in Fraser's River.

Captain Simpson died at Nass after a short illness of 13 days of an inflammation of the lungs. Please present my respects to Charlotte, Miss Flora and the little ones. Believe me to be with much respect Your obt Servant,

JAMES DOUGLAS[4]

Promotion, however, was by no means quick in coming; yet on the Company's lists of its employees in this area his name began moving toward the top—a sign that he was considered a possibility for greater things. Sir George Simpson, for nearly thirty years the chief overseas officer of the HBC and tireless inspector of even its remoter posts, recorded his candid opinion of Douglas in a private "Book of Servants' Characters" (now in the HBC archives in London):

A Scotch West Indian; about 33 Years of Age, has been 13 Years in the Service.—A stout powerful active man of good conduct and respectable abilities:—tolerably well educated, expresses himself clearly on paper, understands our Counting House business and is an excellent Trader.—Well qualified for any Service requiring bodily exertion, firmness of mind and the exercise of sound judgment, but furiously violent when roused.—Has every reason to look forward to early promotion and is a likely man to fill a place at our Council board in course of time.[5]

This was promising (had he known of it); but meanwhile another change was silently taking place, destined to affect his life decisively. Year by year, settlers were moving into the area from other parts of the United States. Their loyalties, if they considered them, were to its government; certainly few of them can have contemplated passing under the aegis of the British crown. Thus it was ever more likely that when the final disposition of the "Oregon Territory" occurred, much of it, and certainly its more southerly parts, would become part of the young republic. The days of the virtually undisputed rule of the Hudson's Bay Company in this region, therefore, were clearly numbered, and this was to be a major factor, as we shall see, in the founding of Fort Victoria. This latter development, however, was still more than a decade away, and in the meantime the headquarters of the Columbia Department enjoyed the last palmy days of its prosperity.

Douglas, as the accountant of this considerable business enterprise, continued to merit the approbation of his superiors. In 1832 and 1833 he crossed the Rocky Mountains, taking the accounts for the year to the senior authorities of the company at York Factory.[6] Here he no doubt made the acquaintance of figures whose word would weigh heavily in promotions. At the meeting of the Council of the Northern Department held in 1832, he was confirmed—but only in the position of clerk!— for another three years, his salary to be £100 a year. During 1833 and 1834 few details exist of his activities, but we can be sure they were satisfactory to his employers, since in 1835 he again made the long journey across the plains to York Factory.

Fortunately, he committed an account of the trip to paper (now in the Provincial Archives, Victoria), and we can thus look through his eyes at his daily progress across first the mountains and then the great central plain of the continent. Some of the features which would dis- tinguish his accounts of his later journeys to Alaska and California—the noting of details of the country, its soil and rock formations, its economic possibilities, the characters of those he did business with—are found here but in embryo; his narrative is thus not of continuous interest, and we may summarize it with some brevity.

As he left Fort Vancouver on March 3, 1835, spring had already come to the Pacific coast. On March 6 he noted:

> No snow in the vicinity of the river, vegetation begins to appear on the sloping hills and the face of nature is everywhere undergoing a rapid change, and the eye of the spectator is continually delighted with the varied beauties just bursting into existence.[7]

As his party made its way up the Columbia into the Interior, however, there were abundant signs that there, at least, winter was not yet over. On March 25 Douglas noted:

> Our progress during this day does not exceed 5 miles, and for a considerable distance below our encampment the ice is still so solid and compact as to remove all probability of its giving way immediately; a circumstance which determines me to push on ahead, leaving the bulk of the Party to come on leisurely with the property. My plan is to proceed with a canoe perfectly light and ten men; in places where the ice has already disappeared, we will use the canoe, and we will

THE SWELLING PROLOGUE TO THE IMPERIAL THEME / 29

either drag or carry our property over the ice wherever we may meet with it.

Soon, changing from travel by water to advancing slowly on snow-shoes, they had crossed the Great Divide and were in what is now the province of Alberta. Douglas noted that "the surface of these Prairies is thickly covered with various grasses, indicating a rich productive soil", but had little else to record of the region, and pushed ahead rapidly. Reaching Edmonton on April 30, he left it on May 2. Progress by boat was soon hampered by the dangerous condition of the waterways:

> The River is so very low that our progress is continually interrupted by the numerous banks of gravel and scattered rocks which are concealed from view by a small depth of untransparent fluid. The Boats are increasingly taking ground on the one or striking heavily upon the others, and the crews on these occasions have no other way of clearing these obstacles but leaping out and dragging them into deeper water, which is certainly not an agreeable pastime on a cold morning with ice forming all around them. We are surrounded on all sides by a fine country possessing all the natural beauties which can be well imagined in a wild uncultivated region.

As his party moved steadily across the vast stretches of the continent, Douglas found time to list the various native tribes of the area and make brief comments on their temperament, customs and beliefs. He goes on to record his arrival on May 30 at Fort Garry. Ten days later, having personally received his commission as Chief Trader and partic-ipated in the Council of the Northern Department, he had left it; on June 17 he had reached Norway House, and on the 24th his journey ended at York Factory. Here he made his reports to his superiors, and after resting and replenishing his supplies, left on the long westward journey with two boats on July 16. The next day he overtook a party of seven boats and continued in their company, making a few brief com-ments in his journal on the flora of the regions they advanced through. On August 2 he was at Norway House, on September 17 back in Edmonton, and soon afterwards he set out once more, this time on horseback, for the Columbia with "24 servants, 6 gentlemen, and 2 females with their attendants". Later, canoes were once again in service for a time. In early October, Douglas noted the first frost, but late in the month, having once more crossed the Rockies on foot, he reached more hospitable climes. The journal stops before the final stage of the long journey, but we may assume that some time in November Douglas was safely back at Fort Vancouver.

He had travelled perhaps five thousand miles; it had taken him the better part of a year to do it; but apparently he saw so little out of the way in this achievement that once it became evident that the journey would end successfully, he had lost interest in recording it.

The next few years were ones of unobtrusive devotion to duty. Fort Vancouver prospered, and Douglas, now assured by reason of his promotion to Chief Trader of a share in the Company's profits, prospered with it. Meanwhile his little family grew, though with no doubt heart-rending setbacks.[8] In 1838 the licence of the Hudson's Bay Company, granting it an exclusive right to trade with the Indians in the vast area from the Great Lakes to the Pacific Ocean, was extended for a further twenty-one years; the *Beaver*, an ugly but serviceable craft, appeared on the northwest coast in 1836,[9] and shuttled industriously among the scattered outposts of the Company. In the absence of McLoughlin, who visited England in 1838-1839, Douglas assumed his powers and responsibilities.[10]

That he viewed them with deep seriousness is evinced by the letter he wrote to Governor Simpson at this time:

> I enter upon the duties of the important charge to which you have been pleased to appoint me, with a degree of diffidence and oppressive anxiety regarding the future interests of the District that I attempt in vain to banish from my mind. These feelings are excited, not by the weight of responsibility properly attached to the charge itself, but proceed from the yearly increasing difficulties which every one acquainted with our affairs must anticipate from the collision of the foreign and independent interests, growing up on every side around us: and I dread being exposed to reproach for results in themselves unavoidable, and that no ability, however great, can hope to avert. Such difficulties, however, will neither discourage from exertion, nor prevent the most strenuous efforts on my part to repay your confidence.[11]

We must by no means assume that Douglas' only interests were in making money for his employers and furthering his own career. The moral and intellectual sides of life were as important to him as the commercial, and this is clearly borne out by the efforts he made to elevate the spiritual standards of both the Indians and the whites under his jurisdiction. Writing to the headquarters of the Company in London during the period when he was in temporary command at Fort Vancouver, he expounded at length his principles and plans. With regard to slavery, he was forced to concede that it would probably be a considerable time before the native tribes were induced to abandon this deeply imbedded feature of their way of life:

> I am most anxious to second your views, for suppressing the traffic of slaves, and have taken some steps towards the attainment of that object. I regret, however, that the state of feeling among the Natives of this river precludes every prospect of the immediate extinction of slavery, unless we resort to the very objectionable plan of a forcible emancipation. With the Natives, I have hitherto endeavoured to discourage the practice by the exertion of moral influence alone, carefully avoiding direct collision either with their selfish feelings or inveterate prejudices, as I do not feel justified in exposing our interests to the shock of excitement and desperate animosity which more active measures on our part might provoke. Against our own people, I took a more active part, and denounced slavery as a state contrary to law; tendering to all unfortunate persons held as slaves, by British subjects, the fullest protection in the enjoyment of their natural rights. I, soon after, seized a favourable opportunity of putting the law into force, by rescuing a runaway slave boy, who had been overtaken by his pursuers and brought here for punishment. He has since enjoyed his liberty, and served the company as a free labourer. These proceedings, so clearly destructive of the principle of slavery, would have roused a spirit of resistance in any people who know the value of liberty; but I am sorry, that the effect has been scarcely felt here, and I fear that all my efforts have virtually failed in rooting out the practical evil, even within the precincts of this settlement . . . The plan I now follow, of considering every person without distinction residing on our premises as free British subjects, who may, at any time, under the Company's protection, assert the exercise of their absolute and legal rights, will greatly mitigate the evils of slavery, by operating as a security against abuse, and making affection the only bond that supports the immoral system.[12]

With regard to education, Douglas had somewhat more hopeful news to report:

The Church and School have been fully engaged in promoting moral and religious improvement, by diffusing the seeds of sound principles and virtuous habits among the members of our own little community, and to a portion of the Native population. Their efforts have not been entirely fruitless, although the effect produced is not of so decided a character as to enable me to speak very confidently with reference to our future prospects.

The juvenile school continues in active operation, exerting on the youth who attend it a powerful and salutary influence, which will become more conspicuous as they advance in years, and attain rank and control over the society around them. The attention of the Revd. Mr. Beaver to the duties of his office has been exemplary, and I think he has succeeded in awakening a more general desire for religious knowledge among the persons of his communion, than existed previously to his arrival. His professional exertions have been unavoidably limited by the multitude of languages Native & Foreign that flourish here, placing almost insuperable obstacles in the way of religious Teachers, and, in a great measure, preventing that general acquaintance, and benevolent intercourse, with the lower classes, which, without degrading, so greatly extends the power & efficiency of the Clergy. While on the subject of morals, I may also mention that a Sunday School, conducted by Dr. Tolmie, who kindly volunteered his services, was opened last winter for the instruction of the Natives, which they attended in great numbers. The weekly lectures were delivered in the Native language, & conveyed some idea of the Divine Attributes, the certainty of a future state of retribution, the moral and social duties of man, illustrated by such familiar and striking images as were most likely to make an impression upon the minds of his rude audience. The more abstruse points of Theology were not introduced, from the difficulty of conveying them in appropriate terms, and besides, this attempt was intended merely as a preparatory step, to a more regular and elaborate course of instruction.[13]

As is evident from this letter, Douglas at first thought highly of the Fort's resident chaplain. Later, however, his opinions were to undergo a complete reversal. This was occasioned by an unfortunate series of incidents. The Rev. Herbert Beaver had been personally selected for his post by Governor George Simpson when on a visit to England in 1835-36; certainly his name seemed highly appropriate, and sailing from London in February 1836 on the *Nereide*, he had arrived via Honolulu at Fort Vancouver on September 6, 1836. One of his first acts had been to unite Douglas and Amelia Connolly in the official bonds of matrimony.[14]

Before long, however, serious difficulties arose. The views of the chaplain were rigid to the point of fanaticism; in particular, he considered the Fort school to be in effect an Anglican parish school, and was determined that its pupils should be taught the Anglican catechism, despite the fact that most of them were French-Canadian Roman Catholics. He also held common-law unions, of which there were many at the Fort, in abhorrence.

On both grounds, the minister objected strongly to McLoughlin. The latter had been baptized a Roman Catholic and was, after a lapse, to die one, and was at all times sympathetic to that faith. In any case, he felt in the position of a father toward his humbler associates, and perceived the turmoil that Beaver's policies were causing in them.

Even more serious in the chaplain's eyes were the numerous unsanctified unions at the Fort. Evidently considering that the rectification of this situation took precedence over Christian charity, he proposed that women not legally married should have their rations stopped and be denied free medical attention.[15] Failing to make progress (by his definition) in this regard, he resolved on a complaint to the highest officials of the Company in London, and in a lengthy letter poured out his grievances. Despite the fact that McLoughlin had been married to his helpmeet by Douglas in his capacity as justice of the peace,[16] and that she was, as Douglas declared in a letter written later to this superiors, "deservedly respected for her numerous charities, and many excellent qualities of heart",[17] Beaver did not hesitate to refer to Mrs. McLoughlin as "a female of notoriously loose character"[18] and "the kept mistress of the highest personage in your service".[19] When this report eventually came to the attention of McLoughlin, the doctor's rage burst its bounds, and, coming on the minister in the Fort grounds on March 19, 1838, he gave him a good thrashing.[20] Soon afterwards, McLoughlin was called away on business and Douglas was left in charge of the Fort for an extended period. However, it was not long before he, too, found himself in a state of icy hostility to the chaplain.

This was occasioned by the minister having declared to the senior officials of the Company in London his horror "when I see the principal house in your Establishment made a common receptacle for every Mistress of an Officer in the service, who may take a fancy to visit the Fort".[21] Douglas, on learning this, immediately asked for an explanation. The chaplain was unable to furnish one, other than to assure Douglas that the latter was not one of those he had in mind. This by no means satisfied Douglas, and he penned a frosty communication to the chaplain on October 2, 1838, saying:

To have given the explanation I requested would have been but an act of simple justice, and your refusal to grant it leaves me but the single alternative of considering your assertions, respecting the inmates of my dwelling, to be equally false in fact, as malicious and slanderous in design.

I remain,
Sir,
Your very obt. servant,
James Douglas.[22]

A few days later, Douglas made a long report to the Governors of the HBC, giving a full account of the whole affair, in which the dignity of his language only formally masked his anger. Among other things, he declared:

I may further add that no person is permitted to make fancy visits, and I neither have nor would suffer any person, of whatever rank, to introduce loose women into this Fort, an attempt which to the honour of every gentleman here, was never made.[23]

Douglas ended his report with a few general reflections:

A clergyman in this country must quit the closet & live a life of beneficent activity, devoted to the support of principles, rather than of forms; he must shun discord, avoid uncharitable feelings, temper zeal with discretion, illustrate precept by example, and the obdurate rock upon which we have been so long hammering in vain will soon be broken into fragments.[24]

The chaplain soon afterwards (November 1838) shook the dust of Fort Vancouver from his feet and returned to London, arriving there in May 1839. His experiences, however, had by no means left him contrite, and he poured out his bile in a long article in the *Church of England Protestant Magazine* for March 1841. He described his effusion as "an exposure of the ramifications of Popery",[25] and said that at Fort Vancouver he had found McLoughlin, whom he labelled "this monster in human shape", permitting the children to be given instruction in the Catholic catechism by a Company employee "living, like himself and most of the other persons at the factory, in open defiance of the laws of God and man".[26] The minister even to some extent regretted his hasty departure, expressing the belief that

> I feel confident that I could, covered by the shield of faith, have taken the Papal bull by the horns; and, aided by the sword of the Spirit, have expelled the hydra-headed monster from the north-eastern Shores of the Pacific . . . [27]

Perhaps not altogether regrettably, at this point the Rev. Beaver disappears from the history of the northwest,[28] and, under Douglas' direction, affairs went forward smoothly until the return of McLoughlin.[29]

Then in 1840 Douglas was again sent on his travels, this time into the mists of the North Pacific. It was thought desirable by the senior officials of the Company that various matters in dispute between the two great fur companies, British and Russian, should be amicably resolved, and to this end Douglas was ordered to proceed to Sitka, Alaska, and there hold discussions with his "opposite number".

Accordingly on April 22, 1840 he set out in the now indispensable *Beaver*. Two days later he was at Cowlitz Farm, and not long afterwards an incident took place which might well have ended his career forever. In the event, however, it was to show not only the moral and physical fibre he was made of, but also, perhaps, prefigure the days of 1858 when in a very different way it was to be shown that in a moment of crisis one man's prompt unflinching action can be decisive.

> From our own ignorance of the road and the culpable negligence of the guide, who loitered all morning at a distance in the rear, we missed the Nisqually Ford, and attempted to gain the opposite shore at

a place where the current ran deep and strong, a mistake that nearly cost the life of one of our leading men, who dashed into the river without any suspicion of danger, and was swept away, after advancing a few steps, into the deepest part of the stream. Dreadfully alarmed I rode out to his assistance, shouting at the same time to a number of Indians present to lend their aid.

The air and water were icy cold, and a huge pile of drift trees a few yards below, under which the stream was urging its furious course, threatened destruction to any who should be hardy enough to approach it. The presence of a danger so appalling daunted the boldest spirits; the contagion weighed upon my own mind, and I confess with shame that I did not feel that cheerful alacrity in rushing to the rescue as at other times. Even then I could not allow a fellow creature to perish before me without an effort to save him while the inactivity of all present was an additional incentive to redouble my own exertions. With a sensation of dread and an almost hopelessness of success I pushed my horse by spur and whip nearly across the river, sprang into the water and rushed towards the spot where the near exhausted sufferer was clinging with his head above water to the end of a tree which had fallen into the river; upon its trunk I dragged myself out on all fours and great was our mutual joy when I seized him firmly by the collar and with the aid of a canoe that arrived soon after landed him safely on the banks where a blazing fire shortly restored warmth to both; and to my latest breath may I cherish the remembrance of Lasserte's providential rescue from a watery grave, as I could never otherwise have enjoyed tranquillity of mind.[30]

Soon afterwards Douglas' party reached Fort Langley thirty miles up the Fraser River. Founded in 1827,[31] it was intended to become a major depot of the Company, and, if the Fraser had been more easily navigable, no doubt would have done so. When Douglas arrived there, he found that a serious fire had destroyed most of the buildings; his party gave what help it could in rebuilding them and then descended the river to the sea, from there proceeding up the western coast of the continent by way of the "Inside Passage". By May 7 he had reached the Indian settlement of Comox on Vancouver Island where he bought fifty beaver skins from the natives noting that they were "numerous, saucy and un-reclaimed by the discipline or influence of the whites". Later he touched at Fort McLoughlin on May 11, where he took on board supplies of food and fuel. Fort Simpson was reached on May 14, Stikine on the 20th, and finally on May 25, he arrived at Sitka.

Here, in his own words, "I held daily conference with the Governor, in a frank and open manner, so as to dissipate all semblance of reserve and establish our intercourse on a basis of mutual confidence". Douglas also recorded that, "We settled the question of boundary in a manner that will prevent any future misunderstanding", and that, "We con-versed on a great variety of business subjects and several exchanges of furs were proposed, which would be a mutual benefit . . . "

Some indication that the present world-wide network of trade was already taking shape may be found in Douglas' account. He noted for example, of the Russian company that " . . . for instance they get remarkably cheap shoes and can give us 200 pairs of boots next autumn at 5/- each, procured on contract from Finland"; also that "their fur trade produced annually about 25,000 beaver & otter and the profits on the business altogether do not exceed 20 per cent upon the capital em-ployed; the furs are sent to the Chinese frontier and exchanged for teas at the rate of 75 roubles or 15 dollars per otter and 15 roubles for beaver skins."

No doubt Douglas' relations with his Russian hosts were friendly; but this did not prevent his shrewd observant eye from noting features of their commercial organization that were, is his opinion, unsound:

> The business of the Russian American Company does not appear to be conducted with system or that degree of well judged economy, so necessary in extensive concerns.
>
> The two establishments I have visited are crowded with men and officers, living in idleness or in employments equally unnecessary and profitless to the business; the officers almost all belong to the Imperial service and besides their pay from Government have an allowance from the Company, and after 5 years service they may return to Europe. They are allowed rations of bread and meat, but every-thing else is provided at their own expense. The labouring servants are brought out on contracts of five years, at 350 roubles per annum with a monthly allowance of 40 lbs. of coarse flour and as much fish as they can use by way of rations; this period of servitude procures them an exemption from 25 years service in the Imperial armies.

A decidedly vicious and ill advised feature in the management of this business is the appointment of naval officers, a class of men ignorant of and by their previous habits of life the most unqualified to manage commercial undertakings, to the principal direction, and these after holding their stations five years, and acquiring some knowledge of business, are withdrawn and replaced by others, who have also everything to learn & who are like manner removed at the moment they are qualified to render efficient service.

On the 29th of May Douglas' party left Sitka; on the first of June, as had been agreed upon during the negotiations, it took possession of Fort Stikine, firing a salute of seven guns and raising the British flag. Then, after touching briefly at Fort Simpson, Douglas proceeded to the mouth of the Taku (or Taco) River, in which area it was proposed to build a new Company trading post. After examining and rejecting several possible sites, a suitable one was found, and on June 23 its construction was commenced.

It is interesting to note the factors which decided the location, since they were to be repeated almost exactly when the time came for Douglas to build a more important post on southern Vancouver Island: " . . . it is well adapted for our purpose, possessing a safe harbour, sufficient level ground for building and abundance of fine building timber; our choice has accordingly fallen here and we will begin operations without delay".

We might note here an unfortunate though not really serious incident that took place at about this time. Douglas describes it in detail and with remarkable vividness; even at the distance of a hundred and thirty years one senses the wounded pride of men "dressed in a little brief authority" and not disposed to discard it:

I will here relate an incident connected with our short stay at Stikine. I mentioned in the entry made on the 31st May that we turned out the hands to take in wood after 5 o'clock, and kept them at work until 7 at night. The Captain appeared unwilling to drive them so hard, as it might make them grumble, and was moreover against the rules of the ship, the general working hours being from six to six. The reason given did not appear to me to possess great weight, and in despite of these consequences of which I stood in no fear, I requested that the hands might be immediately put to work and was obeyed. The following day being Sunday the men were allowed to rest; the Captain early in the day went ashore and remained there till night.

We had prayers on board between 1 and 2 o'clock at which many of the men attended; we assembled for the purpose on the quarter deck and there being appearance of rain, I told the mate to get the awning spread and after service to remove it. At four o'clock in the afternoon, my anxiety to hasten our departure overcoming religious scruples, I ordered the mate, the Captain being still absent, to set all hands to take in wood, and we brought off nearly all we wanted before night. On the following morning I observed the Captain sitting in the cabin in low spirits, as if suffering from some painful impression; he hastily addressed himself to me, saying, in an agitated tone of voice, Mr. Douglas, if you interfere with the duties of the ship, I will leave her as soon as we get to Fort Simpson. In what instance, Sir, have I interfered with the ship's duties? In ways which I cannot exactly remember, but still you have done so. You would oblige me, Sir, by more explicit information; it was never my intention to do anything on board of this ship to diminish the respect due to you; however in my ignorance of naval routine I may have inadvertently tres-passed on some point of etiquette, that I wish you to point out, in order to avoid it in future.

Why the mate an hour ago inquired of me, whose orders am I to obey, yours or Mr. Douglas. Aye, call him. Mr. (*word missing*), why did you put such a question to the Captain, repeating what he had said. Because, Sir, you gave me several orders yesterday when the Captain was on shore; you told me to furl and unfurl the awning, and to send the men for wood. Did I ever tell you, sir, to disobey the Captain's orders? No Sir, well Sir, you have acted very improperly, in a manner more becoming an inmate of the forecastle than a Gentleman and Officer; I have supported you, sir, against the wishes of others when no one would have you, perhaps to the prejudice of more deserving men. Well, Captain McNeill I refuse duty, sir, and with that pert remark he left the cabin. Irritated at his conduct, I hurried, a minute afterwards, on deck after him, and ordered him to the cabin; he obeyed reluctantly, I seized him by his jacket collar, but recollecting myself on his shouting you lay violent hands on me, I released him instantly, and he followed me quietly into the cabin. I then stated that though I had no intention of interfering with the duties or management of the ship, my orders must under any circumstances be obeyed, by every person in the Company's service here, whether Master or Mate; at the same time, addressing myself to the Mate, you are, at present, under the Captain's orders and you, sir, would have acted more in character had you on receiving my orders, said you were ready to attend to them, but thought that in doing so, you interfered with the rules of the ship.

I would, in such a case, have referred you to the Captain; but ignorant as I was of these rules until this moment, I naturally made Application to the Officer on board for such things as I wanted done. This is the only solitary instance which can be produced of any thing which can the most remotely be construed into an act of intermeddling on my part, and had I suspected it would cause any unpleasant feeling I would have taken another course, but such a reflection never occurred to me, and truly in a person at the head of affairs, who bears the weight of responsibility and whose mind is on the rack devising ways and means to expedite our over backward operations, methinks such trifles, light as air, are like feathers in the balance.

This contretemps was not the only regrettable aspect of the voyage. Poor weather, so common on the north Pacific coast, dogged Douglas' party during the erection of Fort Taku, and even though it was midsummer, for days the sky was overcast or wet. On July 25, Douglas recorded that

. . . it is so long since we had a view of the bright blue sky, or the sun's cheerful face, that we feel an indescribable longing for the sight, which in process of time we may feel a disposition to register among the remarkable events of the period.

The next day was hardly better, but fortunately it was Sunday, and no work had to be done:

Raining very slightly. Peace and stillness in our camp, we have prayers in the French language every Sunday evening.

Two days later, the weather finally improved:

Dry weather. Enjoyed the singular felicity of seeing a dim outline of the sun, as the rays of light struggled to break through the masses of vapour that were intercepting their passage to the earth.

Finally on the fifth of August, Fort Taku (sometimes known as Fort Durham) was completed, with two bastions and a stockade. Soon afterwards Douglas sailed away, leaving a small garrison at the Fort to trade with the Indians and struggle with the climate. Late in the month he was briefly at Fort Stikine, early in September at Fort McLoughlin,[32] in the middle of the month at Texada Island (then called Feveda), and finally on September 21 at Fort Langley. Here he took on board some cattle for Fort Vancouver, arriving there October 2.

The voyage had, indeed, been highly successful. Not only had a useful agreement been made with the Russian company; a substantial quantity of beaver and otter pelts had been purchased from the Indians, two forts had been added to the chain of HBC posts along the coast, and much information about Russian ways of business had been gleaned. It seemed only fitting that some suitable reward should be given to the man who had furthered so notably the affairs of his employers, and this now fell to his lot. Waiting for him when he returned to Fort Vancouver was his commission as Chief Factor.

Little time was accorded him, however, to rest on these newly won laurels. He had just returned from the fiords in the northern mists; now, with hardly time for a "breather", he was to find himself under the harsh glare of a southern sun. He received instructions to proceed to California and there conduct negotiations with the Mexican authorities on various matters in dispute. Obedient as always to the orders of those above him, he set out almost immediately, once again keeping a detailed journal of everything he thought important. His first entry is dated Thursday, 3rd December, 1840:

> Left Fort Vancouver this morning at 8 o'clock with Mr. Wood and six men with two Indians, to join the "Columbia" at Fort George; we are afterwards to proceed with an adventure of goods to California, with the view jointly of purchasing the produce of that country and forwarding a large herd of live stock by the overland route to the Columbia, under escort of a party of 30 officers and men now on board the vessel.
>
> We have also other objects of a political nature in view, which may or may not succeed according to circumstances, but in the event of success, the results will be important.[33]

Poor weather was encountered on the voyage, and Douglas, no sailor, was soon meditating gloomily while the anchored ship rode out a storm:

> To us landsmen the prospect around is sufficiently gloomy, danger on every side, and our safety depending on a chain, one defective link in which might prove our destruction.

Christmas Day was passed at sea, with Douglas so overcome with *mal de mer* as to be incapable of the usual celebrations. However, on New Year's Day 1841 the ship came safely into harbor at Monterey, and soon afterward Douglas began his delicate negotiations with Governor Alvaredo, whom he described as "a middle-sized man, rather stout, good looking, with a harassed jaded air".

At first there seemed a certain coolness in the atmosphere, which Douglas wisely resolved to bear patiently:

> He received us with a sort of reserved courtesy, that made us feel rather uncomfortable; I saw there was something wrong, some lurking suspicion of fancied encroachments, or meditated deception on my part, and I prepared to remove them; to resent such conduct would have been more manly and was the first impulse of my own feelings; but second thoughts are best and in this instance I found the truth of the adage as in course of conversation this stiffness of manner wore off, and he insensibly entered with great spirit into the matters under discussion.

Douglas' negotiations with Alvaredo dealt with three main matters: the activities of HBC fur-traders in California, the exclusive use of Mexican ships for coastal shipping, and the purchase of cattle for Fort Vancouver.

In the case of the first of these, we can sense in the background the advancing frontier and its corollary, the retreat of the wilderness. The previous year, Douglas had received a letter from a Captain Souter (or Sutter), telling him to move HBC trappers away from the coastal valleys of California and back into the hinterland; as Douglas had seen no reason to admit Sutter's authority, he had ignored his orders. Alvaredo, however, declared that he had authorized Sutter to act in this manner, and Douglas now agreed that he would accede to these instructions.

Douglas on his part complained that only Mexican vessels were permitted to engage in trade between Mexican ports. Alvaredo, however, refused to give way on this point, explaining that he was merely acting on orders from higher authority. Douglas from his own experience well understood the force of this argument, but "warmly contested the justice of this proceeding". Eventually a compromise was reached by which the HBC could engage in coastwise trade provided its ships had Mexican captains and sailed under the Mexican flag.

As regards the third matter to be discussed, agreement was quickly reached. Alvaredo sold Douglas a number of good cattle, though at high prices, and arrangements were made for a party of Douglas' men to drive them northward to the Columbia.

So ended this successful mission, but, as in the case of the similar one to Alaska, not before Douglas had made careful notes of his brief but shrewd insights into the Californian government, economic conditions, and national character. He recorded, for example, the uneasy rivalry between the civil and military authorities that has been a persistent feature of Latin American affairs:

> The Government of California is administered by a Governor-in-chief and a General of the Forces; the former possesses a nominal control which the latter does not in all cases submit to. These appointments are held under the supreme Government of Mexico. The Customs and Commissariat Departments are managed by officers also holding distinct appointments from the supreme government, and who exercise their peculiar powers independently of the Governor.
> The sole legislative power of the country is vested in a Junta Departmental or Deputation, annually convened at Monterey. It consists of seven members, being one for each district elected by committees of citizens, chosen for the purpose by the general body of house-holders in each District. The Junta possesses great power, its decisions can be reversed only by an act of the supreme Government, the local authorities having no power to do so, the Governor having merely the honorary privilege of presiding at their meetings without a voice in their decisions . . .
> The judicial authority is that of Alcalde or Justice of the Peace, an office seldom adequately filled by persons of education or a competent knowledge of the existing laws . . . There is no judicial

organization in the country beyond the appointment of Alcalde, and an inferior officer in the country for deciding disputes arising between farmers about their cattle. Courts of Justice are unknown, so that crimes remain unpunished or are visited with instant vengeance by the decision of the Governor . . .

The annual expenses of Government are 100,000 Dollars, the import duties vary from 40 to 60,000 Dollars, the balance the persons in office must scrape together the best way they can by despoiling the missions and disposing of public property; as Mexico does not contribute a real to the support of California.

As to what commercial policies the HBC should pursue in this area, Douglas had come to a firm decision. It should not, as various business firms were doing, engage in direct sales to individuals, which meant employing an army of travelling salesmen and being saddled with numerous bad debts.

. . . we ought to confine our attention to a wholesale business, supplying the country merchants with goods, and receiving payments from them in hides, tallow and grain. By pushing this plan we would be secure from great risks, a much less expensive establishment would be necessary, the presence of a vessel would not be constantly required on the coast, and with these advantages we might calculate on doing a safe and profitable business, whereas the retail trade would involve us in heavy expenses, and we have no people competent to carry it on and compete with the clever active men now engaged in it, who speak the language fluently, and know almost every person in California.

Finally, after a series of notes on prices and wages in the region, Douglas concludes this section of his journal with some general observations. His views on the national character seem to suggest that in this respect the passage of a century and the transfer of sovereignty have not perhaps effected a total revolution:

The Californian is proud, lazy and passionate; but kind and hospitable; the vices and virtues of a badly regulated but generous mind.

There were, however, two clouds in this otherwise clear southern

Sir James Douglas, Governor of Vancouver Island, 1851 - 1864, and of British Columbia, 1858 - 1864

John Tod, in charge of Fort McLeod where Douglas arrived in 1825

Sir George Simpson, Governor of the Hudson's Bay Company in North America

Dr. John McLoughlin, *Chief Factor of the Hudson's Bay Company on the Pacific coast*

sky. One was the remarkably high number of murders committed every year; the other was a certain lack of linguistic propriety:

> I hear from the most inexceptionable authority that the Ladies in California are not in general very refined or delicate in their conversation, using gross expressions and indulging in broad remarks which would make modest women blush.

These, however, were only minor blemishes, and the general impression that Douglas received was highly favorable:

> California is a country in many respects unrivalled by any other part of the globe; it enjoys a pleasant salubrious climate, a serene sky in summer, while in winter copious rains moisten and fertilize the earth; the soil is of various kinds and excellent in all, the valleys are extensive and divided by lines of mountains and green hills furnishing streams of water which diffuse fertility among the plains beneath . . . There is no country that has more attractions than California.

Indeed, it seems possible that at stray moments during his visit there, Douglas was tempted not to leave. This at least is the suggestion left by a letter written on his return to a friend:

> . . . I would nevertheless cheerfully become a citizen of that country provided that I could do so in company with a party of friends respectable from their numbers, and powerful enough to restrain oppression . . . In fact, I could have obtained a handsome grant of land on a simple application; but my views are not yet fixed as to the future.[34]

Yet the moment of temptation clearly soon passed—perhaps if Douglas had not had a recent important promotion the struggle might have been harder—and he returned once more to his duties at Fort Vancouver in the spring of 1841, no doubt glad to rest from his travels.

His rest was not to be a long one. Sir George Simpson had decided on yet another tour of inspection of the far-flung HBC empire; leaving London in March, he had arrived in the course of time on the Pacific coast, where Douglas, in the absence of McLoughlin, received him at Fort Vancouver on August 25, 1841. After inspecting the Company farm at Cowlitz, Simpson, accompanied by Douglas, set out for

Sitka, where conversations were held with Russian officials concerning matters of common interest. The voyage naturally gave Governor Simpson many opportunities to judge the character and abilities of the Company's rising star in the northwest, and also to make decisions regarding its future operations in that area. Among these were that Forts Stikine and Taku should be abandoned, and their functions taken over by the *Beaver*, which could be sent on an annual trading expedition.

It was also in this period that it was decided to establish a new post in the southern part of Vancouver Island. As early as 1837 Capt. McNeill[35] had explored this area in the *Beaver*, and found an excellent harbor and fertile soil. Now Governor Simpson, writing to his superiors from Honolulu on March 1, 1842, outlined his views:

> The southern end of Vancouver's Island, forming the northern side of the Straits of De Fuca, appears to me the best situation for such an establishment. From the very superficial examination that has been made, it is ascertained there are several good harbours in that neighborhood; no place, however, has yet been found combining all the advantages required, the most important of which are, a safe and accessible harbour, well situated for defence, with water power for grist and saw mills, abundance of timber for home consumption and exportation and the adjacent country well adapted for tillage and pasture farms on an extensive scale. I had not an opportunity for landing on the southern end of the Island, but from the distant view we had of it in passing between Puget's Sound and the Gulf of Georgia and the report of C.F. McLoughlin and others who have been there, we have every reason to believe there will be no difficulty in finding an eligible situation in that quarter for the establishment in question.[36]

Simpson also saw two other advantages in the location: it would be a convenient centre for whale and salmon fishing, and would strengthen Great Britain's claim to the whole of Vancouver Island. Although he was nominally the subordinate of Sir John Pelly,[37] in London, Simpson's recommendations had the force of law, and the decision was not opposed. All that was needed was to assign the most competent man available to survey the area and report his findings. Inevitably, the choice fell on Douglas.

And so it was that in the summer of 1842 he came at last to where his eventual destiny awaited him—and where in due course his bones would one day rest. It would still be nine years before he became the first servant of the Crown in the colony of Vancouver Island; sixteen before —largely through his wisdom, energy and force of character—the final disposition of that Island and a large part of the nearby mainland would be decided. But the stage was set, the curtain was rising; soon the high drama would begin. The body hardened in the northern winters and on the long trail; the mind made shrewd by commerce, deep by study, wide-ranging by contact with many sorts of men; the will that had borne him into the unknown unflinching; all these he would now bring with him to new tasks and trials. He was not yet forty; yet already he could say, in the words that on the other side of the world Tennyson was writing of the ancient Greek voyager Ulysses:

> I am become a name:
> For always roaming with a hungry heart
> Much have I seen and known; cities of men
> And manners, climates, councils, governments,
> Myself not least but honoured of them all.

So in the long summer days of 1842, a new chapter opened in the life of Douglas. The volume's later pages were as yet unturned, but to him this was no deterrent. Obedient to his superiors and to the larger unseen power behind events, he did what he had always done: his duty and the task at hand. Often before he had faced challenges; each time he had met them in fair fight and conquered them. Now, once again, destiny and duty called. He was ready; he would go.

NOTES

[1] Some of his ideas were decidedly advanced. On Feb. 27, 1841 he wrote to a friend: ". . . I am certain that the time must come when even the House of Lords in Britain will be elected" (letter to Edward Ermatinger in Ermatinger Papers, Provincial Archives, Victoria). McLoughlin also approved of Papineau, one of the leaders of the rebellion of 1837, a fact that did not endear him to his superior, Sir George Simpson.
Useful books on McLoughlin are *John McLoughlin: Father of Oregon* by Robert C. Johnson, Metropolitan Press, Portland, Oregon, 1935; *The white-headed eagle* by Richard G. Montgomery, Macmillan, New York,

1934; *Dr. John McLoughlin the Father of Oregon* by Frederick V. Holman, Arthur H. Clark Company, Cleveland, Ohio, 1907; *Letters of Dr. John McLoughlin, 1829-1832* by B. B. Barker, Bintfords and Mort, Portland, Oregon, 1948; E. E. Rich (ed.), *The letters of John McLoughlin, first series, 1825-1838*, Toronto, Champlain Society, 1941.

2 Bancroft, *History of British Columbia*, San Francisco, 1890, p. 300.

3 Bancroft, *History of Oregon*, San Francisco, 1890, pp. 7-8.

4 Quoted in *Washington Historical Quarterly*, Vol. II, No. 1, October 1907, p. 43.

5 Douglas MacKay, *The Honourable Company*, McClelland and Stewart, Toronto, 1936, p. 200.

6 York Factory was on Hudson's Bay, between the mouths of the Hayes and Nelson Rivers. It was founded in 1682 by Pierre Radisson and Medard Grosseilliers. Located almost at the centre of Canada, it could be reached by sea from Europe; yet, with portages, it was connected by water as far as Edmonton, 1000 miles to the west. The post was shut down on June 29, 1957. See article in the Victoria *Colonist* for April 13, 1958.

7 Douglas was always much interested in natural phenomena. Dr. Helmcken reported, "I have heard Mr. Douglas expatiate on the beauties and flowers, and how much he was enamoured by his first exploration of Victoria District and Beacon Hill." (Reminiscences, III. p. 39)

8 The full list of Douglas' 13 children, as taken from the family tree in the Provincial Archives, is as follows:

Amelia	1829-1830
Alexander	1831-1834
John	1833-1833
Maria	1834-1835
Cecilia (Mrs. J. S. Helmcken)	1834-1865
Ellen	1836-1837
Jane (Mrs. A. G. Dallas)	1839-1909
Agnes (Mrs. Arthur Bushby)	1841-1928
Alice (Mrs. Charles Good)	1844-1913
Margaret	1846-1848
Rebecca	1849-1849
James	1851-1883
Martha (Mrs. Dennis Harris)	1854-1933

9 A model of it may be seen in the Provincial Archives at Victoria, and a photograph in my *Victoria: The Fort* (Mitchell Press, Vancouver, 1968). It was eventually wrecked off Prospect Point near Vancouver in 1888. See "The Advent of the Beaver" by W. K. Lamb, *BCHQ*, Vol. II, No. 3, July 1938, pp. 163-179.

10 Peter Skene Ogden technically "outranked" Douglas, but he was usually absent with the fur brigades. See W. N. Sage, "James Douglas on the Columbia, 1830-1849", *Oregon Historical Society Quarterly*, XXVII, 1926, p. 379.

11 Douglas to Simpson, March 18, 1838. Provincial Archives, Victoria.

12 Douglas to Governor and Committee, Oct. 18, 1838. PABC.

13 Douglas to Governor and Committee, October 18, 1838.
William Fraser Tolmie, M.D., was born in Inverness, Scotland, in 1812

and came to Fort Vancouver in 1833. He eventually became a Chief Factor of the HBC, and came to Victoria in 1859, dying there in 1886. His diary has been published by Mitchell Press of Vancouver under the title *William Fraser Tolmie, Physician and Fur Trader.*

14 They had already had six children, of whom four had died in previous years, and another died at about this time. The date of the ceremony was Feb. 28, 1837, and the marriage licence is in the Provincial Archives at Victoria. A photograph of the page of the marriage register recording Douglas' marriage may be seen in the *BCHQ*, Vol. VI, No. 1, January, 1942, facing p. 22.

15 "The James Douglas Report on the 'Beaver Affair', ed. W. K. Lamb, *OHSQ*, XLVII, No. 1, March 1946, p. 22.

16 The McLoughlins were later married again by the Roman Catholic Bishop Blanchet.

17 Lamb, *Op. Cit.,* p. 21.

18 *Ibid.,* p. 17.

19 *Loc. Cit.*

20 See in this connection a letter by John Work to Edward Ermatinger, dated Sept. 10, 1838, in the *Washington Historical Quarterly* for April 1908, pp. 261-262.

21 "The James Douglas report on the 'Beaver Affair', ed. W. K. Lamb, *OHSQ*, XLVII, No. 1, March 1946, p. 23.

22 Lamb, *Ibid.,* p. 24.

23 *Ibid.,* p. 25.

24 *Ibid.,* p. 28.

25 "Experiences of a Chaplain at Fort Vancouver 1836-1838", by Herbert Beaver. Reprinted in *OHSQ*, March 1938, p. 22.

26 *Ibid.,* p. 25.

27 *Ibid.,* p. 37.

28 Beaver's subsequent career may be traced in G. Hollis Slater, "New Light on Herbert Beaver", *BCHQ*, VI No. 1, January 1942, pp. 13-29.

29 We might note that during this period Douglas welcomed to the Fort the Roman Catholic fathers Blanchet and Demers. The latter was destined in the course of time to become Bishop of Vancouver Island.

30 This, and the other quotations dealing with this expedition, are from an unpublished manuscript in the Provincial Archives, Victoria.

31 And in restored form a well-known tourist attraction today. The site of the Fort was moved a short distance not long after it was founded.

32 This appears to be a depressing spot. Charles Ross, destined to become the first Chief Factor of Fort Victoria, wrote to a friend from Fort McLoughlin on April 24, 1843: "Than our way of life in this dreary wilderness nothing can be more dark and insipid. The posts we occupy, though many, are far between, and seldom have any intercourse with each other oftener than once a year, and then for the most part it is for the purpose of exchanging cargoes of merchandise for cargoes of furs. There is no society—that is, the person in charge must divert himself the best way he can with his own thoughts". (*BCHQ*, Vol. VII, No. 2, April 1943, p. 109). Sir George Simpson, who had seen all the Company's posts, agreed in a letter to Ross that " . . . it was decidedly the most dismal, gloomy place I was ever in, & surrounded by the most cut-throat looking rascals I think I ever met with." (*Ibid.,* p. 117).

[33] This and other quotations dealing with this expedition are taken from an unpublished manuscript in the Provincial Archives, Victoria. See also in this connection Dorothy Blakey Smith, *James Douglas in California, 1841*, The Library's Press, Vancouver, 1965.

[34] Douglas to A. C. Anderson, April 20, 1841. PABC.

[35] McNeill eventually built a house on the shores of McNeill Bay, Victoria (named after him), and died there on Sept. 3, 1875. He held, we might note, one rather interesting theory: "From wrecks of Chinese junks discovered by him and found years ago, he had no doubt of the discovery in ages gone of this continent by the Chinese and Japanese". (Angus McDonald, "A few items of the west", *Washington Historical Quarterly*, July 1917, p. 219). Douglas in a letter to his daughter Martha, dated May 30, 1873, says that a Japanese junk was wrecked at Cape Flattery in 1834.
McNeill Bay later became generally known as Shoal Bay. Shortly after the end of the first world war, a petition was organized by his grandson, D. H. McNeill, and signed by numerous residents of Oak Bay, asking that the name be officially gazetted as McNeill Bay. The Geographical Board of Canada sanctioned this move (see *Colonist* for Feb. 15, 1919), and the area is listed as McNeill Bay in the *Gazetteer of Canada* (1953 edition).

[36] Transcript in PABC. McLoughlin made his only visit to Vancouver Island in the fall of 1839. His name is commemorated by McLoughlin Point in Victoria Harbor.

[37] Pelly was born in 1777, became Governor of the HBC in 1822, and died in 1852. Pelly Inlet in Victoria Harbor is named after him.

CHAPTER FOUR

The Founding
Of Fort Victoria

THE SUMMER of 1842 saw the final preparations for the founding of the new outpost of the Company on Vancouver Island. Sir George Simpson, with the reluctant concurrence of John McLoughlin, had decided that such a step must be taken. Americans were flooding into the "Oregon Territory", and it now appeared inevitable that the area would soon form part of the expanding Union. Of the parts of the Northwest unlikely to fall under American control, the mouth of the Fraser had already been considered and rejected as the new headquarters of the Company on the Pacific coast, a decisive factor being the virtual impossibility of navigating the river's fierce inland rapids as well as the changing channel in the shallow estuarial basin. This pointed to Vancouver Island as the best location for the new trading depot, and this conclusion was formalized by the Council of the Northern Department of Rupert's Land, which passed a resolution in 1842 that "an eligible site for such a Depot be selected, and that measures be adopted for forming this Establishment with the least possible delay". The Council also decided "that the New Establishment to be formed on the Straits of De Fuca to be named Fort Victoria be erected on a scale sufficiently extensive to answer the purposes of the Depot; the square of the Fort to be not less than 150 yards, the buildings to be substantial and erected as far apart as the grounds may admit with a view to guarding against fire". Another decision of the Council was that "Chief Factor McLoughlin take the necessary steps for abandoning the posts of Fort McLoughlin and

Taku in summer 1842, and the post of Stikine in summer 1844; and for fitting the *Beaver* steamer to secure the trade usually collected at these abandoned establishments".

Accordingly, Douglas set out in the summer of 1842 with six men in the schooner *Cadboro*, with orders to make a thorough investigation of the southern part of the Island, and to submit his findings to his superiors. His report to John McLoughlin,[1] dated July 12, 1842, is an illuminating document, revealing not only the methodical and rational nature of the Chief Factor's mind, but also the considerations which he weighed in deciding among the various possible sites for the new depot.

Four possible locations particularly engaged his attention: those which he called by their Indian names (as he understood them) of "Sy-yousung", "Metsho-sin", "Is-whoy-malth" and "Camosack", but which are today known as Sooke, Metchosin, Esquimalt and Victoria. Each had some attractions, but in each case except the last Douglas felt that these were outweighed by their disadvantages.

In the case of "Sy-yousung", Douglas reported that it was

> . . . a spacious inlet extending more than two miles into the country; where shipping may lie at all seasons of the year in perfect safety, as it is protected from every wind; there is however a strong current setting through the entrance, with the flood and ebb that might detain and prove inconvenient to vessels entering or leaving port; otherwise it is unexceptionable as a harbour.
>
> A shallow rivulet 30 feet wide, which takes its rise from a lake in the interior of the Island, falls into the north end of the Inlet, remarkable as being the largest and only fresh water stream capable of floating a canoe that we found on this part of the Island.
>
> It can however hardly be called navigable, as during a short excursion I made upon it, we had to drag our canoe over banks of gravel that traverse the bed of the stream at every hundred yards. An extensive mud flat also lies off its mouth, which is nearly dry and impassable in the smallest craft at low water. It has also the reputation of being a good fishing stream, and as far as I could learn from the natives of the place, a considerable quantity of salmon is caught there annually; a consideration which would make it exceed- ingly valuable to an establishment. These are the only good points of this harbour, which the character of the country in its vicinity render

to no avail, as the place is totally unfit for the purpose, the shores being high, steep, rocky, and everywhere covered with woods. In ranging through the forest we found one small plain containing 3 or 400 acres of land at the distance of one mile from the harbour; but the rest of the country in its neighbourhood appeared to consist either of wood land or rocky hills.

"Metsho-sin" was also, in Douglas' opinion, unsuitable:

Metsho-sin is an open roadstead one and a half miles east of the former port. It is a very pretty place, and has a small fresh water run near it. There is however no harbour and the anchorage is exposed and must be insecure in rough weather; in addition to that dis- advantage, the extent of clear ground is much too small for the demands of a large establishment, and a great part of what is clear is poor stony land with rolling surface, so that on the whole it would not do for us.

"Is-whoy-malth" seemed more promising, but it, too, had serious drawbacks.

It is one of the best harbours on the coast, being perfectly safe and of easy access; but in other respects it possesses no attraction.

Its appearance is strikingly unprepossessing, the outline of the country exhibiting a confused assemblage of rock and wood.

More distant appear isolated ridges thinly covered with scattered trees and masses of bare rock, and the view is closed by a range of low mountains which traverse the island at the distance of about 12 miles. The shores of the harbour are rugged and precipitous, and I did not see one level spot, clear of trees, of sufficient extent to build a large Fort upon. There is in fact no clear land within a quarter of a mile of the harbour, and that lies in small patches here and there, on the aclivities and bottoms of the rising ground. At a greater distance are two elevated plains, on different sides of the harbour, containing several bottoms of rich land, the largest of which does not exceed 50 acres, of clear space, much broken by masses of limestone and granite.

Another serious objection to this place is the scarcity of fresh water. There are several good runs in winter, but we found them all dried up, and we could not manage to fill a single breaker in the harbour.

Much more suitable than any of these three sites was that of "Camosack", since it had a good anchorage, extensive nearby land suitable for farming, abundant timber, and a convenient location for possible sawmills or flour mills. In the words of Douglas:

. . . at Camosack there is a pleasant and convenient site for the establishment, within 50 yards of the anchorage, on the border of a large tract of clear land, which extends eastward to Point Gonzalo[2] at the south-east extremity of the Island and about 6 miles interiorly, being the most picturesque and decidedly the most valuable part of the Island that we had the good fortune to discover . . .

More than two thirds of this section consists of prairie land and may be converted either to the purposes of tillage or pasture, for which I have seen no part of the Indian Country better adapted; the rest of it with the exception of the ponds of water is covered with valuable oak and pine timber. I observed, generally speaking, but two marked varieties of soil on these prairies, that of the best land is a dark vegetable mould, varying from 9 to 14 inches in depth, overlaying a substrate of grayish clayey loam which produces the rankest growth of native plants that I have seen in America. The other variety is of inferior value, and to judge from the less vigorous appearance of the vegetation upon it, naturally more unproductive.

Both kinds however produce abundance of grass, and several varieties of red clover grow on the rich moist bottoms.

In two places particularly we saw several acres of clover, growing with a luxuriance and compactness more resembling the close sward of a well managed lea than the produce of an uncultivated waste.

Being pretty well assured of the capabilities of the soil as respects the purposes of agriculture, the climate being also mild and pleasant we ought to be able to grow every kind of grain raised in England. On this point however we cannot speak confidently, until we have tried the experiment and tested the climate, as there may exist local influences, destructive of the husbandman's hopes, which cannot be discovered by other means . . . We are certain that potatoes thrive and grow to large size, as the Indians have many small fields in cultivation, which appear to repay the labour bestowed upon them, and I hope that other crops will do as well.

The canal of "Camosack"[3] is nearly six miles long, and its banks are well wooded throughout its whole length, so that it will supply the establishment with wood for many years to come, which can be conveyed in large rafts, with very little trouble, from one extreme of the Canal to the other.

I mentioned in a former part of this letter that I proposed to erect any machinery required for the establishment at the narrows of this Canal, about 2 miles distant from the site of the Fort, where there is a boundless water power, which our two millwrights Crate & Fenton think might, at a moderate expense, be applied to that object. . .

The natural supply of fresh water will probably be found scanty enough for the Establishment in very dry seasons, but I think that between a small stream at the distance of 300 paces, and its feeder, a lake 800 yards from the site of the Fort, we may always depend on having at least a sufficiency of this indispensable element. The labour of carting it from a distance of even 800 yards would however be very great, and I would therefore recommend that wells should be dug within the Fort, of sufficient depth to yield a constant and regular supply at all times. This I have no doubt will be found the cheapest plan in the end, besides the importance of having water at hand in case of fire, or in the event of any rupture with the natives.

Douglas concluded his report by repeating his decided conviction that this was by far the most suitable location for the new depot:

I think your opinion cannot vary much from my own respecting the decided superiority of Camosack over the other parts of the Island, or of the continental shore known to us, as a place of settle ment. The situation is not faultless or so completely suited to our purposes as it might be, but I despair of any better being found on this coast, as I am confident that there is no other sea port north of the Columbia where so many advantages will be found combined.

The new outpost was not, however, actually founded till the following year. It was in the spring of 1843 that Douglas set out from Fort Vancouver, calling briefly en route at Fort Nisqually and New Dun geness. On the afternoon of the 14th of March the *Beaver* dropped anchor in Shoal Bay, and the following morning Douglas went ashore at Clover Point. Fortunately for us, he kept a diary (still preserved in the Provincial Archives) of the first few days of Victoria's existence, and we are able to follow developments in some detail:

Wednesday 15th March.

Went out this morning with a boat and examined the wood of the north shore of the harbour; it is not good being generally short, crooked and almost unserviceable. On the south shore, the wood is of a better quality and I think we will have no difficulty in getting enough for our purpose. Small wood for picketing is scarce, particularly cedar which answers better than any other kind for that purpose from its lightness and greater durability under ground. We will probably have to bring such as we require from a distance . . .

I am at a loss where to place the Fort, as there are two positions possessing advantages of nearly equal importance, though of different kinds. No. 1 has a good view of the harbour, is upon clear ground, and only 50 yds. from the beach, on the other hand vessels drawing 14 feet cannot come within 130 feet of the shore, we will therefore either have to boat cargo off and on at a great destruction of boats, and considerable loss of time or be put to the expense of forming a jettie at a great amount of labour. No. 2 on the other hand will allow of vessels lying with their sides grazing the rocks, which form a natural wharf, whereon cargo may be conveniently landed from the ship's yard, and in that respect would be exceedingly advantageous, but on the other hand, an intervening point intercepts the view so that the mouth of the Port cannot be seen from it, an objection of much weight in the case of vessels entering and leaving Port, another disadvantage is that the shore is there covered by thick woods to the breadth of 200 yards so that we must either place the Fort at that distance from the landing place, or clear away the thickets which would detain us very much in our building operations. I will think more on this subject before determining the point. The weather rather cloudy, but dry, and beautifully clear in the afternoon.
Thursday 16

The weather clear and warm. The gooseberry bushes growing in the woods beginning to bud.

Put 6 men to dig a well and 6 others to square building timber. Spoke to the Samose[4] today and informed them of our intention of building in this place which appeared to please them very much and they immediately offered their services in procuring pickets for the establishment, an offer which I gladly accepted, and promised to pay them a blanket for every forty pickets of 22 feet by 36 inches which they bring . . .

Friday 17th

Clear warm weather. Frost last night . . . Saw a luminous streak in the heavens this evening, which lasted from dusk until 9 o'clock, when the moon rose and obscured it . . . We cannot account for this phenomenon, unless we may suppose that it is produced by the reflexion of the waters in the Straits of De Fuca, although it is difficult to account for its existence even on any such principle . . .[5]

Six men digging the well.

Saturday 18th.

Men employed as yesterday. The well is now about 11 feet deep. The luminous appearance still visible in the same position as occupied last night. It faded away about 11 o'clock.

Sat. 18 ⎫
Sun. 19 ⎬ Fine weather. Luminous column still visible in its former
M. 20 ⎭ position.
T. 21

Douglas' account has no further entries, and it is presumed that this reflects his departure for Fort McLoughlin on Millbank Sound and Fort Durham (also called Fort Taku) on Taku Inlet, to remove the stores and personnel from those depots. With these reinforcements, Douglas returned to the partially completed Fort and the work went ahead more rapidly. As soon as it was evident that the project would be successful, Douglas returned to Fort Vancouver, leaving Charles Ross in charge, with Roderick Finlayson as his second-in-command.

Ross evidently found his new post a pleasant change from the damp mists of Fort McLoughlin. Writing to a friend early in 1844, he declared:

The climate is perhaps too fine, of which you may judge, when I tell you that from June to Novr. we had scarcely anything else, than bright sunny days! Yet we were by no means oppressed by the heat, for the close vicinity of the sea & the cooling breezes blowing thence, made it very bearable. At present we have occasional showers & slight frosts—but nothing like what might be called bad weather for the time of year. Such, my dear sir, is Camosun, alias Fort Albert, alias Fort Victoria.[6]

The next few years were ones of steady progress for the new outpost of the Hudson's Bay Company. There was occasional trouble with the local Indians, the first curious visitors from the outside world made their way to the new settlement, and the area saw the beginnings of both farming and lumbering. These developments, however, are not central to our story, and we must redirect our attention to Fort Vancouver and the "Oregon Territory", where Douglas had yet to spend another six years.

NOTES

[1] Douglas' report, from which the following quotations are taken, is printed in full in the *Beaver* for March 1943. See also R. Haig-Brown, *Fur and Gold*, Longmans, Toronto, 1962, p. 35.
It appears that Douglas at one time had believed that the best location on the Island would be at Port Hardy (then called Neweete), as being closer to the fur-bearing areas of the northern interior.

[2] Ten Mile Point.

[3] i.e., the Gorge.

[4] Douglas apparently believed this to be the name of the tribe. Actually it was Songhees or Songhish.

[5] This was in reality the "Great Comet of 1843", seen throughout the Northwest.

[6] Charles Ross to Donald Ross, January 10, 1844. (Quoted in *BCHQ*, April 1943, p. 111) This letter has of course provided ammunition for the long controversy over whether Victoria ever had any other name. I have given some outline of the arguments in my *Victoria: The Fort* (Mitchell Press, Vancouver, 1968, pp. 70-71).
Some additional sidelights on the question of the name of the new settlement may be given: if George IV had lived longer, the fort would possibly have been named after Queen Adelaide (see *BCHQ*, April 1943, p. 76), while Douglas in a letter to J. S. Helmcken, dated March 20, 1867, says: "Touching the enquiries made, it is unquestionably by permission that Victoria has the honor of bearing the Queen's name; and I have heard it asserted on good authority that Her Majesty in Council often referred to it with regard, and expressed a lively interest in its welfare. (Sir James Douglas, Correspondence Outward, PABC).
We might also note that J. R. Anderson, a very early resident of the Victoria area, declared in his old age: "Prior to, and after my residence in Victoria in 1850, I never heard the name of Camosun mentioned by anyone, including Mr. Douglas, Mr. Finlayson, Mr. MacKay, Mr. Staines, or any other." (Notes and Comments, unpublished MS in Provincial Archives, p. 149).
Ross, like Douglas, was married to a half-breed. They had five sons and four daughters. His wife, who gave its name to Fowl Bay (as it is more correctly known) died in St. Ann's Convent in 1885. Ross himself died, apparently of appendicitis, on June 27, 1844. Finlayson assumed direction of the post.

CHAPTER FIVE

The Fur Trade
Moves Northward

THERE CAN BE little doubt as to the central feature of the next few years, so far as the "Oregon Territory" was concerned. It was the steadily growing tide of immigration from the more eastern parts of the United States into the fertile valleys of the Pacific Northwest. This was to have results of great importance, both political and economic. Not only did it foreshadow the end of the somewhat indefinite status of the area, but it also meant the eventual replacement throughout the region of fur-trapping by agriculture. Both developments were to focus the attention of the HBC on Vancouver Island and New Caledonia (as central and northern British Columbia was then called). The Governor and Committee in London and their energetic chief lieutenant in North America, Sir George Simpson, saw the necessity for developing to their fullest the resources of these areas; while some, at least, of those in charge of the political destinies of the empire that was once again expanding after the vicissitudes of 1776-1783, perceived the key position of the north Pacific coast and its hinterland as a link in the larger imperial chain.

In the meantime, however, Fort Vancouver was still the main HBC depot on the Pacific coast. It had been located on the north bank of the Columbia, in case that river should be chosen as the eventual line of demarcation between British and American territory.[1] There was now little hope of this, yet despite the mounting signs that its days of glory were numbered,[2] it continued to be the point at which the furs from a large area of the continent were collected to be shipped to the markets of the world, and through which were received the necessities which only the more advanced parts of the globe could provide. The route taken by the fur brigade was from Fort Alexandria (in what is now the northern Cariboo) to Kamloops, down the shores of Lake Okanagan to Fort Okanagan (or Okanogan) on the Columbia. Here it was joined by another brigade bearing the furs from the Upper Columbia and Kootenay areas. From there the furs were sent down the Columbia by boat to Fort Vancouver. This route was first used in 1812 by the Pacific Fur Company, and followed continuously till 1847.

Supplies from the outside world were frequently lost, however, almost at the end of their long voyage; a dangerous bar at the mouth of the Columbia was a constant menace to shipping, the annual supply ship from London, the *William and Ann*, being wrecked on it in 1829, and the *Isabella* the following year. Such losses were disastrous, and it was hardly surprising that as early as 1844, only one year after the founding of Fort Victoria, the supply ship was ordered to proceed there rather than to Fort Vancouver.

Meanwhile, the tide of American immigration continued to roll on. The question of forming some sort of government had inevitably risen, and in May 1843 a group of settlers had come together[3] and formed a provisional government. They made little secret of their belief that before long they expected to become part of the American Union.

This naturally raised the question as to what attitude the HBC authorities in the area should adopt toward this new development. A policy of co-operation with the inevitable seemed indicated, and after some minor incidents in which Chief Factor McLoughlin attempted to take a "hard line" toward some of the newcomers to the district,[4] an amicable agreement was reached. It was formalized in "Articles of Compact", acceded to by McLoughlin and Douglas in 1845. The latter "recognized" the provisional government, though maintaining their own allegiance to the British crown, as well as the rights of the Company in the area. Douglas accepted the post of district judge for a term of three years in the new administration, and some other HBC officials also agreed to serve in it.

This, however, was merely a "half-way house", a temporary solution. Sooner or later—and with the ever growing tide of immigration it would clearly be sooner—the area must become either a wholly British or wholly American possession. Neither government can have been in any real doubt as to which it would be, but for a year or two the former saw fit to hint that it had not yet given up hope of holding the Columbia basin. A few British warships were sent out to hover in the vicinity— H.M.S. *Modeste* was on these coasts in 1844 and 1845, H.M.S. *America* in the latter year, and H.M.S. *Fisgard* in 1846.[5] These were, however, more a bluff than a threat—it having been borne in on the British Government twice in living memory that the United States was no "paper tiger"—and events moved swiftly to their inevitable conclusion. In 1840 there had been, according to one estimate, only 137 Americans and 63 Canadians (mostly French-speaking) in the Oregon Territory, the latter being largely content with the status quo.[6] In May 1843, however, a party of 875 persons left Independence, Missouri, and reached the west coast in the fall. In 1844 another 1400 arrived, and in 1845 over 3000. The servants of the fur company became by comparison a mere handful; the area was American *de facto* and all that remained was to make it American *de jure*. On June 15, 1846, the Oregon Treaty was signed, under which the 49th parallel became the line dividing British and American possessions on the mainland, with the Gulf of Georgia and the Straits of Juan De Fuca the boundary in the waters off the coast. Thus Vancouver Island and the new HBC outpost on its southern tip remained, as its more prescient officers had hoped, under the British flag.

The same year also saw another important change in this area. Largely because of basic disagreements, both personal and administrative, with Sir George Simpson, John McLoughlin, "The Emperor of the Columbia", decided to retire, and his position as chief officer at Fort Vancouver was assumed by Douglas.[7]

For another three years the rapidly rising star of the HBC presided over the waning glories of the Columbia fur trade, with Peter Skene Ogden as his associate.[8] Even before he moved north to Victoria, however, Douglas began laying the groundwork for solving the problem which he saw would soon be facing him. With the Columbia basin now in American hands, and Victoria destined to become the chief depot for the vast hinterland known as New Caledonia, it was clear that a means must be found of connecting the fur-trapping grounds of the Interior with Fort Langley near the mouth of the Fraser and the new post on Vancouver Island. The extreme hazard of navigating the Fraser had long been known, and it was plain to Douglas that some way must be discovered of circumventing its dangerous rapids.

Accordingly, with the approval of Sir George Simpson, Douglas sent one of his most trusted subordinates, Alexander Anderson, to find a safe route from New Caledonia to the navigable waters of the lower Fraser. Setting out in May 1846 with five companions into the rugged interior of what is now British Columbia,[9] he made his way painfully through the valleys and across the endless mountain ranges of the area. Before long he had charted a trail that led by way of a chain of lakes from Lillooet to Harrison River, thence to the Fraser River and along its banks to Fort Langley, which he reached on May 24. The total distance from Fort Alexandria, the most important collection point for furs in the northern interior, to Fort Langley was 230 miles, and took Anderson nine days to cover.

On his return journey to the interior, Anderson investigated another route; leaving the Fraser River near the present town of Hope and travelling eastward, he ascended the Coquahalla River, crossed the Cascade Mountains, and so made his way northward across the interior plains to Kamloops. This trip took him thirteen days. Anderson reported, however, that for much of the year the trail would be impassable. In Douglas' eyes this was a serious drawback, and he ordered that a fresh start be made to find a more suitable route.

So, in May 1847, Anderson once again set out through this almost totally uninhabited region. Proceeding westward from Kamloops, he followed the south bank of the Thompson River for a considerable distance. This did not at first seem too promising, but eventually he found a possible way through the sea of mountains. It meant going south from Kamloops to Nicola Lake, up the Coldwater River, across the Cascade mountains, and then by way of Anderson River to Kequeloose, a point on the Fraser about six miles above Spuzzum. From there it was hoped that the Fraser could be navigated to Fort Langley, or, if that proved impossible, portages could be made around the most dangerous parts of it.

Douglas himself now made a personal investigation of Anderson's findings, and as a result decided that the best solution to the problem was to ferry the fur convoys (they would sometimes number two hundred horses) across the river at Spuzzum and proceed down the western side of the Fraser along a new trail to be constructed. A new post, Fort Yale, was to be built in 1848 on the west bank of the Fraser, and the trail extended northward from it to the crossing point near Spuzzum. In a letter to the London headquarters of the Company, dated November 6, 1847, Douglas and John Work[10] explained the new proposal:

> Since we had the honour of addressing you from Fort Vancouver on the 20th of September, I have made an excursion to Fort Langley chiefly for the purpose of putting matters in train, for the passage of the Brigade by the contemplated new route to the interior, mentioned in the 18th paragraph of that letter. Accompanied by Chief Trader Yale, and Mr. William Sinclair, leaving Chief Factor Work during the absence of the former in charge of Fort Langley, we proceeded with an Indian canoe up Fraser's River to the Saumeena village, where the horse road to Fort Kamloops falls upon the river about 100 miles beyond Fort Langley. We spent several days in examining the chain of rapids known as "The Falls" which constitutes the chief obstacle of that route. With a few intervening spaces of smooth water, these rapids extend from the Saumeena to the upper "Teat Village" a distance of 13 miles, and we are of the opinion that they will be found exceedingly dangerous at every season, and absolutely impassable in the summer freshets, when the river is full and attains a level of 60 feet above the low water mark in autumn. The rapids occur at a spot where Fraser's River forces a passage through the Cascade Mountains, and stretch from side to side of that stupendous barrier. It is impossible to conceive anything more formidable or imposing, than is to be found in that dangerous defile which cannot for one moment be thought of as a practicable water communication for the transport of valuable property. We propose to avoid that part of the River entirely by extending the horse road about 13 miles to the lower end of the rapids from whence the navigation is unexceptionable to the sea coast distant 130 miles. This extension of the horse road must be carried through the mountains in a narrow

winding defile on the north side of Fraser's River which runs nearly parallel with it. Though neither smooth nor level it is practicable, and when the timber is cleared away will make a much better road than we expected to find in so rugged a section of country. It has moreover the important advantage of being perfectly safe, and is infinitely preferable to the most perilous piece of water communication in the Indian country.

That it was realized that this route was far from perfect, and that it was hoped that some better one might yet be found, is shown by a later section of this letter:

Among other points of valuable information obtained from the Indians whom we saw in the course of our journey, they pointed out another route to the Interior considerably to the southward of those already explored, which falls upon Fraser's River 25 miles above Fort Langley. This would be of immense advantage in many ways, and relieve us of the expense of maintaining a fleet of boats exclusively for the river transport. A party of men with an Indian guide have been sent to examine that route, and as soon as we receive their report we will make our final arrangements for opening one of these two roads as soon as possible; it being now made clear that one or the other must become the highway of commerce to the Interior, and we confidentially expect to have everything in readiness for the passage of the Brigades by the new route in the summer of 1849. We will thereby escape the exactions of the United States Government, and have it in our power to supply the Interior with British goods free of import or transit duties.

Despite his lack of complete enthusiasm for the route involving the crossing of the Fraser near Spuzzum, Douglas ordered Chief Trader Yale, in charge at Fort Langley, to proceed with its construction.[11] This he did, but in a letter to HBC headquarters in London dated December 5, 1848, Douglas and Work explained some of the difficulties involved:

The preparations for opening the new road to the Interior for the passage of the summer Brigade threw much additional work upon the establishment of Fort Langley, as besides making the road from Keque-loose to the Ferry, and from thence through the Portage to the lower end of the Falls of Fraser's River, a distance of 18 miles, through a wooded country, levelling and siz-zaging the steep ascents, bridging rivers, there were stores erected for the accommodation of the Brigades above and below the Falls, boats and skows built for the ferry, and seven large boats for the navigation from Fort Langley to the Falls, there was the heavy transport of provisions to the latter place, and a vast amount of other work connected with that object which it required no common degree of energy and good management in Chief Trader Yale to accomplish with 20 men in the course of a severe winter.[12]

The route via Spuzzum and Fort Yale was followed in 1848, but losses in the crossing of the river were considerable. Reluctantly, Douglas abandoned this solution (though, no alternative being as yet available, this route was used again in 1849), and reverted to a modification of the original way first discovered by Anderson in 1846. The route finally agreed upon was up the Coquahalla River, over the Cascades into the Similkameen Valley and so across the interior plains to Kamloops. A new post, Fort Hope, was constructed at the mouth of the Coquahalla River, and Fort Yale (not a fortified place, despite its name) was more or less abandoned.[13]

This route, used for the first time in 1850, was not ideal, but it had to do, as there was an irresistible economic pressure at work which more than counterbalanced its drawbacks. All goods imported into New Caledonia via Fort Vancouver were now being charged customs duties by the American authorities; moreover, the Indian tribes in what is now the State of Washington were becoming hostile to the whites, and on one occasion killed fourteen of them near Walla Walla. Thus the same forces that had been responsible more than three centuries before for driving Columbus to find a route to the Indies that would circumvent the Moslem lands of the Near East, had now operated in this distant corner of the new world he had discovered, and in response to them, in the latter case as in the former, trade would soon be flowing through new channels.

Later observers would see in these convoys of pack trains, wending their way slowly through the mountain passes, the threads of empire being woven. Such a view would, objectively, be right; without a connection between New Caledonia and the lower Fraser, British Columbia could hardly have come into being; without a path "from sea to sea", the Dominion of Canada, even had it come into existence, could not long have survived; without the Dominion of Canada, there would have been no "All Red Route" around the globe. Thus, though it is now a century and a quarter since Douglas and his lieutenants sought out the difficult and often dangerous way that even-tually joined the fur trapping grounds to the markets of the world, we who come after them still remain in their debt. They toiled with an eye to the balance sheet, but they built better than they knew.

Si monumentum requiris, circumspice.

So the decade drew toward its close. Meanwhile, a series of events was unfolding, destined not only to have an important effect on the history of the Pacific Northwest, but also to provide for Douglas a role on the stage of history in which his character and talents would be amply and publicly demonstrated. Not long after the signing of the Oregon Treaty, the British Government was approached by the Hudson's Bay Company with a request that large areas in what is now British Columbia be granted to the Company. At one time the great fur trading enterprise hoped to secure "all the territories belonging to the Crown which are situated to the north and west of Rupert's Land".[14] The British Government, however, (represented by Lord Grey, the Secretary of State for the Colonies) was not inclined to be so generous with such a considerable section of North America, but in the end it did accede to the granting of Vancouver Island to the Company under certain clearly specified conditions.

The Royal Grant, dated January 13, 1849, stipulated among other things that the Company must establish a colony of settlers on the Island and agree to sell them land at a reasonable figure. The Company was to be allowed to retain ten per cent of all the revenue it derived from the sale of land, coal mining, or similar sources, and the remainder was to be devoted to helping the colonists in their daily life. If the Company did not fulfil the terms of the Grant within five years, then the British Government could resume possession of the Island, and in any case could repurchase it in 1859, at which time the Company's exclusive right of trading with the Indians west of the Rocky Mountains, granted in 1838, would expire.[15]

The Grant was not made without considerable opposition in England. This came from a variety of sources. There were those who had some sort of personal grudge against the Company; there were those who wished to colonize Vancouver Island themselves;[16] there were those who suspected that the Company was secretly against colonization, as spelling the certain doom of their profitable fur trading industry;[17] and there were those who felt that the whole tenor and theme of the burgeoning century of free enterprise was being negated by this reversion to the era and tenets of monopoly. None of these voices of dissent was heeded, however, and the Grant was sustained in the British House of Commons in the summer of 1849.

One important matter remained to be decided; who should be the chief representative of the Crown in the new colony. Earl Grey wrote to Sir John Pelly, asking him to nominate a suitable Governor. Pelly favored the appointment of Douglas, pointing out that he was a man of property, a Chief Factor, and a member of the HBC Board of Management at Fort Vancouver. He prudently conceded, however, that in view of his connections with the Company this should be only a temporary arrangement. Once again, though, the British Government showed itself unwilling to accede to every Company request; perhaps a further eruption of protest was envisioned. At all events, an almost unknown and completely inexperienced young barrister, Richard Blanshard, was selected for the post of first governor of Vancouver Island.[18] His arrival did not take place until the spring of 1850; in the meantime, in June 1849[19] Douglas was transferred to Fort Victoria, there to take up his duties as chief officer of the Company in this comparatively new outpost of its far-flung empire. The usual fate of servants of the HBC was to have "no continuing city", and little could Douglas have foreseen that henceforth, except for brief intervals, this would be his home until he died. From here he would direct the operations, make the decisions, and grasp the visions which would assure for him a permanent, and indeed the prime place in the history of what had not yet been named British Columbia.

NOTES

1 The southern boundary of the Oregon Territory was 42° N. Mexico held control below this line.

² They were actually remarkably brief. Astoria (founded on April 12, 1811 by J. J. Astor's Pacific Fur Company) was originally the main depot for the fur trade on the Pacific coast. During the war of 1812 it was captured by the British, and the American post purchased by the North West Company, but in accordance with the treaty of Ghent (Dec. 24, 1814) restored to American control in 1818. The North West Company, however, continued to use it as their headquarters. Fort Vancouver was built in 1825, a year after John McLoughlin took control of HBC affairs west of the Rocky Mountains, and the headquarters of the Company moved there. The General Council of the HBC, meeting at York Factory on July 2, 1825, decided that beginning in 1826 the trade of New Caledonia should move through Fort Vancouver (instead of, as previously, eastward through Montreal). The Fort was abandoned in 1860 (Sage, *Douglas*, p. 155).

³ The "Champoeg Meeting". For details regarding it, see three interesting articles in the *Oregon Historical Society Quarterly* for 1912: "A Brief History of the Oregon Provisional Government and what caused its formation", by F. V. Holman (pp. 89-139); "Oregon's Provisional Government 1843-1849" by Leslie M. Scott (pp. 207-217); "Truth and Fiction of the Champoeg Meeting" by Russell B. Thomas (pp. 218-237).

⁴ See Bancroft, *History of Oregon*, San Francisco, 1886, Volume I, pp. 459-462.

⁵ Her commander was Captain John Alexander Duntze, after whom Duntze Head is named. She was a sailing frigate of 1069 tons, carrying 42 guns. The first lieutenant of the *Fisgard* was John Rashleigh Rodd, after whom Rodd Hill and Rodd Point are named.

⁶ See "A brief history of the Oregon Provisional Government and what caused its formation" by F. V. Holman, *Oregon Historical Society Quarterly*, XIII, No. 2, June 1912, p. 105.

⁷ McLoughlin's last letter to his superiors, dated November 20, 1845 (printed in full in the *American Historical Review*, Vol. XXI, No. 1, October 1915) is a sad document. He clearly felt that through no fault of his own, he was leaving the Company's service under something of a cloud, and this letter is a long vindication of his policies.

There has been some speculation (which may some day be resolved) as to the part played by Douglas in the disputes over policy between Simpson and McLoughlin. Douglas was indebted to McLoughlin for much of his rise in the ranks of the Company; on the other hand, he was aware that Simpson was the ultimate master he would have to please. When McLoughlin died in Oregon City in 1857, Douglas' comments were noticably restrained; he was, it seems fair to say, at no time an enthusiast for lost causes.

⁸ Ogden was born in 1794, joined the North West Company in 1811, and in 1834 was in charge of the district of New Caledonia. Soon afterward he was promoted to the rank of Chief Factor. He died Sept. 27, 1854 at Oregon City. Ogden Point, Victoria, is named after him.

⁹ It did not receive this name until 1858.

Anderson's personal day-to-day account of his explorations in 1846 and 1847 may be found in his "History of the North West Coast" (unpublished MS in Provincial Archives, Victoria, 1878). There is an interesting article, "Brigade Trails of B.C." by E. P. Creech in the *Beaver* for March 1953.

10 For an interesting article on Work, see Henry Drummond Dee's "An Irishman in the Fur Trade; the Life and Journals of John Work", *BCHQ*, Vol. VII, No. 4, October 1943, pp. 229-270. Work's name is commemorated in Victoria by Work Point Barracks.

11 James Murray Yale was born in 1800. He entered the service of the HBC at the age of 16 and died at Victoria in 1871. He is buried in the old Quadra Street cemetery.

12 Fort Langley Correspondence, PABC.

13 See F. W. Howay, "The Raison D'Etre of Forts Yale and Hope", *Transactions of the Royal Society of Canada*, Third Series, XVI, 1922, Section II, pp. 49-64.

14 Sir John Pelly to Grey, March 5, 1847.

15 The terms of the Grant are printed in full in Howay and Scholefield, *British Columbia from the earliest times to the present*, Vancouver, 1914, Vol. 1, pp. 676-680.

16 An elaborate scheme was drawn up by a certain James Edward Fitzgerald to this effect. See *B.C. Archives Report for 1913*, pp. 54-62. There was also a plan to establish a Mormon settlement on the Island. (Sage, *Douglas*, p. 140).

17 It seems likely enough that this was indeed the case. Many observers expressed this opinion at the time, and certainly remarkably few colonists were ever encouraged to come to the new settlement. It is more than probable that the ultimate aim of the Company was to keep Vancouver Island as a sort of geographical shield for its lucrative operations on the adjacent mainland. See J. S. Galbraith, *The Hudson's Bay Company as an Imperial Factor, 1821-1869*. U. of Toronto Press, 1957, pp. 284-285.

18 Dr. Sage, in his *Sir James Douglas and British Columbia*, (U. of Toronto Press, 1930) says that Blanshard "had already seen service under the Colonial Office in the West Indies, in British Honduras and in India", (p. 148); but this is incorrect.

19 The month which also saw the death at Montreal of Mrs. Douglas' father, William Connolly.

CHAPTER SIX

The Governor and
The Chief Factor

WHEN DOUGLAS arrived in Fort Victoria in the summer of 1849 to take up his duties as Chief Factor of the depot whose construction he had supervised six years before, there was little sign of the remarkable future that was in store both for him and the settlement on the southern tip of Vancouver Island. Considerable progress, however, had been made in creating a community which should be, so far as possible, self-supporting, while the trade in furs with the natives was expanding satisfactorily. Its first chief officer, Charles Ross, had died in 1844, but Roderick Finlayson had since guided the destinies of the Fort with a sure hand. Occasional difficulties with the natives had been overcome by a shrewd combination of tact and firmness, there were at least three dairies, large tracts of the arable land around the Fort were under cultivation, and grain was already being shipped to points as far distant as Sitka, Alaska. There was also a sawmill at Millstream.

The Fort itself had been constructed on a scale in keeping with the important role envisioned for it. It consisted of a quadrangle about three hundred feet square surrounded by a stockade some eighteen feet high, with various buildings for housing the personnel, storing provisions, and preserving the precious furs.

Already a few visitors from the great outside world had made their way here. Some were mere private citizens, like the artist Paul Kane, who has left us an interesting account of his observations;[1] others were on official business, like the two British army officers, Warre and

Vavasour, who were sent out by the Imperial Government to make a report on the military and economic potentialities of the new outpost. They were inevitably much struck by the abundance of fish and game and the great stands of timber, and also commented favorably on the Company policy of forbidding the sale of intoxicating liquor to either whites or Indians.[2] The occasional warship was also to be seen in the vicinity, H.M.S. *America*, under the command of the Hon. John Gordon, brother of the Earl of Aberdeen, at that time Foreign Secretary of Great Britain, arrived in 1845, and its captain sampled, though without enthusiasm, the local hunting and fishing.[3] The following year the survey ships *Fisgard* and *Pandora* arrived to begin the charting of Victoria and Esquimalt harbors. Other vessels in the vicinity during this period were H.MS. *Herald*, the steam vessel *Cormorant*, and the HBC supply ship *Vancouver* (eventually wrecked on the Columbia bar in 1849).

Yet, though the Fort had attracted enough attention to be "written up" in the *Illustrated London News* (issue of August 26, 1848), it was far from the main trade routes of the world, and its handful of inhabitants must have often felt themselves marooned. Despite this, they tackled their duties with zeal and efficiency, conscious that there was no outpost of the HBC so remote as not to be under the constant eye, if not of the Governor and Committee in London, at least of Sir George Simpson, the chief figure of the Company in North America.

The year in which Douglas arrived to assume direction of the destinies of the Fort saw a noticeable quickening of the tempo of its life. Not only did it become a Crown Colony, as well as (under the Royal Grant of January 13, 1849) a sort of fief of the Hudson's Bay Company, but it welcomed its first independent settler, its first schoolmaster and (for a few days) its first gold-miners.

The settler was Captain Walter Colquhoun Grant, who arrived in the summer of 1849 in the *Harpooner* with eight workmen and a variety of disparate equipment. This included sets of carriage harness (though the Island had as yet no carriages), cricket equipment, and a belief that he could both operate a farm and perform his duties efficiently as the official surveyor of the Colony. Disillusionment in this last regard was soon to cast its pall over both himself and his employers, but in the meantime he added at least variety to the small world of the newly created colony.[4]

A less engaging newcomer was the Rev. Robert John Staines, who arrived with his wife in the same year. He had been employed by the Company to minister to the spiritual needs of the Colony, as well as to operate a school for the children of fort officials.[5] The rudimentary quarters in which he and his wife were forced to lodge were not at all to his liking, but he set about his duties with enthusiasm, and though his pupils were often subjected to the vagaries of his uncertain temper, they undoubtedly acquired—so essential to life on the frontier—a good knowledge of Latin grammar.[6]

A third set of visitors to the Fort also made their sudden appearance in 1849, not long before Douglas' arrival. Roderick Finlayson was still in charge, and was much amazed when a shipload of miners from San Francisco suddenly appeared in the Harbor and offered to exchange gold for goods. Finlayson, indeed, at first took them to be pirates, but eventually gathered that they had "struck it rich" in the California gold-rush and were merely anxious to buy such necessities as boots, blankets, and cooking equipment.[7] Having done this, they departed, leaving the surprised residents of the Fort unaware that they had been given a preview of events still some nine years in the future.

Douglas himself arrived at the Fort in June, and the transfer of authority proceeded smoothly. Affairs went forward without untoward incidents; the year waned and died; and in due course it was 1850. The winter was severe, and snow was still a foot deep when on the 11th of March H.M.S. *Driver* appeared in the harbor and, to the accompaniment of a salute from the Fort guns, the first Governor of the Crown Colony of Vancouver Island stepped ashore to assume his duties —or, as some would say, into the lion's den.

It will soon be apparent why this metaphor is used, when we consider the situation that now existed. Although the young barrister was automatically the First Citizen of Vancouver Island, this was largely an empty honor. The affairs of the Company were firmly in the hands of Douglas, and as little else existed in the colony, it was not at all clear in what field the new Governor was expected to exercise his prerogatives.

The secretary to the Governor and Committee in London, Archibald Barclay, had explained to Douglas the dividing line between the two jurisdictions. Douglas was to be "agent to the Company for all matters relating to the territory of Vancouver's Island", while Blanshard would be "confined to the administration of the civil government of the colony and to military affairs".[8] These latter duties, considering that Captain Grant was the colony's sole settler, scarcely promised to be onerous, while no important military operations seemed in prospect.

Inevitably, an awkward situation was soon created, one that was not to be satisfactorily resolved until the dismayed and disillusioned Blanshard had left the Colony forever in the fall of 1851. Douglas was well aware that he had been considered for the governorship himself, and that his superiors believed him well deserving of it; that a man younger than himself (Blanshard was then 32, and Douglas 46), so lacking in experience, so unaware of the problems of the settlement, should have been given the highest post in the new colony, must have been galling indeed. However, the ingrained habit of obedience to authority, reinforced perhaps with reflections about giving people enough rope, combined to produce in Douglas an attitude of respectfulness toward the Governor which may or may not have mirrored his true feelings. A week after the arrival of the new Governor, Douglas reported the event to a friend in studiously correct language:

> Her Majesty's sloop "Driver" arrived here on the 11th instant with His Excellency Richard Blanshard Esq. Governor of Vancouver Island on board. Mr. Blanshard has neither Secretary nor troops, being accompanied by a single body servant. I have not had time to become much acquainted but I may say that his quiet gentlemanly manner is prepossessing. He has not yet entered upon his executive duties, further than reading his commission to the assembled states of this colony.[9]

Almost from the beginning, however, difficulties developed. No official residence was available for Blanshard, and he was forced to remain aboard the *Driver*. Douglas had been instructed to build a house for the Governor,[10] and did the best he could with what resources were available to him. His best, however, did not seem good enough to Blanshard, who complained about the matter in writing:

> I find that the labourers who for the last few days have been employed on the cottage which has been commenced for my residence have again been withdrawn.
>
> During the four months I have been in this colony, the work at the cottage has been totally discontinued with the exception of a few days when labourers varying in number from one to three have been employed.
>
> I request that you, as representative of the Hudson's Bay Company in this colony, will inform me whether it is the intention of that company to supply proper labour to complete the work at my cottage, which I was informed by the Directors I should find ready on my arrival, or whether I am no longer to rely on their doing so.[1]

This letter apparently did not produce noticeable results, for in August Blanshard again wrote to Douglas:

> I find that three of the Kanakas and one of the workmen have been withdrawn from my cottage, leaving one solitary man to carry on work that has already been loitered over for more than five months. I beg to state that you are at liberty to withdraw him also, as the labour of a single man is a mere mockery, and I will consider such withdrawal as proof of the inability or unwillingness of the Hudson's Bay Company to furnish me with lodging.[12]

The house was, however, at the cost of about $1600[13] eventually completed, and Douglas, describing it as "on the whole the best finished building in Oregon",[14] made a report on the whole affair to Barclay. He was evidently much put out by the Governor's criticism, describing it as "excessively mortifying", and saying that it had given him "more pain than I can describe". He also took issue with the accuracy of some of the Governor's charges:

> You will observe by his letter of the 5th August that he speaks of only *one man* being employed at the "Cottage" while my reply of the same date shows that no fewer than ten workmen were then actually employed about it.[15]

In his outline of the difficulties which had caused the delay, we note reference to a double set of loyalties, or priorities:

We have done everything in our power to forward the building; but unfortunately it was impossible, with our limited means, to keep pace with his wishes, without altogether neglecting the Company's business and making it a secondary object, or hiring mechanics in the Columbia at the enormous rates paid there for labour, and I did not feel at liberty to adopt either of these expedients.[16]

Douglas suggested, however, that the shortage of skilled labor in the colony should be rectified:

I beg to recommend in the event of any other public buildings being contemplated, that mechanics may be sent out to erect and finish them, as we have not a single house carpenter or joiner at this place, our own work being done by the rude self-taught carpenters of the country, who are not capable of turning out a neat job.[17]

Others problems, however, were less easily resolved. Blanshard had been under the impression that he would be granted a country estate of a thousand acres; it transpired that in practice the thousand acres would be attached to the office, not the man, and would "belong" on the same terms to the next Governor. "He might select, subdue, and beautify the tract for his successors, should he so please, but he could not sell nor pocket any of the proceeds of it".[18]

This was by no means the full measure of his disillusionment. The Company had a system of prices, by which its own employees were able to buy supplies fairly cheaply. Blanshard, however, was not an employee of the Company, and was, therefore, charged the top price. As the cost of living was much higher than he had expected, and he was already out of pocket for his passage,[19] he soon began to feel the pinch, especially as he had no firm commitment from anyone regarding salary. To add to his problems, his health began to deteriorate.

Despite all this, this "comparatively young man, of medium height, with aquiline aristocratic features, set off by a large military mustache"[20] struggled on, making regular reports to Earl Grey. These dealt with a variety of topics: he reported on the natural resources of the colony (which contained for a time but a single colonist, Captain Grant, and when he for a time went elsewhere in search of El Dorado, not even that); he attempted to mediate between the Company and its employees, and to this effect appointed Dr. J. S. Helmcken (who had recently arrived in the colony in the *Norman Morison*) as magistrate at the coal mining settlement at Fort Rupert, in the northern part of the Island;[21] he went to Fort Rupert himself to investigate conditions;[22] and on November 18, 1850, only eight months after his arrival at Victoria, he sent a letter of resignation to Lord Grey. The reasons he gave were the state of his health and his finances; but no doubt the awkwardness and virtual superfluousness of his position were also factors. Many months, of course, would have to elapse before an answer to his letter could be received, and in the meantime he did his best to carry out his duties as he saw them.

Nor did he hesitate to stand up to the Company and its chief representative in the colony. On occasion he seems to have been precipitous, as when he reported his suspicions that three British subjects (deserters from the navy) had been murdered by Indians with the connivance of the HBC;[23] in a later despatch, however, Blanshard conceded that he had probably been misinformed.[24]

In some other matters, however, he felt himself on surer ground. He suspected that the company was appropriating to itself a much larger parcel of land in the vicinity of the Fort than it was entitled to, and complained about this not only to Lord Grey[25] but also to Douglas' superior, Sir John Pelly. Douglas, however, according to Blanshard, blandly professed "ignorance of every arrangement"[26], and Sir John could not apparently find the time to answer his mail.

In the meantime, Douglas also acted according to his lights, which in his case meant the promotion of the interests of his employers the Hudson's Bay Company. In December 1849 Archibald Barclay, Secretary of the Company, writing from London, had outlined the views of the Governor and Committee of the HBC regarding the purchase of the land surrounding the Fort and in other areas:

> With respect to the rights of the natives, you will have to confer with the chiefs of the tribes on that subject, and in your negociations with them you are to consider the natives as the rightful possessors of such lands only as they are occupied by cultivation, or had houses built on, at the time when the Island came under the undivided

sovereignty of Great Britain in 1846. All other land is to be regarded as waste, and applicable to the purposes of colonization. Where any annual tribute has been paid by the natives to the chiefs, a fair compensation for such payment is to be allowed.

In other colonies the scale of compensation adopted has not been uniform, as there are circumstances peculiar to each which prevented them all from being placed in the same footing, but the average rate may be stated at £1 per head of the tribe for the interest of the chiefs paid in signing the Treaty . ..

The principle here laid down is that which the Governor and Committee authorize you to adopt in treating with the natives of Vancouver's Island, but the extent to which it is to be acted upon must be left to your own discretion and will depend upon the character of the tribe and other circumstances. The natives will be confirmed in the possession of their lands as long as they occupy and cultivate them themselves, but will not be allowed to sell or dispose of them to any private person, the right to the entire soil having been granted to the Company by the Crown. The right of fishing and hunting will be continued to them, and when their lands are regis-tered, and they conform to the same conditions with which other settlers are required to comply, they will enjoy the same rights and privileges.[27]

Douglas acted promptly on these instructions and reported the results to Barclay:

> I summoned to a conference the Chiefs and influential men of the Songees Tribe, which inhabits and claims the District of Victoria from Gordon Head on Arro Strait to Point Albert on the Strait of De Fuca as their own particular heritage. After considerable dis-cussion, it was arranged that the whole of their lands, forming as before stated the District of Victoria, should be sold to the Company, with the exception of village sites and enclosed fields, for a certain remuneration, to be paid at once to each member of the tribe. I was in favour of a series of payments to be made annually but the proposal was so generally disliked that I yielded to their wishes and paid the sum at once . . .
>
> I subsequently made a similar purchase from the Clallum Tribe, of the country lying between Albert Point and Soke Inlet. In con-sequence of the Claimants not being so well known as the Songhees, we adopted a different mode of making the payments, by dealing

exclusively with the Chiefs, who received and distributed the payments, while the sale was confirmed and ratified by the tribe collectively. This second purchase cost about £30.0.8.

I have since made a purchase from the Soke Tribe of the land between Soke Inlet and Point Sheringham, the arrangement being concluded in this, as in the preceding purchase, with the Chiefs or heads of families who distributed the property among their followers. The cost of this tract which does not contain much cultivable land was £16.8.8[28].

Altogether, Douglas disbursed to the Indians, in addition to some trade goods, the sum of £150.3.4[29]. This may not seem to us an unduly large amount for so much valuable land, but the natives were evidently satisfied with it, as Douglas soon received other offers of territory:

. . . The Cowetchin and other Tribes have since expressed a wish to dispose of their lands, on the same terms; but I declined their proposals, in consequence of our not being prepared to enter into possession, which ought to be done immediately after the purchase, or the arrangement may be forgotten, and further compensations claimed by the natives.[30]

It should be noted that the purchase of their land by no means meant that the Indians had to vacate it:

I informed the natives that they would not be disturbed in the possession of their village sites and enclosed fields, which are of small extent, and that they were at liberty to hunt over the unoccupied land, and to carry on their fisheries with the same freedom as when they were the sole occupants of the country.[31]

As these figures suggest, Douglas was not inclined to be wasteful with the Company's money, and his dealings with the Indians resulted on one occasion in a few penetrating questions from the Governor. Blanshard subsequently gave his version of the affair to Lord Grey:

The Agent of the Hudson's Bay Company has presented me an account for signature, being a voucher of the balance between the amount expended by the Hudson's Bay Company on the Colony, and the receipts of duties, sales, royalties collected in the Colony.

The account asserts that they have expended $2736 (Dollars) of which $2130 (Dollars) are for goods paid to Indians to extinguish their title to the land about Victoria and Soke Harbour, the remainder also for goods paid also to Indians for work done for the Colony, provisions and ammunition for the same Indians. The receipts amount to $1489 (Dollars) (from which 10 per cent is to be deducted according to the Charter of Grant to the Hudson's Bay Company) and consists entirely of Royalties on Coal for the last two years, land sales there are none, as I have previously informed your Lordship. On examining the account I found that for the goods paid to the Indians a price was charged three times as great as what they are in the habit of paying them at for their own work; respecting this and some inaccuracies I detected in the Account I addressed a letter to the Agent; he corrected the errors but made no alteration in the prices, and in the course of the conversation gave me to understand that they did not expect the Charter of Grant to be renewed at the expiration of the five years (January 1854) and that they would be entitled to a reimbursement of their expenditure. At this rate they may continue for the next three years paying away a few goods to Indians to extinguish their claim to the soil, and by attaching an ideal value to their goods they will at the end of that time appear as creditor of the Colony to an overwhelming amount, so that the foundation will be laid of a Colonial debt, which will for ever prove a burden.[32]

This was not the only occasion on which the two principal figures in the Colony were at odds. When Blanshard discovered that the Chief Factor was signing the registers of sea-going vessels, he summoned Douglas and pointed out to him that this privilege was that of the Governor.[33]

Other points of difference arose from time to time between the two major figures in the Colony. In a letter dated March 21, 1851, Douglas outlined some of them to Barclay.

I have done everything in my power to meet Governor Blanshard's views and to support his authority in the Colony; but there are certain points on which we may be allowed to differ in opinion without necessarily involving a breach of harmony. The Governor for instance was always opposed on public grounds to the reserves of land held for the two company's[34] and in favour of having a military force in the colony—for the protection of the inhabitants and in reference to these subjects he still maintains the same opinion, while I am bound as a servant of the Company to follow the committee's instructions and to study on every point to protect their interests. It was with the object of meeting Governor Blanshard's views without materially compromising the interests of the Company that I took the liberty of recommending the formation of a rural police to be effected by granting a certain number of 20 acre lots on the Fur Trade reserve to the company's retiring servants, a measure which I still hope the committee may sanction as it will meet the demand for protection at very small expense.

We should not, however, picture Douglas as occupied exclusively with piling up money for his employers. The spiritual and intellectual side of life were as important to him as the economic, and no amount of derisory comment about Victorian hypocrisy should be allowed to obscure this fact. Religion and education were throughout his life matters to which he accorded the most zealous attention. While still at Fort Vancouver he had set down in a note book four tasks which he hoped to achieve. These were:

The moral renovation of this place.
Abolition of slavery within our limits.
Lay down a principle and act upon it with confidence.
The building of a church of Christ in this place.[35]

Pursuant to these aims, in 1844 he had attempted to establish a boarding school where children from the smaller posts in the Columbia valley could be educated.[36] No churches yet existed in the new colony of Vancouver Island—a cause of vexation to Mr. Staines—but soon after Douglas' arrival there a school was in existence, directed by the reverend gentleman, which attracted pupils even from the mainland. One of these, James Anderson (son of the Alexander Anderson who had explored the routes to the interior) lived on till 1930,[37] and still remembered in the evening of his days the alarming voyage across the straits from Fort Langley to become one of the school's first students:

Oh, the misery I endured; what with my recent parting, the terror of the rough sea, the savage crew and their terrifying canoe songs, I never expected to see land again. A bed was made for me in the centre of the canoe, when after hours of torture, in my futile attempts to balance the rocking of the canoe, exhausted nature at length came to my relief and I fell asleep. A phenomenon which perplexed my young mind, I was only nine years old, was the phosphorescent glow at each stroke of the paddle. I looked in vain, even for a lighted pipe, but could discover nothing to account for the curious occurrence. I was awakened early by the water, which owing to the increased violence of the wind, the canoe was taking in. The Indians by signs asked for one of my blankets; with this a sail was improvised and we made better time, entering Plumper Pass as the sun rose and we landed on the little pebbly beach on the right close to the big bluff. With what feeling of joy I landed can be imagined, wet, cold, and miserable as I was. Then I began worrying about Mr. Douglas and my sister as they had not arrived. However, after some time they put in an appearance and we had breakfast. After a good rest we made a start in the afternoon and put ashore on the Saanich beach for dinner. I was awakened the next morning by water being sprinkled on my face by my sister and found their canoe alongside just off Beacon Hill. This eminence was so named on account of a beacon on its summit in the shape of a pole surmounted by a barrel. Soon we landed at the little jetty and I was hoisted on the shoulders of a stalwart Kanaka and deposited at Mr. Douglas' house where we found the family assembled who gave us a hearty greeting.[38]

It is interesting to read the letter written by Douglas to the father of the two Anderson children recording their safe arrival at the Fort. It discloses aspects of his character that, already formed, were not henceforth to alter: his ability to note and remember detail and then set it vividly before the reader's eyes, his awareness of the realities of this harsh world,[39] and his sympathy with the young who must some day make their way through it.

I have no doubt you are anxious about your dear little ones whom you resigned to my care with so much reluctance last summer, and I regret that there has been no opportunity of communicating with you before now. I am happy to say that they are both well and decided favourites with the Staines. They were a good deal affected on leaving you but strove to hide their grief from me by conversation and the novelty of travelling over a country they had never before seen, their attention was attracted to other objects and their thoughts diverted from scenes of home. The first night we encamped on board the "Cadboro" near the River's mouth where mosquitoes in countless swarms riveted every thought on the best means of escaping their annoying stings. The day following a storm drove us to the shelter of Point Roberts where we spent the day, the remainder of the voyage was unmarked by any important incident, wind and weather being favourable. After arriving at this place there was amusement enough to keep their spirits up and they soon fell into the ways of the place.

They remained with me until accommodations were provided for them in school and I believe it was not until they were finally separated from my family that they felt the bitterness of parting. The next time I saw Eliza was in school and she could not refrain from shedding tears. James has his own troubles in school and has had to fight his way in that arena of the great world, an exercise useful to the future man.[40]

Despite his difficulties with Governor Blanshard, Douglas was beginning to put down roots in his new home. He built a house for himself on the shores of James Bay, and having debated in his mind as to whether £1 an acre was too high a price to pay for land, decided in the end that it was not, and acquired a considerable tract of property near the Fort.

Other areas in the vicinity of the Fort were coming under cultivation. It had long been Company policy that each settlement should be self-supporting, and to this end it now established Viewfield Farm in 1850 and Colwood or Esquimalt Farm in 1851. The former was located in what is now Esquimalt and comprised 600 acres, and the latter was near Colwood. Here sheep, cows and pigs were raised, and even the humblest members of the colony were able to have a more varied diet than they would have enjoyed at home.

The whole question of colonization, however, was somewhat at cross purposes. The Company, by the terms of the Royal Grant, had agreed to bring out settlers and sell them land; and in compliance with this covenant it did so. To the extent that this prevented the cancellation of the Grant, aided the production of food for the Fort, or provided essential craftsmen such as blacksmiths and carpenters, the interests of the Company were served; but on the other hand, the conversion of the frontier wilderness into an urbanized economy was the very last of its wishes. Douglas himself had at one time been well aware of this. In a letter to the Governor and Committee in London he wrote:

The interests of the Colony and Fur Trade will never harmonize; the former can flourish only through the protection of equal laws, the influence of free trade, the accession of respectable inhabitants; in short, by establishing a new order of things, while the fur trade must suffer by each innovation.[41]

Now, however, he no longer seemed to see matters in this light. It is possible that he was drawing a lesson from his experiences at Fort Vancouver. The valleys of the Columbia had been lost not only to the Company but also to the Empire, largely because they were being peopled by Americans, not Britons; perhaps, he seems to have reasoned, a like fate would eventually overtake Vancouver Island if its land was not, so to speak, held down by settlers from the British Isles. He was, in other words, perhaps now thinking in imperial rather than economic terms, and seeing himself as not merely the servant of a fur trading company but as the proconsul of an empire.

At all events, a modest trickle of emigrants began reaching the Island. The *Harpooner* had arrived in 1849 with a few colonists, including James Yates, a shipwright by trade, who was eventually to become a merchant and to give his name to an important thoroughfare in the city of Victoria. Also on this ship was Dr. Alfred Benson, who was, however, assigned to Fort Vancouver, and the Muir family, who soon left for Fort Rupert.

In 1850, the *Norman Morison* brought out eighty men (nearly all miners intended for the Company workings at Fort Rupert), but including Dr. J. S. Helmcken, destined in the course of time to become Douglas' son-in-law and to live on into the age of the motor car and the aeroplane.[42] The following year the *Tory* brought 130 settlers, mainly laborers to work on the Company farms, but including some figures who would someday be well-known residents of the area. Mr. and Mrs. Blinkhorn became the first settlers at Metchosin, Richard Golledge was someday to be Douglas' private secretary, Edward Langford was appointed overseer of Colwood Farm, and William John Macdonald was eventually to fill a variety of distinguished positions, including those of mayor of Victoria and member of the Senate of Canada.

Evidence that the Company would have no great objection if some of these newcomers moved on is given by one of Governor Blanshard's despatches:

> The ship "Tory" has just landed about one hundred and twenty persons, all with two exceptions servants of the Hudson's Bay Company; some have already been sent to Oregon, and some to other posts of the Company; no preparations had been made here for their reception beyond erecting a couple of log houses or rather sheds. In these the remainder are huddled together like cattle as I have seen myself, to the number of thirty, or thirty-five in each shed, men and women, married and single without any kind of screen or partition to separate them. As may be supposed, great discontent exists already and will most certainly increase—the result will probably be that they leave the colony and seek employment in Oregon.[43]

So the term of Governor Blanshard, who reigned but did not rule,[44] drew to its unhappy end. While waiting for permission to return to England, he continued to perform what he conceived to be his duties, and in his spare time

> . . . used to ride in solitary state about the country, and did not seem to make any friends. Indeed, there were few with whom he could associate on an equal footing, and they seemed to hold aloof.[45]

For Douglas, too, it does not seem to have been an altogether propitious period, as he was continually faced with problems which he was forced to deal with unaided, and for which his previous experience had not always prepared him. Writing to a friend a week after Blanshard's arrival, he noted that

> The barque "Cowlitz" from England arrived here a few days ago and we are now busy discharging her cargo. Nearly all the seamen on board ran from her at the Sandwich Islands from whence she came on with Sandwich Islanders who made a shift to get here but cannot be trusted on a coasting voyage. Two more ships are expected out in the course of this season with about 70 servant colonists whom we shall have trouble enough to keep and feed. The anxiety and suspense of this life is torturing . . .[46]

Later in the same year, the Chief Factor received somewhat discouraging news:

We have letters from England up to 24th June, a dividend had been declared—a paltry affair of some hundred pounds, just about enough to keep us in tobacco money. I hope the next will be more respectable or the sooner we cut and run the better.[47]

Almost inevitably, the subterranean clash of interest between the Company and those settlers who were, or wished to be, independent of it, took shape in action. A group slowly formed whose basic aim was to effect a change in the fundamental conditions of life in the Colony—to move it, in effect, into the mainstream of the nineteenth century. When this group learned that Blanshard would soon be leaving the Colony and that Douglas would be his successor, they were sufficiently aroused to compose a petition to the retiring Governor which catalogued their grievances, expressed their fears for the future, and suggested changes in the government of the Colony. The petition (which Dr. Helmcken thought Blanshard himself had some hand in composing)[48] is perhaps worth quoting in full:

To His Excellency Richard Blanshard, Esquire,
   Governor of Vancouver Island.
May it please your Excellency:
   We, the undersigned inhabitants of Vancouver Island, having learned with regret that your Excellency has resigned the government of this colony, and understanding that the government has been com- mitted to a chief factor of the Hudson Bay Company, cannot but express our unfeigned surprise and deep concern at such an appoint- ment. The Hudson Bay Company being, as it is, a great trading body, must necessarily have interests clashing with those of indepen- dent colonists. Most matters of a political nature will cause a contest between the agents of the Company and the colonists. Many matters of a judicial nature will undoubtedly arise, in which the colonists and the Company, or its servants, will be contending parties, or the upper servants and the lower servants of the Company will be arrayed one against the other. We beg to express in the most emphatical and plainest manner our assurance that impartial decisions cannot be expected from a governor who is not only a member of the Company, sharing its profits, his share of such profits rising and falling as they rise and fall, but is also charged as their chief agent with the sole representation of their trading interests in this island and the adjacent coasts.

Furthermore, thus situated, the Colony will have no security that its public funds will be duly disposed of for the benefit of the colony in general, and not turned aside in any degree to be applied to the private improvement of that tract of land held by them, or otherwise unduly employed. Under these circumstances, we beg to acquaint your Excellency with our deep sense of the absolute necessity there is, for the real good and welfare of the colony, that a council should be immediately appointed, in order to provide some security that the interests of the Hudson Bay Company shall not be allowed to outweigh and ruin those of the colony in general.

We, who join in expressing these sentiments to your Excellency, are unfortunately but a very small number, but we respectfully beg your Excellency to consider that we, and we alone, represent the interests of the island as a free and independent British colony, for we constitute the whole body of the independent settlers, all the other inhabitants being, in some way or other, connected with and con- trolled by the Hudson Bay Company, as to be deprived of freedom of action in all matters relating to the public affairs of the colony, some indeed by their own confession, as may be proved if necessary. And we further allege our firm persuasion that the untoward influences to which we have adverted above are likely, if entirely unguarded against, not only to prevent any increase of free and independent colonists in the island, but positively to decrease their present numbers.

We therefore humbly request your Excellency to take into your gracious consideration the propriety of appointing a council before your Excellency's departure; such being the most anxious and earnest desire of your Excellency's most obedient and humble servants, and Her Majesty's most devoted and loyal subjects.[49]

Blanshard, who in his first few weeks as Governor had informed the British Government that he could not see his way to implement their directive to establish a Council to aid him in his tasks (there being virtually no genuine colonists to draw it from),[50] now, in his last days of office, appointed a council of three. Its members were Douglas, John Tod and James Cooper, and it met for the first time on August 30, 1851. Thus the first faint beginnings of a more representative form of government were already in existence when on the first of September Douglas formally became what it might be claimed he already was in practice: the Governor of Vancouver Island. A few days more, and Blanshard had embarked on a British warship for San Francisco, from which point he was left to find his own way back to England as best he could. An era was over, a new one had begun.

It is easy to criticize Vancouver Island's first governor, but perhaps he deserves instead our sympathy. He had no real training for his duties, the colony over which he attempted to preside was still in its infancy, and his superiors in London seemed to have but scant appreciation of his difficulties. His health was not robust, and he was forced to live in the shadow of one of the most capable men in the history of the Northwest—a man, moreover, who undoubtedly believed himself more than equal to combining the two highest offices in the colony.

Certainly those who knew Blanshard remembered him with respect. Dr. Helmcken, for example, declared many years later that "he was a very intelligent and affable man".[51]

Yet now his short term of office was over, and the capable hands of the Chief Factor held all the reins of power. True, many tasks confronted him in the years ahead. He would have to supervise the fur-trading operations of the Fort, expand its auxiliary activities such as farming, provide for the physical, intellectual and spiritual needs of the Company's employees, and protect them against both the native tribes and the forces of foreign powers.

These, however, were problems which in one form or another he had faced before; there would soon be others, though, which would present a greater challenge. Already, as the petition to his predecessor had made clear, there were some premonitory signs. No longer was every member of the community an employee of the HBC, bound by its authority in almost every aspect of his life. There was now a body of independent settlers; these had crossed the wide oceans in search of a life of their own, and were by no means disposed to bow the knee before the Company or its autocratic Chief Factor. Moreover, their ranks were slowly but steadily augmented by new arrivals. It seemed certain that they would eventually constitute the great majority of the inhabitants of the colony; a consciousness of common interest would imbue their outlook, and this in turn would issue in a demand for a reorganization of the government of the colony along lines more congenial to their needs and outlook. They would, in plain words, call for a much greater degree of democracy in the affairs of the settlement; and this, by reason of his background, his character, and the economic interests of the Company which in one of his two capacities he represented, would rouse but scant enthusiasm in James Douglas.

This was not the sole problem the new Governor would face; another, closely allied to it, would also in course of time obtrude itself. Not only was the almost feudal organization of the colony soon to be challenged by the rising tide of nineteenth century democracy, but its economic basis, fur trading, would steadily yield to a more diversified and urbanized network of relationships. This trend had not yet begun when Douglas succeeded to the governorship, but before he laid it down thirteen years later it would be an irreversible feature of the colony's life.

In both these cases, Douglas would face the choice between vainly essaying to turn back the tide of history and steering the colony as it was borne upon its swiftly flowing waters into a hitherto uncharted sea. It is a measure of the man that rather than turn the governorship into the home of "lost causes and impossible loyalties", he used it to facilitate the great changes that he knew must come.

There was also another force that eventually he would be forced to grapple with: the advancing tide of American nationalism and expansionism. Spreading out across the continent, it had already in his lifetime crossed the illimitable prairies and flooded into the valleys of the Columbia; before it, the outposts of British influence had been submerged forever. What would happen if some new source of wealth should suddenly make Vancouver Island or the adjacent mainland an El Dorado for eager adventurers from the ever more powerful republic to the south? Would the same story be repeated? This problem, too, would one day face James Douglas, and, as we shall see, standing in the "hot gates" of history and geography, he would hold the pass.

Thus, though he now enjoyed sole sway in the young colony, the years ahead would clearly not be easy ones. Yet always before, as we have seen, entrusted with responsibilities, he had shown himself deserving of them. Now, once again, their burdens as well as their glory would be his; now, once again, he would not fail.

NOTES

1 In *Wanderings of an artist among the Indians of North America*, The Radisson Society, Toronto, 1925, Chapter XIV.

2 Their report is printed in full in *Miscellaneous Papers relating to Vancouver Island 1848-1863*. Great Britain, Colonial Office.

3 Finlayson, *Biography*, Victoria 1891, p. 15.

4 See W. E. Ireland, "Captain Walter Colquhoun Grant, Vancouver Island's First Independent Settler", *BCHQ*, Vol. XVII, Jan.-Apr. 1953; also J. R. Anderson, Notes and Comments (unpublished MS in Provincial Archives) pp. 157-8.

5 It is possible that his school was not the first to be operated in the colony, and that the Catholic missionary, Father Lampfrit, preceded him. This controversy may be pursued in D. L. MacLaurin, "Education before the gold rush", *BCHQ*, October 1938; also in *A Century of Service 1858-1958*, by Sister Mary Margaret Down, Morriss Printers, Victoria, 1966, pp. 23-25.

6 For further details of Staines' background and career see G. Hollis Slater, "Rev. Robert John Staines; Pioneer Priest, Pedagogue & Political Agitator", *BCHQ*, Vol. XIV, Oct. 1950. For reminiscences of one of the school's first pupils, see J. R. Anderson, Notes and Comments, (unpublished MS in Provincial Archives), pp. 158-168.

7 See R. Finlayson, *Biography*, Victoria, 1891, pp. 21-22.

8 Barclay to Douglas, Aug. 3, 1849. PABC.

9 Douglas to A. C. Anderson, March 18, 1850. Quoted in J. R. Anderson, Notes and Comments, pp. 132-133.

10 The instructions issued to Douglas by the HBC perhaps unconsciously reveal its fundamental attitude to Vancouver Island's first representative of the Crown: "A house will also have to be provided for him, but a very temporary one will answer the purpose for the present, and until funds arise from the sale of land and other property". (Barclay to Douglas, Aug. 3, 1849).

11 Blanshard to Douglas, June 26, 1850. PABC.

12 Blanshard to Douglas, Aug. 5, 1850. PABC.
It is surely a fair inference, considering the facilities for face-to-face discussions between the two men, that they both already sensed a certain tension in their relationship.

13 W. K. Lamb, "The Governorship of Richard Blanshard", *BCHQ*, Vol. XIV, Jan.-Apr. 1950, p. 3.
It stood at what is now the corner of Yates and Government streets.

14 Douglas to Barclay, Sept. 10, 1850. The house was 40 x 20 feet, with a kitchen 18 x 12 attached.

15 Douglas to Barclay, Sept. 10, 1850.

16 *Ibid.*

17 *Ibid.*
18 Bancroft. *History of British Columbia,* San Franscisco, 1890, p. 270.
19 Unlike many of the earliest arrivals in Victoria, he did not come round the Horn. By this time it was possible to take a steamship to Panama, cross the isthmus, and then complete the journey on another ship. See F. V. Longstaff, *Esquimalt Naval Base,* Clarke and Stuart, Vancouver, 1942, pp. 22-23.
20 J. S. Helmcken, *Colonist,* Christmas Number, 1887.
21 Fort Rupert was named after the first Governor of the HBC, Prince Rupert (1619-1682).
22 And was promptly presented by the Admiralty with a bill for £47. 15.0 for his transportation. He was forced to inform the Colonial Secretary (Despatch No. 20, August 11, 1851) that he no longer had any available funds.
23 Despatch No. 5, August 18, 1850. PABC.
24 Despatch No. 7, October 19, 1850. PABC.
25 Despatch No. 9, November 18, 1850. PABC.
26 Despatch No. 10, Feb. 3, 1851. PABC.
27 Barclay to Douglas, December 1849. PABC.
28 Douglas to Barclay, May 16, 1850. PABC.
29 *Ibid.*
30 *Ibid.*
31 Douglas to Barclay, May 16, 1850. PABC.
32 Blanshard, Despatch No. 11, Feb. 12, 1851. PABC
33 Bancroft, *History of British Columbia,* San Francisco. 1890, pp. 277-278.
34 The HBC and its subsidiary, The Puget Sound Agricultural Company.
35 B. A. McKelvie, "Douglas: a new portrait", *BCHQ,* Vol. VII, No. 2, April 1943, p. 95.
36 *Ibid.,* p. 97.
37 He was struck by a motor car at the corner of Transit and Newport, Oak Bay, on the evening of April 9, 1930, and died instantly. See the *Colonist* of April 10 for an account of his career.
It gives some idea of the comparatively short span of British Columbia history to note that Anderson in his childhood had known at Fort Vancouver an old Kanakan who claimed to have eaten part of Captain Cook (J. R. Anderson Notes and Comments, pp. 209-210), and that Anderson in his turn was pronounced dead by Dr. D. M. Baillie, who still lives and flourishes in the neighborhood of Victoria.
38 Anderson, Notes and Comments, pp. 140-141.
39 "There is no escaping from trouble in this world". (Douglas to Jane Dallas, Sept. 5, 1869).
40 Anderson, Notes and Comments, p. 142.
41 This letter, written Oct. 18, 1838, is quoted from J. S. Galbraith, *The Hudson's Bay Company as an Imperial Factor 1821-1869,* U. of Toronto Press, 1957, p. 12.
42 Born in 1824, he died in 1920. His home, built in 1852 and still standing, is a well-known tourist attraction.
43 Blanshard, Despatch No. 16, June 10, 1851. PABC.

[44] The historian Bancroft puts the matter with some accuracy: "Though backed by the greatest nation on earth, he was more helpless than the seventh wife of a savage". (*History of British Columbia*, San Francisco, 1890, p. 277).
[45] J. R. Anderson, Notes and Comments, p. 156.
[46] Douglas to A. C. Anderson, March 18, 1850. For complete version, see J. R. Anderson, Notes and Comments, p. 133.
[47] Quoted in J. R. Anderson, Notes and Comments, p. 192.
[48] Helmcken, Reminiscences, III. p. 105.
[49] Sage, *Douglas*, pp. 168-169.
[50] Blanshard, Despatch No. 2, April 8, 1850. PABC.
[51] *Colonist*, Christmas number, 1887.
Although the British Government never employed him again, he did not disappear entirely from the stage of history at this point. A parliamentary committee inquiring into the affairs of the HBC in 1857 heard testimony from him regarding his experiences. Blanshard was understandably unsympathetic to the Company, and partly as a result of this enquiry the monopolistic position of the HBC was terminated. See Bancroft, *History of British Columbia*, pp. 376-381.

CHAPTER SEVEN

The Colossus of
the Narrow World

THE NEXT six years were to be busy ones for Douglas. Almost alone, he had to supervise and direct every aspect of the Colony's develop- ment. Moreover, he had to do so in the service of two masters. In his capacity as Governor of Vancouver Island, he was responsible to the Secretary of State for the Colonies, while as Chief Factor of Fort Victoria he owed allegiance to the Governor and Committee of the Hudson's Bay Company. Both of the authorities from whom he received his instruc- tions resided in London, but this did not much simplify the situation. His two sets of superiors inevitably saw the world from different angles, and it was not always possible to reconcile their views. In such cases, it was by no means clear what Douglas was expected to do; when dis- loyalty was unthinkable and exclusive loyalty impossible, a dilemma was indeed created. This is reflected in a letter from Douglas to the Secretary of the HBC, written in the last few days of Governor Blanshard's term of office. In it, Douglas declared:

> I accept the office of Governor of Vancouver's Island solely in obedience to the Company's wishes, and I shall not fail to do every- thing in my power to promote the interests intrusted to my charge.[1]

A man who accepts a public responsibility "in obedience" to the wishes of a private commercial enterprise must have a remarkable degree of confidence in his ability to avoid any conflict of duties. Whether Douglas quite realized this is unclear; certainly he seems to have noticed no ambiguity in the phrase "the interests intrusted to my charge".

It is remarkable in the circumstances that he was nearly always able to satisfy both groups of superiors, and to advance the interests of both the Colony and the Company without undue friction—especially as two distinct factions were crystallizing in "The Fort", one composed of the HBC and its employees, the other of the independent settlers.

The variety of tasks which confronted Douglas was formidable. Roads and bridges were necessary to unite the Fort with the outlying settlements; efficiently operated farms were essential if the colonists were to eat; schools were needed that young minds might not lie fallow; and churches if religion was not to decay. Defenses must be looked to, with one eye to the native tribes and the other to foreign powers; money must be found to carry these projects forward; all this while keeping a supervising eye on the chain of trading posts that stretched from the shadow of the Rockies to the Pacific coast, and fulfilling in what time remained the duties of a husband and a father.

Each of the varied tasks which Douglas dealt with in the next six years could here be considered separately. Yet though this privilege is the historian's, it was far from that of Douglas. Life presented itself to him in no neat categories, labelled and tied for his inspection. Rather it came to him in an endless intermingled stream of problems and challenges, new ones continually arising before the old ones were fairly settled. This being so, it is surely better if they are dealt with here in the same way; certainly it will enable us more easily to put ourselves in the position of the man who, after thirty years in posts of hardship or responsibility, now guided the destinies of Vancouver Island.

One of his earliest letters to the headquarters of the HBC in London after assuming undivided control of the colony reveals the diversity of the tasks confronting him. Roads and education, for example, both required prompt attention. With regard to the former, Douglas outlined what was perhaps the first step toward the creation of Vancouver Island's present network of highways:

> I have received a petition from the settlers at Soke Inlet about 25 miles west of this place praying to have a road opened by the sea coast to their settlement, as they are now put to a great expense for canoe hire for want of a good horse road. I think favourably

of the object of their petition, and beg to recommend it to the favourable consideration of the Governor & Committee, as it will contribute greatly to the convenience of the inhabitants and otherwise promote the interests of the Colony.[2]

I have lately had the line of road examined by competent persons, and think that such a road as is at present required may be made at an outlay to the Colony of £50, in payments to Indians who would chiefly be employed in the work, the principal labour being cutting the trees and clearing the ground of stumps. By carrying the road through Victoria, Esquimalt, Metchosin & Soke, the principal settlements would be connected by a convenient land communication which would greatly facilitate intercourse, add to the security of detached settlers, and advance the colonization of the country by throwing open valuable tracts of immediately cultivable land which are now surrounded by dense forest.[3]

Turning to education, a subject always of close concern to him, the Governor suggested steps which might be taken to further it:

I will also take the liberty of calling the attention of the Governor & Committee to the subject of education by recommending the establishment of one or two elementary schools in the Colony, to give a proper moral and religious training to the children of settlers, who are at present growing up in ignorance and the utter neglect of all their duties to God and to Society.

That remark applies with peculiar force to the children of Protestant parents; the Roman Catholic families in this country having had until lately a very able and zealous teacher in the Rev. Mr. Lampfrit, a French priest of the Societé des Oblats, who is now living with the Indians in the Cowetchin valley. One school at Victoria and one at Esquimalt will provide for the present wants of the settlements, and a fixed salary of £50 a year to be paid by the Colony, with an annual payment by the parents of a certain sum, not to exceed thirty shillings for each child, with a free house and garden, is the plan and amount of remuneration I would propose to the Committee. In regard to the character of the teachers I would venture to recommend a middle-aged married couple for each school of strictly religious principles and unblemished character, capable of giving a good sound English education and nothing more, these schools being intended for the children of the labouring and poorer classes, and children of promising talents, or whom their parents may wish to educate further, may pursue their studies and acquire the other branches of knowledge at the Company's school, conducted by the Revd. Mr. Staines.

I would also recommend that a good supply of school books, from the alphabet and upwards, with slates and pencils, be sent out with the teachers, as there are very few in this country.[4]

As we noted earlier, Douglas had not only to inform his superiors in the Company of the progress of its affairs on Vancouver Island, but also to communicate with the successive Secretaries of State for the Colonies regarding matters of interest and importance. In one of his earliest despatches, Douglas began by acknowledging his appointment in language that some might think bordered on obsequiousness:

I have the honour to acknowledge the receipt of your Lordship's communication of the 19th May 1851, transmitting a commission under the Great Seal of the United Kingdom, appointing me to be Governor and Commander in Chief in and over the Island of Vancouver, and its dependencies, together with instructions under the Royal Sign Manual and Signet for my guidance in the administration of the Government thereof, and also a Commission under the Seal of the High Court of Admiralty, appointing me to be Vice Admiral of that Island and of its dependencies, all which Instruments were duly received by me on the 30th of October.

I beg through your Lordship to convey to Her most Gracious Majesty my humble thanks for those distinguished marks of confidence which it shall be my endeavour to prove are not misplaced. The Royal Instructions will be faithfully executed, and in the exercise of the powers and authority vested in me by the Royal Commission, it shall be my study to promote, to the utmost of my ability, the honour and advantage of the Crown, as well as the interests of Her Majesty's subjects in this Colony.[5]

These formalities duly recorded, Douglas turned his attention to public affairs in the colony. He noted that he had added Roderick Finlayson to his Council, describing him as "a gentleman of worth and great experience". In a more sombre vein he reported the capture and execution by their own people of the three Indians responsible for murdering some white men near Fort Rupert in the term of Governor Blanshard, informing Lord Grey that:

The mangled remains of the criminals were taken to Fort Rupert, and after being identified by the Chiefs of the Quakiolth Tribe, were interred near the Fort, so that there is no doubt as to their having met the fate they so justly deserved.[6]

The arts of peace as well as war were also chronicled, Douglas declaring himself

... happy to inform your Lordship that the grain crops throughout the settlement were abundant this season, and were secured in fine con-dition, though, singular to say, in the American settlements about Nisqually and on the Columbia River the harvest was remarkably wet, and it is estimated that at least one third of the grain of this season perished in the fields, and a larger proportion was much dam-aged by the wet, a circumstance which tells greatly in favour of the climate of Vancouver Island.[7]

The native tribes also engaged Douglas' interest, and he had sug-gestions to make regarding them:

I shall probably take the liberty of calling your Lordship's attention hereafter to the best means of improving the condition of the aborigines of this Island, who are, in many respects, a highly interesting people, and I conceive worthy of attention. They will become under proper management of service to the Colony, and form a valuable auxiliary force in the event of war with any foreign power. From my long experience of Indian character, and of the tribes on this coast in particular, I am led to regret that the missionary societies of Britain, who are sending teachers to so many other parts of the world, have not turned their attention to the natives of Vancouver's Island.[8]

In a later despatch, Douglas touched on a complex question—that of accepting Indian testimony in disputes. Here he found himself in a logical dilemma. He felt that Indians, as not being Christians, could not be sworn; yet it seemed a *reductio ad absurdum* to conclude from this that as witnesses they were automatically worthless. His own feeling was that the testimony of Indians should be accepted whenever either or both parties to a dispute were of their race; but not when both were whites.[9] We should not conclude from this, however, that Douglas thought of the natives with contempt, or was indifferent to their grievances. He was careful in the same despatch to Lord Grey to make this clear:

I would take the liberty of remarking to your Lordship, how very important it is to the peace and security of the settlement that instant attention should be paid to the complaints of Indians, and their wrongs receive speedy redress, as nothing will tend more to inspire confidence in the governing power, and to teach them that justice may be obtained by a less dangerous and more certain method than their own hasty and precipitate acts of private revenge.[10]

A note was sounded in this early despatch, however, which would be repeated at intervals in succeeding years. This was one of uneasiness regarding the occasional incursions of Americans into areas north of the boundaries agreed to in 1846. Two American ships, for example, touched briefly at Victoria on their way to the Queen Charlotte Islands, where it was rumored that gold had been found. Even in the first few months of his governorship, Douglas seems to have sensed that this was not just an incident, but a portent:

Their presence on the coast will, I fear, be productive of much evil, and lead to serious difficulties with the native tribes.[11]

This was not the only occurrence of its kind to give Douglas some misgivings; the Governor reported two others to the HBC:

The "Exact", an American schooner, arrived here yesterday from Nesqually, bound to the Queen Charlotte's Islands with 32 passengers, all of whom are Americans, on board, being the second party of Americans who have gone this autumn to the gold mines. I could take no measures to prevent their going, neither does it appear to me advisable to do so at present, as they will assist in exploring the gold district and may be dismissed whenever Government may choose to eject them.[12]

A subsequent disquieting American action in the summer of 1852 was also reported to the Company:

I have just received information to the effect that the master of the American brig "Susan Sturges" lately cut, and carried off, a cargo of spars from Queen Charlotte's Island, a liberty that no British vessel would be permitted to take on the American coasts.[13]

Douglas feared that an important discovery in these remote islands might cause serious economic dislocation in the colony. Even the rumor of one, he reported:

. . . led to much excitement among the laboring classes in this colony, and I fear that many of them will in consequence leave their present employment to become gold hunters, a circumstance which will for a time retard the progress of the settlement.[14]

As a precautionary move, Douglas sent the HBC brig *Recovery* to the Islands, and took immediate possession of "the only surface gold vein in Gold Harbour", informing Lord Grey that he had done so "with the consent and approbation of the native Indians".[15] He evidently did not feel that matters in that area were entirely settled by this action; expressing his belief that any good discovery would bring Americans to the area in some number, he noted soberly that

. . . it will be no easy matter to eject them when firmly established.[16]

He also put forward a suggestion to the Company which he hoped would to some extent counteract any possible loss of population from the colony:

I herewith transmit copy of a letter lately received from John and Andrew Muir containing a proposition, which I promised to lay before the Committee for bringing out 10 persons, their connections in Scotland, to this country.

As this is the first application of the kind that has yet been made for the introduction of settlers unconnected with the Company's service, the Committee will probably see the advantage in making the charges for the passage to this country as moderate as possible, more especially as several of the parties expected by the Muirs are young unmarried women of good character who will be a great acquisition to the Colony.

I may further add that the Muirs are now the only settlers at Soke with the exception of Munro, the tenant on Captain Grant's property, the other white residents having all abandoned the settlement, some with the view of residing at Victoria, but generally speaking with the intention of proceeding by the first chance to Queen Charlotte's Island to try their fortune at gold digging. It is therefore, I think, very desirable that the Muirs should have every inducement to remain there.[17]

Colonists were also in prospect from another source than the British Isles, Douglas reported in a later letter to HBC headquarters:

William R. Pattle, whose name appears on the statement of applications for the purchase of land, arrived here in the early part of last month, from San Francisco with the schooner "Honolulu", of which he is master, and the reputed owner. It is his present intention to become a colonist, and to raise pigs for the California market. He has now two white men and several Indians employed in clearing away timber and making other improvements upon his claim.

Mr. Pattle is a native of New Brunswick in British North America, and reports that there are many of his countrymen in California who would gladly settle upon Vancouver's Island if they met with the smallest encouragement, or were even assured of finding employment here until they could collect funds sufficient to enable them to purchase land for themselves.

As a laboring population they would, I have no doubt, from the experience they have had in their own country, be found admirably adapted for a new colony. I shall take the earliest opportunity of letting them know that all well disposed and industrious men will be kindly received, and meet with every encouragement on Vancouver's Island.[18]

It is interesting to note that Douglas also mentions in this period a private venture which he thought might prove in time a public benefit. This was the formation of a company to erect and operate a saw mill "on some part of the coast". Douglas reported that he himself had invested £200 (out of a total capitalization of £2000), and felt that there was "every prospect of its becoming a good investment". This was not in fact to prove the case, but it is noteworthy as evidence that Douglas had sufficient faith in the colony's future to invest some of his own savings in it.

Later, he had more to say regarding the progress of this project. Writing to the headquarters of the HBC, he reported having made a move in which once again private and public interests and benefits were inextricably intertwined:

The steam saw mill Company having selected as the site of their operations the section of land marked upon the accompanying map north of Mount Douglas, which being within the limits of the Sanitch country, those Indians came forward with a demand for payment, and finding it impossible to discover among the numerous claimists the real owners of the land in question, and there being much difficulty in adjusting such claims, I thought it advisable to purchase the whole of the Sanitch Country, as a measure that would save much future trouble and expense. I succeeded in effecting that purchase in a general convention of the Tribe; who individually subscribed the Deed of Sale, reserving for their use only the village sites and potato patches, and I caused them to be paid the sum of £109.7.6 in woollen goods, which they preferred to money.[19]

By the spring of 1852, education had also made good progress:

Mr. Charles Bailey, the young man who acted as schoolmaster for the emigrants during the outward voyage of the "Tory", having conducted himself with great propriety since his arrival here, and not being particularly useful as a mere labourer, I have opened a day school for boys, the children of the Company's labouring servants at this place, who are growing up in ignorance of their duties as men and Christians.

It is now attended by 18 boys, who are making fair progress in learning. The parents furnish books and stationery, and pay £1 annually for each child, which goes into a fund for the support of the schoolmaster, and he also receives his wages and provisions from the Company, who are put to no other expense for the institution.

I beg also to inform the Governor and Committee that Mr. Langford is desirous of opening a young lady's school at his establishment with the view of bettering his circumstances, and has written to a young lady of his acquaintance, a Miss Scott, who has had much experience as a teacher, to join him in this country, provided she can obtain a free passage in any of the Company's ships. May I take the liberty of asking the aid of the Governor and Committee in promoting that important object so far as to allow that lady a free passage in the "Norman Morison" to this country, should she feel disposed to undertake the voyage.

This would be a great boon to the country, and another proof of the deep interest felt by their Honors in the progress of education.[20]

In the same letter, Douglas reported at length about a complaint made to the British Government by Admiral Moresby, R.N., who had called at the Fort for supplies and had, in his opinion, been forced to accept high-priced goods and watery rum. Douglas maintained that, as in the case of Governor Blanshard, the navy were not Company employees and were thus entitled to no discounts, and that the rum, far from being watery, was in fact "33⅓ per cent over proof".

> The rum is of better quality than is generally used in the Navy, and it would probably be advisable to send out a cheaper article for their supply, as they appear to regard the price more than the quality.[21]

Douglas did, however, suggest that some facilities should be provided at the Fort for regularly supplying ships of the Royal Navy with needful articles. This, he declared, once again with an eye on each of his two masters

> would be a great saving to the Government, and there would of course be some profit on the transaction to cover risk.[22]

Douglas also threw out a suggestion in which it is not unfair to discern the faint outline of the great naval base of our own day:

> Much advantage, both as regards the protection of the Colony and the increase of general sales, would, moreover, be derived in another way from making this part of the coast the occasional rendezvous of the Pacific squadron.[23]

In the same letter Douglas reported that J. Despard Pemberton, the surveyor, had made good progress in surveying the district. His account incidentally reveals that no possible saving was too small to be considered:

> I herewith forward a Tin Case containing various Drawings and plans from Mr. Pemberton as per accompanying list, which to save the expense of postage I have consigned to J. Perry, Esquire, British Consul, Panama, and requested him by letter to forward the same without delay.[24]

It is perhaps only fair to state at this point that Douglas throughout his career showed a vigilant interest in the slightest financial advantages, and that this was not always confined to those which would benefit the authorities he served. He was, in plain words, anxious to do as well as he could for himself, and this is illustrated by the efforts he now initiated to secure "back pay" for the period from May 12, 1849 to March 9, 1850, when, to his way of thinking, or at least argument, he, and not Richard Blanshard, had been the first governor of Vancouver Island. In support of this somewhat surprising thesis, he referred to a private letter, dated June 29, 1849, which had been sent to him by Sir George Simpson, informing him of his appointment as governor pro tempore, at a salary of £300 per annum. The Governors of the HBC were evidently ready to consider this claim, and accordingly on March 12, 1852 the Secretary of the Company, Archibald Barclay, sent a letter to Douglas, requesting the necessary tangible evidence for his assertion:

> With respect to the salary of £300 for the time you held the office of Governor of Vancouver's Island previous to the appointment of Mr. Blanshard, the Governor and Committee do not in any degree doubt the correctness of your representation on the subject, but as no copy of the official letter to which you allude can be found, you are requested for the sake of regularity to transmit a copy of it.

On June 22, 1852, Douglas forwarded to Barclay an extract from Simpson's letter which appeared to confirm his assertions regarding his appointment as Governor in 1849 at a salary of £300 per annum. Simpson in his letter to Douglas had enclosed some material from the "general despatch" of 1849 from the North American to the London headquarters of the Company, which recommended that as a reward for their exceptional services Chief Factors Ogden, Douglas and Work should be given additional compensation. It was suggested in this despatch that Ogden and Work should henceforth receive an extra £200 per annum, but that "the salary allowed to Mr. Douglas as Governor of Vancouver's Island ought, in the estimation of the Council, to satisfy that Gentleman's expectations".

Douglas appeared, then, to have some support for his claim, and was for some time to press it with his superiors. They, however, felt that they had acted correctly toward him, and eventually declined to grant him any additional compensation.[25]

This, however, was merely a minor facet of a complex character; compared with the services he was rendering to both the fur trade and the Crown, it need not long detain us. Certainly in the larger arena of events, under his guidance the year had been one of progress. The industrious Mr. Pemberton commenced a survey of the Sooke and Metchosin districts, and the road to those areas was gradually hewn through the wilderness. Thirty pounds had already been spent on it, and Douglas estimated that for another seventy pounds it might be made passable, if not for carriages, at least for pedestrians and cattle.[26] Coal in good quantities was found near Wentuhuysen Inlet, which was now given the name of Nanaimo.[27] The Governor personally travelled by canoe to the area, where he found the Indians friendly and was supplied by them with "fresh salmon and excellent potatoes". On viewing the large deposits of easily mined coal, his customary reserve evidently for a moment relaxed, and he wrote to the Colonial Secretary that

> . . . it was impossible to repress a feeling of exultation in beholding so huge a mass of mineral wealth, so singularly brought to light by the hand of nature.

He envisioned as a result of the discovery a bright future for the colony.[28]

Thus, though there were some clouds on the horizon—the remoteness of Vancouver Island from the main world trade routes was one— Douglas surveyed the scene with some satisfaction:

> As the white population increases in number, the Indians will under prudent management become submissive, and all apprehension of danger will cease; but in the meantime it is necessary to maintain our influence, which mainly depends on the belief of our ability to punish offences, by a display of physical force capable of supporting the laws, and of repressing the evil disposed.[29]

It must have come as something of a shock when late in 1852 a serious crime was committed within a few miles of the Fort. Two shepherds, Peter Brown and James Skea, were in charge of the Company's sheep farm at Lake Hill (also known as Christmas Hill). On the morning of November 5, Skea came upon the dead body of his companion. Douglas gave his superiors a vivid picture of the scene:

> The body was still warm and was surrounded by a pool of blood, and death had been evidently caused by two gunshot wounds, one of which had penetrated the chest from the right side where the ball had entered; the other had taken effect on the left side, about the region of the heart, and must have caused almost instant death. The door of the house was open, and several articles of property, including two guns and four blankets, were missing . . .

A fire bag, looking glass, a wooden comb and pipe of Indian manufacture, which they had evidently left behind in the hurry and alarm of their retreat were also found in and about the house, a fact which adds strength to the conviction arising from the other circumstances observed, that the deed was committed by natives, and most probably those who stopped at the station in the morning. One of those parties is well known here, having been lately em- ployed as a shepherd at that station, and I have no doubt we shall soon discover the real authors of the outrage, who it is supposed had no other motive than the desire of plunder. Having just returned from the scene of the murder, I have not had time to arrange any plan for bringing the criminals to justice, a measure absolutely necessary as an example to others.[30]

Douglas, however, on the same day that the crime was committed, decided on his response to it:

I propose in the first place despatching messengers to the chief of the Cowegin Tribe tomorrow, to inform them of the foul deed that has been committed, and to demand the surrender of the criminals if as suspected they belong in their tribe. I shall also offer a reward for their discovery and apprehension, and should those measures fail in their object, I shall be under the painful necessity of sending a force to seize upon the murderers, in whatever place they may be found. The great point in such cases is to avoid implicating the whole tribe in the guilt of individuals, and if we succeed in that object the parties will be brought to justice without much trouble or expense.[31]

In accordance with this plan of action, Douglas himself led the expedition which left Victoria on the fourth of January.[32] It consisted of the *Beaver*, another HBC ship, the *Recovery*, and the boats of H.M.S. *Thetis*. Douglas had reason to believe, as a result of information gathered from the local natives, that one of the murderers was of the Cowichan tribe, and accordingly the little flotilla anchored off the mouth of the Cowichan River. Douglas and his party (consisting of a force of 130 seamen and marines under the command of Lt. Sansum of the *Thetis*, as well as 11 half-breeds, servants of the Company) then went ashore.

Despite the size of this force, it was easily outnumbered by the Indian tribesmen who soon collected in their war-canoes. These included

. . . two large canoes crowded with the relatives and friends of the murderer, hideously painted, and evidently prepared to defend him to the last extremity; the criminal himself being among the number.[33]

A young naval officer, John Moresby, recalled the scene over half a century. On the one hand were marshalled

. . . over 200 tall warriors, their height exaggerated with head-plumes, faces terrifically painted with ochre, decked with loin-ropes of shells which met their deer-skin leggings and clattered with every movement . . .[34]

On the other hand, distinctive features of the white man's civilization were also displayed:

. . . a small tent was pitched for the Governor, where were deposited presents for the tribe, beside his pistols and cutlass, the use of either to depend on circumstances. [35]

After a long parley, while the disciplined forces of the whites stood ready for any word of command, the tribe was induced to surrender the guilty man. Douglas thereupon

. . . assembled the Indians and spoke to them long and seriously on the subject of their relations with the Colony, and the rules which must govern their conduct in the future.[36]

The expedition then proceeded to Nanaimo, where, after being hunted through the woods, the other fugitive was run to earth. A jury, the first ever seen on Vancouver Island, was then convened on the *Beaver*, and, as the prisoners admitted their guilt, there could be only one verdict.

They were sentenced to be hanged, and the execution took place in the presence of the whole tribe, the scene appearing to make a deep impression upon their minds . . ..[37]

Not all the events of this period were so sombre as these; the peaceful economic development of the colony also went forward steadily. Increasing quantities of coal were discovered at Nanaimo; Douglas described the supply as "boundless", reported that a ready market could be found for it in California, and suggested that the Company send out at least an additional twenty miners from England without delay.[38] There was as yet not much protection for the little settlement, but Douglas had already planned the construction of a stockade and one or more bastions;[39] in the meantime he made use of the *Cadboro* and the *Recovery*, keeping one or other of them stationed in the vicinity as symbols of the white man's power.

A few months later, Douglas decided on a personal inspection of the coal mines. Setting out in the *Otter* in August 1853, he covered the 80 miles in just under ten hours. He found that work was proceeding steadily, if not at a furious pace; this he attributed to the fact that the men had contracted to produce one ton of coal for each day's work. By offering to pay a premium on quantities mined in excess of that amount, Douglas was able to stimulate their energies.[40]

The discovery of this valuable natural resource inevitably raised the question of assuring its undisputed legal possession by the white man. Douglas was prompt to take note of the instructions that had been given him in this regard by his superiors in the Company:

> I observe the request of the Governor and Committee that I should take an early opportunity of extinguishing the Indian claim in the coal district, and I shall attend to their instructions as soon as I think it safe and prudent to renew the question of Indian rights, which always gives rise to troublesome excitements, and has on every occasion been productive of serious disturbances.[41]

Nevertheless, as at Forts Vancouver and Victoria, Douglas' interests in Nanaimo embraced much more than the purely economic aspects of its life. Education and religion, even in this remote and tiny settlement (only "twelve dwelling houses, a forge, 1 lumber store and a bastion are finished or in progress") were matters of keen concern to him, and (though not without a side glance at a possible connection between morality and economy) he reported his findings and recommendations to his superiors in London:

> While at Nanaimo, I had much conversation with the miners, and other married servants of the Company, on the subject of opening an elementary school for their children, who have been much neglected, and are growing up in ignorance of their duties as Christians and as

men. Seeing that they all expressed an ardent wish to have the means of educating their children, I transferred Mr. Baillie, who has for some time been employed as teacher of the Victoria Day School, but who is not now required here, to the Establishment of Nanaimo, where he has since opened School. His emoluments are the same as formerly, say £40 a year with board from the Company, and one pound sterling per annum for each child under his tuition, to be paid by the parents, who are also to provide books and stationery at their own expense.

I will also take the liberty of suggesting to the Governor & Committee the propriety of sending out a Clergyman for Nanaimo. The expense of that appointment will be richly repaid by its influence in improving the morals of the people, and the saving in police charges, while in many other respects it will redound to the honour and advantage of the Company.

The party selected for that office should be a member of the Free Kirk of Scotland, the miners being generally of that persuasion, and not disposed to receive instructions from the clergy of any other denomination.[42]

Meanwhile, at the southern end of the Island, the Company's farms were becoming sizable and flourishing operations. "Craigflower Farm" (whose manor house still stands) was under the capable management of Kenneth McKenzie; it soon had its own carpenter's and blacksmith's shops, sawmill, flour mill, brick kiln and slaughter house. Constance Cove Farm, two miles away in what is now the town of Esquimalt, was also producing valuable foodstuffs for the colony. Thomas Skinner was its overseer, and, because of the great oak trees in the district, called his home "Oaklands". The Governor was often a visitor at these farms, especially "Craigflower", and round the blazing fireplace would hear from visiting naval officers the news (as of three months previously) of the great world beyond the seas.[43]

The lumbering industry was also becoming an important feature of the colony's life, Douglas reporting that

The export of timber to California is now beginning to attract attention, several American vessels having lately called here for cargoes of piles . . .[44]

Meanwhile, in her own sphere, the Governor's wife reigned unobtrus-

James Murray Yale, Chief Trader at Fort Langley

Richard Blanshard, first Governor of Vancouver Island, 1849 - 1851

Dr. J. S. Helmcken, pioneer colonial physician, son-in-law of Governor Douglas

Col. Richard Clement Moody, Commander of the Royal Engineers and Chief Commissioner of Lands and Works

THE COLOSSUS OF THE NARROW WORLD / 109

ively. One event over which she presided would, seven decades later, still be vividly remembered:

My first experience of a real picnic was on the occasion of one given by Mrs. Douglas to the school children at the North Dairy Farm. Dump carts, waggons and any other rough vehicles and horses were put into requisition for the conveyance of the guests on this memorable occasion. Can I ever forget the lurid happiness of that delightful day? In my boyish imagination I could not conceive anything grander, more luxurious or extravagant could be done in this world. The glorious day, the unrivalled scenery, at that time unspoilt by the hand of man, the wealth of floral beauty, the thorough enjoy- ment of the drive in the rough vehicles, the rich milk and cream from the dairy, the jam tarts with twisted ropes of crust over them, the cookies and unlimited bread and butter were to my mind the acme of extravagant luxury, and lastly, the drive home in the evening con- cluded this never to be forgotten day of happiness.[45]

Nor were these the only delights of the young. Voyages of exploration up the Gorge in canoes with the Rev. Mr. Staines; watching the tribal ceremonies of the local natives or the public whipping of a recalcitrant seaman; greeting the occasional ships that found their way to the harbor, bringing such treasures as toys, oranges or fire-crackers; running along the plank bridge that crossed the head of James Bay or just "lying at full length thinking of the beautiful country";[46] even (for there was a reward) trapping the rats which infested the Fort dormitory: all these had their time and place.[47]

Thus slowly but surely the life of the colony was ramifying. John Work was added to the Governor's Council and four magistrates (E. E. Langford, Thomas Skinner, Kenneth McKenzie and Thomas Blinkhorn) were appointed. More schools were opened—one near Craigflower[48] and one about a mile from the Fort. The town of Victoria grew steadily if not spectacularly; by the fall of 1853 it contained "87 dwellings and store houses".[49] It was still without a church, but, considering the acute shortage of labor, Douglas did what he could; one was begun in 1853, though before it was finally completed it would be 1856.[50] Douglas also at this time reported the arrival in the colony of the Roman Catholic Bishop of Vancouver Island, Bishop Demers, with several priests.[51]

As the functions and responsibilities of government expanded, so, of course, did the need for revenue. The income tax had not yet been invented, and Douglas, casting about for some source of funds, hit on a way of combining a steady income for the Colonial Government with the moral improvement of the Colony. He had long been disturbed by the amount of drinking in the settlement, informing the Colonial Secre- tary on one occasion that

> Drunkenness is now the crying and prevalent sin of this colony, and will, I fear, continue to be so, until a better and more responsible class of people are sent to the country, or a great improvement takes place in the moral tone of the present population.[52]

Moreover, it was apparent that liquor vendors were making remarkably large profits by their trade. For American whiskey which had cost them five shillings a gallon, they were charging 7½d. for a glass holding half a gill[53]. Under these circumstances, the saloon keepers seemed well able to contribute to the public purse, and after a long debate with a some- what reluctant Council, the Governor decided to impose a stiff tax.

In a letter to HBC headquarters, Douglas expounded its terms and advantages:

> Two classes of licences for the sale of spirituous drinks are to be issued, Wholesale and Retail Licenses, the Duty to be levied on the former is fixed at £100, on the latter at £120 per annum. This is not too high when it is considered that there are no customs nor excise duties nor any public burdens whatever borne by the people of this colony. I do not suppose that the duty will put a stop to drunkenness, but it will at least take from the tippler a part of the means devoted to intemperance, and that part will be applied to the substantial improvement of the country and to counteract in some measure the influence of his evil example.[54]

Later in 1853, Douglas reported evidence that this new measure had been a wise one; there was, he informed the Secretary of the Company, much less public drunkenness, and the Colony was now on a sounder financial basis.[55]

It was in this period that Douglas made a suggestion to the British Government in which it is possible to see a larger vision taking shape:

May I take the liberty of suggesting to your Grace how very usefully the carpenters and seamen of H.M. Ships might be employed while stationed here, at a very small additional expense to the public, in erecting store houses for the use of H.M. Navy in the magnificent harbour of Esquimalt about five miles distant from Victoria, where there is a site admirably adapted to that purpose. This I conceive would result in a great saving of expense to the Government, as the stores and provisions wanted for the cruizers stationed on the northern Pacific might be shipped from England direct for the Naval store houses at Esquimalt, and remain there until required, instead of being first landed, as by the present arrangement, at Valparaiso, and reshipped from thence to this country in vessels chartered for the purpose, thus involving the risk and expense of a reshipment and of landing and storage at Valparaiso, which might in whole or in greater part be saved by a direct shipment from England to Van-couver's Island. That plan, if adopted, would, besides the aforesaid saving of expense, prove a great convenience to the public service, and enable H.M. ships to remain longer on the coast, without being detached to the ports of California or elsewhere for supplies. It would also be a very popular measure with H.M. subjects in this country, and would greatly tend to the progress of colonization, and therefore chiefly I have submitted it for your Grace's consider-ation.[56]

Unfortunately, this proposal did not receive the approval of the Imperial authorities, and it was not until after the outbreak of the Crimean War a year later that anything was done to implement it.

A matter which was to be a subject of international dispute for the next twenty years also engaged Douglas' attention at this time. This was the question of the ownership of the smaller islands between Vancouver Island and the mainland. The language of the Oregon Treaty, which was intended to fix the boundary between British and American posses-sions in the Pacific northwest, seemed difficult to interpret, but Douglas had no doubt that all these islands (which he called the Arro Archipel-ago) belonged to the British Crown. For some years he was not only to assert this thesis both publicly and in writing, but also, so far as he was able, enforce it in practice. Thus late in 1852 he had bluntly announced his policy to the British Government:

I shall assert the sovereignty of Great Britain to all the Islands in the Arro Archipelago.[57]

A year later, he reported to the Company that:

Two several attempts have been made by roving Americans to squat there, but I managed to get rid of them without creating any disturbance. The decision of a question of so much importance should, however, not be left to chance.[58]

A few weeks later, Douglas outlined his reasons for considering the matter a vital one:

The question of right is clearly in favour of the claims of Great Britain, and the necessity of the case demands that those claims should be maintained; as "Vancouver Strait" is the present navigable outlet from the Gulf of Georgia, and if it be surrendered to a foreign state, that noble inland sea bounded on every side by the Territories of Great Britain will be, in a measure, sealed to British commerce.[59]

Nor was he content merely to write letters in support of the British claim. Late in 1853 he informed the HBC that

A canoe party under the orders of Captain Stuart will be despatched today for the purpose of taking possession of Lopez Island and of marking that act by some permanent improvements.[60]

At about the same time, the Company sent a party to San Juan Island. Its employees had landed there briefly in 1845 and claimed possession, and there had been a company fishing station there since 1850. Now it established a farm there, which, under the management of Charles Griffin, soon prospered, there being at one time above two thousand horses, cattle and sheep on the Island.

These actions were given the approval of the Company, and there for a while the matter rested. That it was by no means permanently settled, however, will be seen as our story progresses. Indeed, as we shall see, a few years later it was for a moment to bring Douglas into the very shadow of what might have been disaster. This, however, still lay hidden in the future, and in the meantime the situation appeared stabilized.

It was in this period that the private life and public duties of Douglas crossed each other. Douglas' sister Cecilia, after an unsatisfactory first marriage, had married David Cameron, a cloth merchant of Perth, who was employed in Demerara, British Guiana. In 1853 the couple, with their daughter Cecilia, moved to Victoria, and Douglas found a clerical position for his new brother-in-law at the Nanaimo coal mines.

This favor to his relative by marriage was soon to be followed by a greater one. For some time, Douglas had realized that some of the magistrates that he had appointed earlier were unequal to their duties; he therefore set up a Court of Appeal, and made Cameron, despite his slender legal knowledge, its first presiding judge, with a salary of £100 a year.[61]

It is at this point that we must start taking note of a sizable opposition to the Governor and his policies. The first signs of this had appeared in the brief term of Governor Blanshard, when a petition, signed by all the independent settlers, had been given the retiring governor for presentation to the British government. The basic thesis of the petition had been that it was unwise to have as Governor a man who was also the chief representative of a private commercial enterprise; a man, moreover, who had no official colleagues, merely subordinates. This latter point had been to some extent answered when Blanshard had appointed his first council; the former, however, remained, and gave uneasiness to a growing number of settlers. Their ranks were reinforced when Dr. J. S. Helmcken married Douglas' daughter and David Cameron his sister. Three important figures in the Colony were now relatives by marriage, causing mutterings about a "Family Compact".

The numbers of the malcontents were augmented by those who for one reason or another had a personal grudge against the Governor. James Yates, the saloonkeeper, was aggrieved by the tax on liquor; James Cooper had earlier been obstructed by Douglas in his capacity of Chief Factor when he had essayed a private venture in cranberries;[62] Langford and Skinner seemed to harbor obscure grievances, while all these dissident voices were blended into a chorus by the tireless agitation of the Rev. Robert John Staines.

This discontented cleric had not entirely neglected his duties as schoolmaster and chaplain. His pupils in Victoria's first school had acquired the rudiments of learning, while among the marriages he had performed were those of John Work, Roderick Finlayson, W. F. Tolmie and J. S. Helmcken. In other respects, though, he had fallen short of expectations. He had devoted much of his time to raising pigs, and had become involved in a lawsuit about them; he was thought by Douglas to be the author of an anonymous letter to the Imperial Government complaining about various defects in the colony's administration; he was even suspected, most damning of all, of "rendering the labouring classes dissatisfied and suspicious". Douglas, though at first inclined to approve of him (as, one recalls, long years before, he had of the Rev. Herbert Beaver), had since come to wish him elsewhere; this view was intensified when two successive petitions were circulated in the colony, demanding far-reaching reforms in its system of government. Among the changes asked for were a more democratic form of government, including an elected House of Assembly, a Governor independent of all commercial ties, and the revocation of the Royal Grant of 1849. The appointment of Cameron as Chief Justice was also viewed with disfavor, since he was a relative by marriage of the Governor, and had had no previous judicial experience.

Douglas, however, informed his superiors that though Judge Cameron "has no doubt his faults like other men. . . I am confident of his firmness and integrity, and fully convinced that he will not wilfully commit an act of injustice." He admitted that Cameron was a HBC employee but declared, "This is however an unavoidable evil, as there are no qualified persons in the Colony for such offices except the officers of those Companies"..[63]

The cantankerous parson was one of the major figures in the preparation of these petitions, and this, among other things, caused Douglas to characterize him as one who

> entertains a most unaccountable and unreasonable dislike to the Company, and has done so ever since his arrival in this country; and he moreover endeavours to fill the minds of every stranger who arrives here with the rancorous feelings of his own breast.[64]

That the views expressed by the petitions were fairly widespread is, however, shown by the fact that the first one was signed by Tod, Tolmie and Finlayson, all old HBC servants, a fact which made Douglas declare that they

> should have had more sense and good feeling for the service than to take part in any proceeding affecting the Company's rights or character.[65]

Two events, however, combined to bring this agitation to at least a temporary halt. As a result of representations by dissatisfied parents of children at the Fort school, and of Douglas himself,[66] the Rev. Staines was relieved of his duties as schoolmaster; shortly afterward, having been selected by the malcontents to convey one of the petitions to the Home Government, he took passage for San Francisco, but lost his life when his ship, the *Duchess of Lorenzo*, went down in a storm.[67]

The second major event was of a very different sort. Tension had for some time been building up between Britain and Russia, and on March 27, 1854, the two countries found themselves at war, France allying herself with Britain in the conflict.

One might have supposed that this conflict, in any case waged for limited objectives, would have produced in a part of the world so distant from the battlefields of the Crimea not much more effect than the customary patriotic glow. Yet such was not to prove the case. This was partly because as fur traders all officers of the HBC on the Pacific coast had long been aware of the Russian presence in Alaska; their most formidable commercial rivals conducted many of their operations from this base, while the products of Vancouver Island, notably grain, had from the early years of that colony been shipped to Sitka.

Moreover, the man who, while remaining a high officer of the HBC, was also responsible for the military affairs of the colony, had acquired an unusual sensitivity to the currents of international politics. No doubt his deep reading had made him aware of the ceaseless ebb and flow of power down the centuries, and his acute intelligence had brought him to realize that it had not yet come to an end. At all events, the war was to produce immediate if varied reactions in Douglas, as a result of which, when the conflict had come to an end, the colony would be found to have acquired a new and important position in the global net-work of the Empire.

News of the great world in this period took a considerable time to reach Fort Victoria, and the war had actually been under way for three months before Douglas received official confirmation of the fact. He had, however, been warned earlier by the British Government that its outbreak was more than likely, and even while he was still unsure whether this had occurred, he had analyzed the situation as it might before long exist. In a despatch to the Duke of Newcastle on May 16, 1854, Douglas outlined what he believed were appropriate mea-sures. First, he considered the problem of defence, and suggested what were, in effect, preparations for guerrilla warfare:

> An irregular force of whites and Indians could be raised here and be made exceedingly useful in harassing and impeding the march of an enemy attempting to leave the sea-coast or penetrate into the country. To arm and equip such a force for the protection of the settlements, is a measure which I conceive should be imme-diately adopted and carried into effect, otherwise the whole coun-try may fall a prey to the first invader or be plundered by any marauding party that may land upon the coast.
>
> I would therefore earnestly recommend that precautionary steps against invasion may be immediately resorted to, and if approved by Your Grace that I may be empowered to carry the same into effect and to draw on the proper Department to defray the expense at-tending such measures.
>
> The accompanying requisitions which will probably be found in-complete, will show what I conceive to be necessary for the equip-ment of any military force raised in the country. A battery with a few heavy guns to defend the entrance of the harbour would also prove of very decided advantage.
>
> Your Grace will I presume order a detachment from the fleet in the Pacific, to be sent hither for the protection of the colony, in addition to the military force raised in the colony itself.
>
> Those defensive measures will involve the erection of Store Houses and Barracks for the accommodation of the Troops, and on the whole lead to a considerable outlay of money, which will not

be lost to the country, as long as protection is afforded to the lives and property of H.M. subjects.

The "requisitions" mentioned by Douglas were fairly substantial. They included 400 muskets, 100 rifles, 500 uniforms, 1000 pairs of military shoes, powder, ball, grape and canister "in quantities necessary", as well as a twelve-months' supply of such essentials as beef, pork, flour and rum.

Douglas, however, was by no means content with a purely defensive role for the colony he governed. Already he envisioned a bold plan for the use of his proposed force:

> I would further remark in reference to the Earl of Clarendon's communication that a very serious injury might be inflicted on Russia by taking possession of all their settlements on the American coast, north of Queen Charlotte's Islands; they are all upon the seaboard and accessible to shipping. Their defences are on a scale merely calculated to cope with savages, and could not be maintained against a regular force of 500 men. The occupation of those settlements may be regarded as an indispensable measure of protection against the piratical vessels of all nations which may seek to prey upon our commerce in the Pacific, and find a refuge there; the enemy will also be deprived by that measure of all their possessions in America, and of a most valuable branch of trade producing a large public revenue, and would thereby sustain a most serious loss.[68]

While he awaited the Duke's reply, Douglas acted on his own responsibility. To raise or equip a force of five hundred men was far beyond the means of the Colony, but in the meantime he did what he could. The inhabitants of Fort Victoria were by this time "much alarmed at the idea of a descent by the Russians, or rather by predatory vessels acting under the authority of letters of marque",[69] so the Governor, after consultation with his council, ordered the arming of the crew of the HBC ship *Otter*. This only added about thirty men to the defenders of the colony, but it apparently had some effect in stiffening morale.

The question as to who would pay for this measure would have to be decided. Douglas told the Duke what he thought:

That measure of defence will cost about £600 a month, which, I presume, will be defrayed by Her Majesty's Government, as in the Grant of Vancouver's Island to the Hudson's Bay Company, it is provided that the Governor and Company are "to defray the entire expense of any civil and military establishments which may be required for the protection and Government of such settlements, (except nevertheless during the time of hostilities between Great Britain and any foreign European or American power)", a provision which directly applies to the present circumstances of the Empire, and I should therefore be happy to have your Grace's directions in reference to the payment of that outlay.[70]

It was to be some time before this question was settled, and in the meantime the Colony girded itself for combat. It must have come as a rather unpleasant surprise when Douglas was told that his suggested force of five hundred gallant defenders was "both unnecessary and unadvisable".[71] British warships, he was informed, would look in at Esquimalt from time to time, and with that he would have to be content.

There was actually sound reasoning behind the decision of the British Government. Unknown to Douglas, an agreement had been concluded between the highest officials of the two great fur trading empires, the HBC and the Russian-American Fur Company, by which if war should break out, neither would molest the trading posts of the other. This agreement had received the blessings of both governments, but was kept a secret from all but a few of the highest officials, among whom Douglas was not reckoned to be one. His fears of a sudden Slavic onslaught on Fort Victoria were, therefore, in reality, groundless, but he was not to be informed of this for some time to come.[72]

Only commercial posts were safeguarded by this agreement; military ones were fair game. It was because of this that a series of events now took place, which would continue to affect the destinies of Vancouver Island long after all the participants were dead.

In the summer of 1854, an attack was made by a combined Anglo-French naval force on the Russian fortress of Petropaulovsk on the coast of Kamchatka. The venture was poorly planned and proved unsuccessful. There were many casualties, who had to be taken to San

Francisco for attention. This was clearly unsatisfactory, and in order to prevent a repetition, early in 1855 Rear-Admiral Bruce, the commander-in-chief of the Pacific Station (whose headquarters were at Valparaiso) wrote to Douglas, suggesting not only that his squadron might need supplies (he casually mentioned a thousand tons of coal, as well as "a full supply of fresh meat and vegetables") but also that a modest naval hospital be constructed near Victoria.

Douglas had well before this been anxious to see some sort of facilities for the navy at Esquimalt. As we saw, as early as July 28, 1853 he had written to the Imperial authorities, suggesting that store houses for the British fleet should be built in that area. This proposal had not at that time found favor and was rejected; a decision which in Douglas' view spelled economic disaster for the colony, and resulted in a despatch to the London government whose tone surely verges on bitterness:

> Deeply interested as I feel in the progress of every measure having a vital influence in the progressive improvement of this Colony, you will perhaps excuse me for remarking that I exceedingly regret this decision of their Lordships, and for the reason that it destroys almost the only existing prospect of being countenanced in our exertions to promote the colonization of Vancouver's Island, with the patronage of Her Majesty's Government. Deprived by its remote position from commercial intercourse with the mother country or any other British possession, and cut off from the advantages of foreign trade by the heavy import duties levied on all the productions of this Colony in the neighboring Ports of the United States, the inhabitants of Vancouver's Island are really placed in the worst conceivable position as regards their general prosperity, and it is very evident that the natural resources of the Colony must, in such circumstances, remain undeveloped, and the country continue an uninhabited waste.

> The Colony has been heretofore mainly supported by the large sums of money expended in house building and other works by the Hudson's Bay and Puget Sound Companies and by the servants of these companies. That resource must necessarily soon fail, and then follows the perplexing question as to what the laboring people in this Colony will find to do. They will then be destitute of employment and having no property nor means of acquiring land, on which

to employ their labour, and there being no foreign outlet for the expansion of general enterprises, they will be unable to earn a livelihood, and the probable consequence will be a general desire for emigration to the American settlements, where grants of land are freely profferred to all parties who become settlers, and improvers of the soil.[73]

Now, however, that was a chance that all might yet be well. Acting at once on the Admiral's suggestion, Douglas sent instructions to Nanaimo for the coal, to the Agent of the Company Farm at Nesqually[74] for "2000 head of sheep and as many beeves as he can manage to purchase", and urged the general public to start raising vegetables. He also in a short time, at a cost of slightly under £1000, erected three buildings to serve as the naval hospital. They were 30' by 50', clean, bright, and airy, and could accommodate a hundred patients.[75] Douglas now felt himself ready—or almost ready, for vegetables do not grow overnight—to receive the Admiral and his men. The only question that bothered him was the matter of who was to pay for all these things, and he cautiously sounded out the Admiral in this regard:

> I have assumed a responsibility beyond the limit of my instructions from Her Majesty, and entirely of a personal nature, but this being done from motives of humanity, and with the view of promoting the interests of the public service, I am in hopes it will meet with the approval of Her Majesty's Government, and I feel assured that you will not hesitate to share that responsibility with me.[76]

As it happened, the need for the buildings did not at first arise. A second Allied expedition to Kamchatka in the summer of 1855 found the fortress abandoned, and only a single casualty—an engineer suffering from scurvy—was admitted to the hospital. Nevertheless, an important step forward had been taken; Esquimalt was still far from a major British naval base, but Douglas' three buildings marked the first step in the great development that was to come.

The Admiral and the Governor found other ways of being useful to each other. In his letter of August 3, Douglas had dropped a suggestion about one of them:

The west coast of Vancouver's Island is still visited by American vessels, who are carrying on an illicit trade in fire arms and spirituous liquors, to the great injury of the country, and I trust you may find it convenient to cast an eye to that quarter.[77]

When the two men met face to face, a much more important subject was discussed. Writing to the headquarters of the HBC afterwards, Douglas reported on this matter, which, as we have seen, had long caused him much uneasiness:

I have this morning had a very interesting interview with Admiral Bruce. He kindly observed that his present visit is intended as a mark of regard for this Colony, and that he will endeavour to protect its interests and render every assistance in his power in respect to the San Juan question.

This is satisfactory and relieves me of much anxiety.[78]

The war did not further seriously affect Vancouver Island, except in so far as it stimulated its economy. Douglas established a committee, consisting of the Rev. Edward Cridge (who had arrived in the colony on April 1, 1855 to succeed the Rev. Staines as Fort Chaplain), Robert Barr the schoolmaster, and his old opponent James Yates the publican. These three raised considerable sums of money to provide comforts for the troops struggling under defective leadership on the distant battlefields,[79] and gradually the inconclusive conflict moved toward its eventual close in 1856.

We must not assume, however, that while the war was in progress all other activities in the colony were in abeyance. It is usual, indeed, for social change to accelerate in time of war, and Vancouver Island in these two years was no exception. A few months after the outbreak of hostilities, Douglas reported to his superiors in the HBC that a variety of projects were going forward. The road to Sooke was progressing, making use of Indian labor at $8 a month; white labor, in Douglas' view, was too expensive, costing $2 to $2.50 a day, with carpenters at $4 to $6. The jail was finished, and a courthouse was envisioned, while the gift or sale of liquor to the Indian population was prohibited.[80]

By this time, moreover, Douglas and his Council were beginning to think in larger figures. The same year, they appropriated £500 for roads, £500 for bridges, and £500 for the needed courthouse; while £1000 was voted toward the construction of a hospital.

As the year drew toward its close, other signs of expansion were apparent. The frame of Craigflower School was completed, while a party of coal miners and their families, after a harrowing voyage aboard the *Princess Royal*, arrived in Nanaimo.[81]

Not all the increase in the population of the colony was due to immigration; this year saw the birth of the Douglases' last child, Martha. She was eventually to be the the last survivor of his children, not dying till the depths of the Great Depression of the 1930's.[82]

The Company farms continued, meanwhile, to prosper, although at "Craigflower" its overseer, Captain Langford, was reprimanded by the Company for entertaining too lavishly. Under the threat of having to find employment elsewhere, he veered slightly in the direction of frugality.[83]

Not only the land but the sea provided a harvest. The resourceful Indians extracted oil from whales and dog fish and sold it to the whites, who then exported as much as 10,000 gallons a year of it to California. There it brought from $2 to $3 a gallon, and was reported as "burning freely in the coldest weather".[84]

It was in 1854, we might note in passing, that Douglas planted a Black Prince cherry stone in his back garden. When it grew old, cuttings were taken from it, one of which became the tree in the grounds of the new Museum and Archives building, which itself stands approximately on the site of Douglas' house.

In the closing weeks of the year, the Governor took some notice of the criticisms of his regime which were being made to the British Government by his opponents in the colony. Asserting that its prime mover, the late Rev. Staines, "unfortunately for himself was a violent party man, and was prudent neither in his conduct nor associations", Douglas declared with some exasperation:

> I really do not understand what the Memorialists refer to in the closing paragraph of that document, as no attempt has ever been made "to deprive them of their just rights" or "to require the

sacrifice of their dearest interests" or "to exercise over them a law-less and arbitrary power".

They have not ventured to specify their "real grievances" nor "the wrongs inflicted upon them" nor "the grievances under which they are deeply suffering", neither have they ever stated them to me. I have therefore come to the conclusion that those grievances are less real than imaginary, a conclusion strengthened by the present prosperous state of the country. The people, moreover, appear happy and contented, the frugal and industrious are rapidly improving their condition in life, there are no taxes nor public burdens, the laws are justly administered, the means of education are extending, intemperance is on the decrease, and crimes are almost unknown; in short, since the departure of the Revd. Mr. Staines and his co-adjutor Mr. Swanston, I have not heard a complaint from any person in this colony, except in regard to the sale price of the public land, which seems to be the only real grievance, affecting the colonists generally, and that grievance I have no power to redress.[85]

The British Government was evidently satisfied with Douglas' administration, for it lent no support to the agitation against it. Rather it continued to give him its cordial and sympathetic assistance, and under these favorable auspices, 1854 passed into 1855.

This year was to prove in most respects a satisfactory one. A census was taken in the colony, which revealed that as of December 31, 1854, there were 774 whites on the Island, of whom 232 lived in Victoria and 151 at Nanaimo. Not yet, clearly, had the area become a haven for the elderly; nearly half the population of the Island was under 20 years of age, and apparently nobody was over 60![86]

On the first of April, 1855, after a long voyage from England, the Rev. Edward Cridge arrived in the colony with his wife on the *Marquis of Bute* to replace the unfortunate Mr. Staines. Born in 1817, he was to live on till 1913, and in 1872 was to become the centre of a doctrinal controversy which would shake Victoria to its foundations. This, however, was still many years in the future, and in the meantime he entered upon his duties with diligence, while his wife opened the first Sunday School in the colony.[87]

The summer of this year saw the formation of the first Colonial

Militia. Designed more for protection against Indians than Russians, it consisted at first of only 8 privates, a corporal and a sergeant.[88] No sudden crisis required the services of this formidable body, however, and late in the year the Governor was able to report with some satisfaction to the Colonial Secretary:

> I have nothing of much importance respecting this Colony to communicate, except the pleasing fact that peace and quietness reigns within its limits, and that an abundant harvest has yielded a bountiful supply of food for the consumption of the white population.[89]

We might note, however, that "south of the line" conditions were far from peaceful in this period. There was open warfare between the Americans and the native Indians, with sizable casualties on both sides. Douglas' attitude toward the situation was a delicate one; if the white men in the territory of Washington were overwhelmed, it might place those on Vancouver Island in a dangerous position; on the other hand, if he seemed to be openly engaged on the side of the Americans, it might lead to a sympathetic uprising at home. He compromised by making firearms and ammunition available to the Americans (at the request of the acting governor of Washington Territory), but otherwise maintaining a judicious and slightly sanctimonious neutrality.[90] As he explained to his superiors in the British Government:

> I do not wish to incense the native tribes, or to become a party in the war. It is, I confess, a difficult game to play; but the same course of policy was adopted with success during the Cayuse war, when we were enabled to save many valuable lives and otherwise to render essential service to the country.[91]

He could not, however, deny himself a few reflections on the war:

> I am of opinion that there must have been some great mismanagement on the part of the American authorities, or it is hardly credible that the natives of Oregon, whose character has been softened and improved by 50 years of commercial intercourse with the establishments of the Hudson's Bay Company, would otherwise exhibit so determined a spirit of hostility against any white people.[92]

Douglas also experienced uneasiness from other sources. During the summer of 1855, about 2000 Indians arrived in the colony, including "a large body of Queen Charlotte Islanders, the most warlike, ignorant and barbarous people on the coast".[93] They were, in the main, seek-ing employment, but this did not prevent Douglas from experiencing "great and unceasing anxiety" at "the presence of so many armed bar-barians in a weak and defenceless colony". However, in the autumn most of them departed, and the Governor reported that:

> They begin in fact to have a clearer idea of the nature and utility of laws, having for object the punishment of crimes and the pro-tection of life and property, which may be considered as the first step in the progress of civilization.[94]

As a precaution, however, he established a police force of "four active men", though he felt that one of twenty or thirty would be even better.

The Americans, unfortunately, were less tractable than the Haidas. In the summer of 1855, a party of them landed on San Juan Island, and attempted to assert the authority of their government. Douglas made an immediate report on the affair to London:

> I beg herewith to transmit for your information copy of a Re-port from Mr. Charles Griffin, detailing the particulars of an out-rage committed by an armed party of American citizens, headed by a person styling himself Sheriff Barnes of Whatcomb County, who landed on the Island of San Juan, and in the name of the United States of America demanded payment of certain local taxes on Brit-ish property there, amounting in all to the sum of about 80 dollars. The demand being refused, they proceeded to make seizures, and succeeded in carrying off with impunity thirty four head of valuable breeding rams, with which they hastily took their departure for the American shore, before the British residents could muster for the protection of their property.
> I despatched a sufficient force to their assistance, but the Amer-icans had left the Island with their booty a few hours before the arrival of that detachment, which unfortunately did not pursue the party, or the property abstracted might have been recovered.
> I have addressed a letter to Mr. Stevens, Governor of Washing-ton Territory, in reference to that subject, and transmit a copy of the same herewith.

The Federal officers of Washington Territory having latterly stood entirely aloof, and taken no part in the boundary dispute, I was in hopes of remaining in quiet possession of the Arro Islands until the question of sovereignty was decided by the action of the Imperial Government, but it appears that the mob of Washington Territory have taken the matter in hand and are disposed to settle it in their own way.

I am very unwilling at the present conjuncture of affairs in Europe to take any steps that may give trouble or disturb our peaceful relations with the Government of the United States, but I fear that consequence will be inevitable unless measures are taken on both sides to prevent unlawful acts, and to enforce the peace of the country.

Outrages on the one side will as a matter of course lead to sharp reprisals on the other, and the result may be very serious to both parties.[95]

Douglas' letter to Governor Stevens, enquiring if this affair had had his sanction or authority, received a somewhat dusty answer, as Douglas reported to Lord John Russell on June 12, 1855:

On those subjects, however, Governor Stevens maintains a guarded reserve, and the whole tenor of his communication is so little explicit, as to leave a strong impression on my mind that the proceedings of the American party on San Juan were certainly not discouraged by the Federal authorities of Washington Territory.

It would clearly be conducive to the best interests of this and the neighbouring American settlements, if the executive authorities on both sides would honestly unite in maintaining the peace; but I am of opinion that no such concert can be looked for from the authorities of the United States, owing partly to a fear of displeasing the mob, and perhaps in some measure to a feeling of their own strength contrasted with our inferior numbers.

I apprehend further difficulties. . .

These "difficulties" did not, however, materialize just yet, and in due course 1855 passed into 1856. This year was to see the completion of Victoria's first church, the expansion of its militia to thirty men (one lieutenant, one sergeant, two corporals and twenty-six privates), and the appointment of the Rev. Mr. Cridge as Vancouver

Island's first school inspector. The colony now had three schools—one in Victoria with 26 pupils, one at Craigflower, also with 26, and one at Nanaimo with 29. There were also six saw mills, three flour mills, and 39 stores and shops on the Island.

Yet it was none of these matters that was to mark 1856 as a crucial year in the history of the colony. Its central event, beyond a doubt, was the giant stride made in that year toward a more democratic form of government.

This had for some time been inevitable. Not only was the broad trend of the age in that direction, but popular participation in the processes of government was steadily becoming the rule in British colonies. The example of the British possessions in eastern North America was plainly one which would have to be followed in the west; it was only a question of time and of degree.

A decision on these latter points was now made in London, and one day Douglas read, evidently with some dismay, a despatch from the Imperial Government[96] in which he was informed that he must now establish a popularly elected assembly to assist the Governor and his council in the direction of the colony's affairs.

Douglas clearly felt no great enthusiasm for the proposed venture into representative government, but he acquiesced in the decision of his superiors, On the 22nd of May, 1856, he wrote to them:

> It is, I confess, not without a feeling of dismay that I contemplate the nature and amount of labour and responsibility which will be imposed upon me, in the process of carrying out the instructions conveyed in your despatch. Possessing a very slender knowledge of legislation, without legal advice or intelligent assistance of any kind, I approach the subject with diffidence; feeling, however, all the encouragement which the kindly-promised assistance and support of Her Majesty's Government is calculated to inspire. . .
>
> I am utterly averse to universal suffrage, or making population the basis of representation; but I think it expedient to extend the franchise to all persons holding a fixed property stake, whether houses or lands, in the Colony; the whole of that class having interests to serve, and a distinct motive for seeking to improve the moral and material condition of the Colony.[97]

A few weeks later, Douglas was still somewhat uneasy about the colony's impending move into previously uncharted waters:

There will be a difficulty in finding properly qualified repre-sentatives, and I fear that our early attempts at legislation will make a sorry figure; though at all events, they will have the effect you contemplate of removing all doubts as to the validity of our local enactments.[98]

After discussing the matter with his council, Douglas went forward with plans for the election. The qualification for voters (which had been left to some extent at his discretion) was to be the possession of twenty acres of land, and for members the ownership of £300 worth of land. There were to be four constituencies: Victoria, with three members; Esquimalt-Metchosin with two; Nanaimo with one, and Sooke with one. The election was duly held, and on the 12th of August the first House of Assembly of Vancouver Island came to-gether. Its members were J. D. Pemberton, James Yates and E. E. Langford for Victoria; Dr. J. S. Helmcken and Thomas Skinner for Esquimalt-Metchosin; John Muir for Sooke, and John F. Kennedy for Nanaimo.[99]

Douglas addressed the new house; his speech was remarkably elab-orate for so small an audience, but gave a comprehensive picture of the prospects of the colony. He did not attempt to disguise the diffi-culties it had thus far labored under: the persistent loss of population caused by the California gold rush; its remoteness from other British colonies; the tariffs placed on its exports by the United States; the threat of serious trouble with the native Indians. On the other hand, he declared, there were also reasons for optimism: it seemed likely that the Imperial Government would soon have negotiated a reciprocity treaty with the United States, by which the products of Vancouver Island would be able to enter that country duty free; it was evident that the colony had abundant natural resources, especially in coal, tim-ber and fish; the continuation of a policy of fair dealing with the In-dians would in all likelihood prevent disorders; while as a precaution, the British government would before long be stationing a ship in the vicinity of the colony. In conclusion, Douglas stressed that despite the absence of the external trappings of grandeur, the occasion was for all that a momentous one:

Gentlemen, I feel, in all its force, the responsibility now resting upon us. The interests and well-being of thousands yet unborn may be affected by our decisions, and they will reverence or condemn our acts according as they are found to influence for good or for evil the events of the future.[100]

With these considerations to ponder, the House then got down to business. Dr. Helmcken was chosen as Speaker; a dispute arose over whether E. E. Langford had the necessary qualifications to be a member; he resigned, and J. W. MacKay was chosen by acclamation in his place.[101]

And with this coming of at least a limited democracy to Vancouver Island, we may perhaps pause a moment and take stock. Five years had now passed since Douglas had assumed the direction of the Colony, and in every respect they had been five years of progress. The little settlement which had looked to him for protection had received it; the products of the soil and sea were beginning to find their way into the markets of the world;[102] roads had been built, a church, a hospital and several schools erected; while the population was slowly being augmented by immigrants from beyond the sea. The few buildings which the Governor had constructed at Esquimalt had not yet expanded into the great naval base of the future, but the first step, so all-important in these matters, had at least been taken. Thus, though so far removed from the centres of civilization, the colonists had occasion to look back on these five years with satisfaction and forward to the days ahead with hope.

The man who had guided the settlers through this period must also have looked back on it with pride. Entrusted with the supreme power in one of the smallest and remotest British colonies, he had not always received the aid or the sympathetic understanding which he believed he merited; yet, nothing daunted, he had done what he could with what he had, and out of very little had created a modestly prosperous community.

Problems, indeed, still faced him. It was by no means certain that the fighting still raging in the American territories between whites and Indians would not spill over the border. Douglas himself, no alarmist, expressed his fears to the home government in sober terms:

> Our situation may however be compared to a smouldering volcano, which at any moment may burst into fatal activity.[103]

Despite this ever present danger, Douglas maintained his policy of upholding law and order. When an Indian attempted to kill a white man near the Fort, the Governor, taking a force of about 400 seamen and marines, plus 18 members of the Victoria Voltigeurs, proceeded northward to the Cowichan district, offered friendship to all except the criminal and those who would shelter him, received the surrender of the wanted man, and in the presence of the whole tribe hanged him.[104]

A few weeks later, he completed a detailed census of the native tribes, estimating that there were 25,873 Indians within the colony of Vancouver Island, with perhaps 8,000 blood relations on the adjacent mainland. When submitting this document to the home government, he also included his own candid reflections on the human beings behind the statistics:

> They are hospitable and exceedingly punctilious in their mutual intercourse, grateful for acts of kindness, and never fail to revenge an injury. Though generally dishonest, they are seldom known to violate a trust. They have all some rude idea of a great first cause, and an intuitive sense of moral good and evil, yet not having been trained in the fear of God, their minds have no ruling principle except the impulse of the moment.[105]

There were, however, signs of a mellowing process at work. This Douglas ascribed to the growing interest of the tribesmen in

> . . . the cultivation of the potatoe, and other agricultural products, which has the effect of softening their character. . .[106]

In general, then, Douglas was modestly hopeful that no serious trouble would occur. The correct policy, he believed, (though he did not state it in those terms) would likely be found in a judicious blend of the Christian and the Machiavellian:

> By retaining their confidence and taking advantage of their mu-

tual animosities, we may therefore always manage to prevent extensive combinations of the Tribes. . .[107]

There was another danger, however, facing the colony and its Governor, which seemed unlikely to yield to such devices. This was the
pressure, sometimes invisible but always felt, of the expanding republic
to the south. Compared with the meagre forces with which he held the
colony, it was a formidable and growing power; and already some of
its citizens were disputing the ownership of the smaller islands at the
larger island's doorstep. Till now, he had held them back; but that a
stronger challenge was likely in the years ahead, he was all too well
aware. Yet already the attitude he would adopt in that case had been
fixed; more than a decade before, he had stated his views without
equivocation:

> When the Legions were recalled from Britain, and other remote
> possessions, the Roman Empire fell rapidly into decay; with a ter-
> ritory nearly as extensive, our dominion would suffer from the same
> course; there is danger in receding; strength, power and safety are
> to be found only in a bold advance.[108]

Such was Douglas' belief; yet the time, the place and the form of
this test of strength and will were still undisclosed. Little did he know
that even before the first meeting of the little seven-man assembly the
shadow of this challenge had already fallen across "The Fort", and
been duly reported (though without a full awareness of its significance) to his superiors in distant London. Yet such, in fact, was the
case. A century later, as one reads through Douglas' despatches to
successive Colonial Secretaries, it can still quicken the pulses when,
turning a page, one comes on the first mention of what within two
years would be the focus of his attention, the main subject matter of
his despatches, and the mainspring of his most far-reaching actions:

> I hasten to communicate for the information of Her Majesty's
> Government a discovery of much importance made known to me
> by Mr. Angus McDonald, Clerk in charge of Fort Colvile, one of
> the Hudson's Bay Company's Trading Posts on the upper Colum-
> bia River District.
> That gentleman reports in a letter dated on the 1st of March

last, that Gold has been found in considerable quantities within the British Territory on the Upper Columbia, and that he is moreover of opinion that valuable deposits of gold will be found in many other parts of that country; he also states that the daily earnings of persons then employed in digging gold were ranging from £2 to £8 for each man. . .

I will not fail to keep you well informed in respect to the extent and value of the gold discoveries made. . .

Several interesting experiments in gold washing have been lately made in this colony, with a degree of success that will no doubt lead to further attempts for the discovery of the precious metal. The quantity of gold found is sufficient to prove the existence of the metal, and the parties engaged in the enterprise entertain sanguine hopes of discovering rich and productive beds.[109]

Such was Douglas' report. Over the next two years, as the importance of the discoveries steadily became more evident, he would write more like it. Eventually, as the news spread down the western coast of the continent, a great tide of humanity, blindly seeking riches, would flood into the colony of Vancouver Island and the adjacent mainland, and by so doing would confront Douglas with the greatest challenge of his career. Then all that he had brought with him to this moment would meet its test; for a time, the issue would hang in the balance; in the end, having both literally and metaphorically "held the fort" and brought those under his protection through many perils safely, Douglas would take his permanent place in the annals of what would some day be the Province of British Columbia and the Dominion of Canada. Yet, as the little colony of Vancouver Island went about its daily tasks in 1856 and 1857, all this was still hidden from even the most perceptive, and meanwhile a score of other matters engaged the attention of the settlers and their Governor. It was not till the spring of 1858 that, clear and loud, the clock of history would strike.

NOTES

[1] Douglas to Barclay, August 26, 1851. PABC.
[2] Douglas to Barclay, October 8, 1851. PABC. "Soke" is always the spelling in early accounts.
[3] Douglas to Barclay, October 8, 1851. PABC.

[4] *Ibid.*

[5] Douglas to Grey, October 31, 1851.

[6] *Ibid.*

[7] *Ibid.*

[8] Douglas to Grey, October 31, 1851.

[9] Douglas to Grey, December 16, 1851.

[10] *Ibid.*

[11] *Ibid.*

[12] Douglas to Barclay, November 24, 1851.

[13] Douglas to Barclay, August 26, 1852.

[14] Douglas to Grey, January 29, 1852.

[15] Douglas to Grey, May 28, 1852.

[16] Douglas to Grey, May 28, 1852. As a response to these developments, in 1853 Douglas was appointed by the Imperial Government Lieutenant-Governor of the Queen Charlotte Islands.

[17] Douglas to Barclay, December 9, 1851.

[18] Douglas to Barclay, April 27, 1852.

[19] Douglas to Barclay, March 18, 1852.

[20] *Ibid.*

[21] *Ibid.*

[22] *Ibid.*

[23] *Ibid.*

[24] Despard Avenue, Oak Bay, is named after him. Pemberton was elected a member of the first House of Assembly of Vancouver Island (1856), and later wrote an interesting book, *Facts and Figures relating to Vancouver Island and British Columbia* (London, 1860). His assistant was B. W. Pearse (1832-1902), whose second wife died at the age of 101 on January 23, 1954.

[25] The above passage is based on material supplied to the author by the Governor and Committee of the Hudson's Bay Company, and is published with their permission.

[26] Douglas to Barclay, May 8, 1852. Douglas estimated labor costs at from $2½ to $3 a day for mechanics, and $1.25 to $2 a day for laborers.

[27] This was an approximation of the Indians "Sne-ny-mo", meaning "the whole" or "a big strong tribe". J. D. Pemberton was apparently responsible for the new name for the settlement, which continued to be known officially as "Colvile Town" until about 1860.
For an interesting article on the founding of Nanaimo, see B. A. McKelvie, "The Founding of Nanaimo", *BCHQ*, Vol. VIII, No. 3, 1944, pp. 169-188.

[28] Douglas to Sir John Pakington, August 27, 1852.

[29] Douglas to Barclay, April 27, 1852.

[30] Douglas to Barclay, Nov. 5, 1852.

[31] *Ibid.*

[32] Before he left, he gave his daughter Cecilia in marriage to Dr. J. S. Helmcken on December 27, 1852. The young couple had actually planned to marry a few months later, but Douglas, aware of the dangers he would face among the Indians on his expedition, was anxious that at least one of his children

should be provided for in case he should not return. See Helmcken, *Reminiscences*, III. 64.

33 Douglas to Barclay, January 20, 1853.

34 Admiral John Moresby, *Two Admirals*, London, John Murray, 1909, p. 130.

35 Moresby, *Two Admirals*, p. 126.

36 Douglas to Barclay, January 20, 1853.

37 *Ibid.*

38 Douglas to Barclay, December 3, 1852.

39 A bastion was finished in the spring of 1853, and is still an object of interest today.

40 Douglas to Barclay, September 3, 1853.

41 Douglas to Barclay, May 16, 1853.

42 Douglas to Barclay, September 3, 1853.

43 Good descriptions of these farms may be found in L. B. Robinson, *Esquimalt: Place of Shoaling Waters*, Quality Press, Victoria, 1947.

44 Douglas to Barclay, May 16, 1853.

45 J. R. Anderson, *Notes and Comments*, pp. 180-181.

46 Anderson, *Op. Cit.*, p. 160.

47 *Ibid.*, p. 166.

48 The schoolhouse at Craigflower (opened in the spring of 1855) is still standing and is the oldest such building in Western Canada. As noted earlier, however, the classes held there were preceded by others in the Victoria area.

49 Douglas to Barclay, October 10, 1853. The first census ever taken in Victoria gave its population at this time as 254 (111 men, 50 women and 93 children).

50 It was totally destroyed by fire in October 1869. However its communion service (engraved with the arms of the HBC) was saved, and is still in use today at Christ Church Cathedral.

51 Douglas to Pakington, March 4, 1853.

52 Douglas to Pakington, November 11, 1852.

53 Douglas to Newcastle, April 11, 1853.

54 Douglas to Barclay, April 8, 1853. The tax on liquor dealers brought in £220 in 1853, £460 in 1854, and £340 in 1855. (Bancroft, *History of British Columbia*, p. 339).

55 Douglas to Barclay, November 4, 1853. The first retail liquor licence was taken out by James Yates.

56 Douglas to Newcastle, July 28, 1853. PABC. Valparaiso, Chile was the base of the Pacific Squadron until it was transferred to Esquimalt.

57 Douglas to Pakington, November 9, 1852.

58 Douglas to Barclay, November 4, 1853.

59 Douglas to Barclay, November 21, 1853.

60 Douglas to Barclay, December 5, 1853.

61 Douglas provided for appeals from Judge Cameron to the Governor-in-council.

62 Dr. Helmcken in his reminiscences speaks of Yates as "a powerful cantankerous being . . . a dark colored Scotsman" (III. 26) and of Cooper as

"a fine looking florid stout able man, but of an irascible grumbling disposition." (III. 101).
63 Douglas to Grey, December 11, 1854. The "Companies" were the HBC
and its subsidiaries.
Cameron remained Chief Justice of Vancouver Island until he was succeeded
by Joseph Needham on October 11, 1865. Judge Needham, who used
to appear "with a full bottomed wig and scarlet robes trimmed with fur"
(W. W. Walkem, *Stories of Early British Columbia*, Vancouver, 1914,
p. 25), resigned in March 1870, was knighted and then accepted a post in
Demerara.
64 Douglas to Barclay, May 27, 1853.
65 Douglas to Barclay, August 16, 1853.
66 Early in 1854, Douglas had written to Barclay, declaring flatly that, "The
Revd. Mr. Staines is a fomenter of mischief and I believe a preacher of
sedition". (letter of January 30, 1854).
67 Staines Point on the south end of Trial Island, near Victoria, is named after
him. See also in this connection Helmcken, Reminiscences, III. 97.
Before deciding that the "malcontents" were a bad lot, we should, I think,
note that nearly all the changes they demanded were eventually brought
into effect.
68 Douglas to Newcastle, May 16, 1854.
69 Douglas to Newcastle, August 17, 1854, PABC.
70 *Ibid.*
71 Grey to Douglas, August 5, 1854.
72 Douglas knew of the neutrality agreement by the fall of 1854, but was only
officially informed of it in September 1855. See "The war scare of 1854:
the Pacific Coast and Crimean War" by Donald Davidson, *BCHQ*, Vol. V,
No. 4, October 1941, p. 251.
73 Douglas to Grey, October 3, 1854.
74 Near the modern city of Tacoma, Washington, U.S.A. The spelling
"Nisqually" is now the accepted usage.
75 The last of these three buildings was only dismantled in the summer of 1939.
See *BCHQ*, October 1942, p. 279.
76 Douglas to Bruce, PABC. Douglas returned to this theme in a subsequent
letter to the Admiral (August 3, 1855). He urged him in his reports to
the Admiralty to "fully represent the great importance of those buildings as
respects the public service; otherwise a question may be raised as to the
payment of the expenses incurred in these erections, and it may be therefore
out of my power to meet your views on other matters."
77 Douglas to Bruce, August 3, 1855. PABC.
78 Douglas to William G. Smith, August 28, 1855. PABC.
79 They included Captain Grant, who had been Vancouver Island's first independent settler. See J. R. Anderson, Notes and Comments, p. 158.
80 Douglas to Barclay, August 26, 1854.
81 See Barrie Goult, "First and last days of the Princess Royal", *BCHQ* III,
No. 1, January 1939.
82 On July 14, 1854, Douglas wrote to W. F. Tolmie: "Mrs. Douglas is
now leaving for Nesqually with James and baby to try the effect of a change

of air. I am afraid they will put you to much trouble, which I will not forget. Have the goodness to supply them with anything they want at Nesqually on my account, as I regret no expense for their good." (*B.C. Sessional Papers,* 1914, Archives Report, p. V104). W. F. Tolmie was in charge of Fort Nisqually for many years. He married Jane Work, eldest daughter of John Work, and died in December 1886 at the age of 74. See *William Fraser Tolmie, Physician and Fur Trader,* Mitchell Press, Vancouver, 1963.

83 An interesting account of Langford's ways and works is to be found in "The Trials and Tribulations of Edward Edwards Langford" by S. W. Pettit, *BCHQ,* XVII, Jan. 1953, pp. 5-40.

84 Douglas to Russell, August 21, 1855.

85 Douglas to Grey, Dec. 11, 1854.

86 The census is reproduced in *BCHQ,* Vol. IV, No. 1, January 1940, pp. 51-58.

87 "I remember also something of the evening and night of that first day; the tea and fresh milk and bread and butter; and how, when settling ourselves to sleep for the night, we saw a large white rat crossing the stovepipe which ran through our bedroom from the great Canadian stove in the sitting room." (*Colonist,* Dec. 22, 1907).
There is a good article on Bishop Cridge in the *Colonist* for Dec. 23, 1917.

88 See B. A. McKelvie and W. E. Ireland, "The Victoria Voltigeurs", *BCHQ,* Vol. XX, July-Oct. 1956.

89 Douglas to Newcastle, Nov. 8, 1855.

90 The resemblance to Canada's policy in the Vietnamese War will not, perhaps, escape the reader's attention.

91 Douglas to Molesworth, November 8, 1855. Douglas later made loans, which eventually amounted to $7000, to Governor Stevens to help finance operations against the Indians of Washington Territory.

92 *Ibid.*

93 Douglas to Russell, August 21, 1855.

94 *Ibid.*

95 Douglas to Grey, May 18, 1855.

96 Labouchère to Douglas, Feb. 28, 1856.

97 Douglas to Labouchère, May 22, 1856.

98 Douglas to Labouchère, June 7, 1856.

99 Douglas' comment on the election was "The affair passed off quietly and did not appear to excite much interest among the lower orders". (Douglas to Labouchère, Aug. 20, 1856).

100 *Miscellaneous Papers relating to Vancouver Island,* House of Commons, 1857.
It is interesting that this long speech contains not a single reference to the HBC.

101 MacKay was to live on till 1901, and his widow till 1914. (Anderson, Notes and Comments, p. 176).

102 Vancouver Island sent samples of its products to the Paris Exposition of 1855.

103 Douglas to Labouchère, July 22, 1856.

104 He also found time on this expedition to notice the scenery, reporting to the

Colonial Secretary that, "I greatly admired the beauty and fertility of the Cowegan Valley, which contains probably not less than 200,000 acres of arable land". (Douglas to Labouchère, Sept. 6, 1856).

As a result of this expedition, Douglas wrote to a London firm: "I wish you would send me a good serviceable sword with a strong belt, of which I felt the want in my late journey". (B. A. McKelvie, "Douglas: a new portrait", *BCHQ*, April 1943, p. 99).

[105] Douglas to Labouchère, Oct. 20, 1856.

[106] *Ibid.*

[107] *Ibid.*

[108] Douglas to Simpson, April 4, 1845. Quoted in Galbraith, *The Hudson's Bay Company as an Imperial Factor, 1821-1869*, p. 216.

[109] Douglas to Labouchère, April 16, 1856.

CHAPTER EIGHT

His Finest Hour

We were compelled in the emergency, by a stern necessity, either to take the initiative, and to give a direction to the masses, or to submit to their dictation.[1]

DURING THE YEAR and a half that separated the beginnings of parliamentary government in Vancouver Island in August 1856 from the great gold rush which began in the spring of 1858, the story of the colony, as reflected in Douglas' despatches, might be called one of counterpoint. The matters with which the Governor had been grappling since 1851—schools, roads, hospitals, farming, fishing, lumbering and defence, to name but a few—were still dealt with and reported on; yet running through them like a glistening thread was the subject which was eventually to crowd them all into the margin: the increasingly important discoveries of gold on the mainland adjacent to Vancouver Island.

It had actually long been known that a certain amount of the precious metal was to be found in the Interior. As early as 1833 David Douglas the botanist (no relation to the Governor) had noticed gold in the Okanagan area;[2] from time to time, Indians had brought nuggets to HBC posts and been recompensed.[3] Yet, as we saw, it was not until the spring of 1856 that Douglas thought there had been a discovery of sufficient importance to report it to the government in London.

A few months later, he had further news of this nature to com-municate:

It may probably interest Her Majesty's Government to learn that some very fine specimens of Scale Gold have been lately discovered in one of the tributary streams of Fraser's River, at a considerable distance from the sea coast. The persons who made the discovery propose to continue the search for gold, as soon as the river which was then in a swollen state falls to its lowest level, and I will do myself the honour of informing you of the result of their ex-plorations.[4]

From this point, the subject would recur with some regularity in Douglas' despatches, yet not at first to the exclusion of all else. The conflict in the American territories immediately to the south between the natives and white settlers, the possibility that this struggle might spread into the British possessions north of the line, the disputed matter of the Arro Archipelago: all these from time to time engaged the Governor's attention, and have some claim on ours.

On the 20th of August, 1856, for example, Douglas reported a serious incident in the colony, and the method he adopted for averting what might have been an outbreak of violence beyond his power to control:

A gang of Queen Charlotte Islanders who had been several months resident here. . . attacked and nearly destroyed a native Cowegin village situated about 50 miles north of this place.

The Cowegins, few in number, fought desperately and were all slaughtered on the spot, and the assailants made off toward their own country with a number of captive women and children.

When tidings of that disaster reached the Colony, the remaining northern Indians, though still numerous, were greatly alarmed, and the Cowegins, incensed by the loss of their friends, were only re-strained from attacking them en masse by their respect for Her Majesty's Government and the dread of giving us offence. They however hovered on the borders of the settlements, and shot every northern Indian, without respect to tribe or person, who ventured abroad.

In those circumstances, it became necessary to apply a remedy, as the excited passions of the hostile savages would have eventually brought on a collision within the limits of the settlements, where the northern Indians had assembled for protection, and they were afraid to leave the Colony, as the route to their distant homes leads directly through the Cowegin country. There was also great cause to fear that so large a number of Indians, united by a common sense of danger, if permitted to leave in a collective body, would in all probability, from a feeling of their own strength, become dangerous, and commit numberless depredations on the less powerful native tribes of Vancouver's Island, who might be surprised and cut off in detail.

I therefore adopted a plan, which, without displeasing the Cowegin tribe, was considered by the northern Indians as a mark of peculiar favour; this was to despatch them on their return homeward under the escort of the Hudson's Bay Company's steamer "Otter", and according to that arrangement fifteen large canoes manned with about 300 northern Indians were sent away from this place on the morning of the 7th of August, and were conducted as far as River de Grullas, about 150 miles north of Victoria, where they were left to make their own way.[5]

In the same despatch, the Governor reported the arrival at Esquimalt on August 11 of Rear Admiral Bruce in the *Monarch*, followed the next day by Captain Houston in the *Trincomalee*.

In October, Douglas mentioned that a few retired employees of the HBC were looking for gold on the upper Columbia;[6] yet two months later he found himself dealing with a very different kind of matter.

This was occasioned by the arrival in Fort Victoria from Bellingham of Lt. Fleming of the American army. He had come on instructions from his superior, Captain Pickett, (later to distinguish himself in "Pickett's charge" in the Civil War), to search for some deserters from the forces of his country who, he had reason to believe, were on Vancouver Island. He proposed that Douglas locate, arrest and deliver these men to the American authorities, or, alternatively, that the Americans be allowed to send a force into the colony to do it for him. Douglas instantly rejected both these courses, pointing out that desertion was not an extraditable offence, and there the matter rested.[7]

Early in the new year of 1857 Douglas was advised by the British Government that he was soon to expect American representatives on another mission.[8] A joint commission of British and American officials had been agreed upon by their respective governments, which, it was hoped, would establish beyond further dispute the boundary line between their possessions in the northwest. The officials appointed for this task appeared in June, Captain James C. Prevost in H.M. steam corvette *Satellite* arriving on the 17th,[9] and Archibald Campbell, the American commissioner, on the 29th in the U.S. paddle steamer *Active*. It was decided that they would commence their labors by determining the exact point at which the 49th parallel reached the Pacific Ocean.

Shortly before this, the inhabitants of Sooke had become alarmed at the presence in their midst of large numbers of northern tribesmen. Douglas made a brief expedition to the area and restored confidence, subsequently explaining his method to the Home Government:

> I advised them to conceal their fears and to assume on all occasions a bold countenance with Indian visitors, in order to impress their rude minds with a feeling of respect for the power and resources of Government.[10]

In July, however, the fateful theme once more recurs:

> It is however certain that gold has been found in many places by washing the soil of the river beds, and also of the mountain sides, but, on the other hand, the quantities hitherto collected are inconsiderable and do not lend much support to the opinion entertained of the richness of these deposits, so that the question as to their ultimate value remains thus undetermined, and will probably not be decided until more extensive researches are made.[11]

Douglas did, however, envisage trouble in the Thompson River district, as the native Indians were opposed to the activities of the white gold miners, preferring to allocate responsibility for the discovery and sale of nuggets to themselves. Foreseeing "the motley adventurers who will be attracted by the reputed wealth of the country from the United States possessions in Oregon",[12] the Governor raised the question with his superiors

> . . .if in that case it may not become a question whether the natives are entitled to the protection of Her Majesty's Government,

and if an officer invested with the requisite authority should not without delay be appointed for that purpose.[13]

Yet as summer passed into fall, the Governor's uneasiness diminished, and in one of his despatches a note of unruffled confidence is— almost for the last time—sounded:

I have much satisfaction in communicating for your information that the Colony continues in a state of profound tranquility, that the native Indian tribes are quiet and well disposed; that the harvest has been housed in good condition, and though the grain crops are not so heavy as in the year 1856, that there is nevertheless an abundant stock of food in the settlements for the consumption of the year.[14]

Yet this was but the calm before the storm. In the closing week of the year, Douglas reported that the Indians, "having tasted the sweets of gold finding, are devoting much of their time and attention to that pursuit".[15] It seemed likely, moreover, that they would soon be joined by numbers of white Americans:

The reputed wealth of the Couteau Mines is causing much excitement among the population of the United States Territories of Washington and Oregon, and I have no doubt that a great number of people from those territories will be attracted thither with the return of the fine weather in spring.[16]

Douglas informed the Colonial Secretary that as a precautionary move he had issued a proclamation

declaring the rights of the Crown in respect to gold found in its natural place of deposit within the limits of Fraser's River and Thompson's River districts within which are situated the Couteau mines; and forbidding all persons to dig or disturb the soil in search of gold until authorized on that behalf by Her Majesty's Government.[17]

Douglas did not conceal the fact that he feared an invasion of Americans, and declared his intention of having his proclamation published in the newspapers of Oregon and Washington. This, he seems to have believed, would suffice:

to place a legal check on the movements of American citizens and to prevent them from entering the British Territory either for mining or other purposes.[18]

Douglas admitted to the Colonial Secretary that, since he was only Governor of Vancouver Island, he had no legal authority at all on the mainland. He expressed the hope, however, that his authority as Chief Factor of the HBC (which did have legal rights in that area) could be stretched to cover the situation, and declared his readiness to visit the mines himself if the Home Government should deem it advisable.

In a later despatch, a very different matter is dealt with. Having heard that a group of Mormons was anxious to emigrate from Utah to Vancouver Island, Douglas, while referring to them as "enterprising fanatics", expressed his willingness to receive them "provided they yield obedience to the laws and avoid public scandals and lead quiet and honest lives".[19]

In the meantime, despite the Governor's announcements in their newspapers, the Americans were beginning to filter into the gold fields, Douglas reporting that

some 70 or 80 adventurers from the American side have gone by the way of Fraser's River to the Couteau Mines, without taking out licences.[20]

This however, was but a trickle; now came the flood. Even its beginning can be dated with some accuracy; it was about mid-day of Sunday, April 25, 1858. Then, to the astonishment of the placid groups of worshippers decorously leaving church, the first ship-load of would-be gold miners disembarked from the *Commodore* at Victoria. Clad in a motley variety of clothing, representing a dozen races and nationalities, they scrambled ashore; over four hundred men, asking only for the provisions, tools and boats that would enable them to reach the gold fields of the mainland and find their fortunes.

Even these, it soon transpired, were no more than the first wave. Soon, nearly every day brought fresh loads of the eager gold-seekers, and Douglas, who once had worried about "70 or 80 adventurers", was now reporting with growing concern the arrival of increasing thousands.

His despatch to the Colonial Secretary of May 8, 1858, gives a vivid picture of the novel and alarming situation that now faced the Governor of what had only a few weeks before been a quiet hamlet of perhaps three hundred souls:

> Boats, canoes, and every species of small craft are continually employed in pouring their cargoes into Fraser's River, and it is supposed that not less than one thousand whites are already at work, and on the way to the gold districts.
>
> Many accidents have happened in the dangerous rapids of that river; a great number of canoes having been dashed to pieces, and their cargoes swept away by the impetuous stream, while of the ill-fated adventurers who accompanied them, many have been swept into eternity.
>
> The others, nothing daunted by the spectacle of ruin, and buoyed up by the hope of amassing wealth, keep pressing onwards towards the coveted goal of their most ardent wishes.

These new arrivals in the Colony were, Douglas conceded, well behaved, there being "not a single committal for rioting, drunkenness, or other offences during their stay here"; moreover, their presence, even when only temporary, gave a sharp financial stimulus to the Colony. Furthermore, if the rumored deposits proved considerable, there would be a bright future for Victoria as a half-way point between San Francisco and the gold fields. Thus, looked at in purely economic terms, the new developments were highly favorable.

However, as Douglas at once realized and hastened to report, there was another side to the matter. The social composition of the colony and the adjacent mainland was changing almost hourly. Once nearly exclusively of British stock, now it was rapidly becoming multi-national, or, considering the point of origin of the gold-seekers, American. Inevitably, these would have scant enthusiasm for British institutions, and would be more likely to try establishing in their new habitat those to which they were already accustomed. It would be, in fact, the history of the Columbia valley all over again. Thus, Douglas declared:

> Taking that view of the question, it assumes an alarming aspect, and suggests a doubt as to the policy of permitting the free entrance

of foreigners, into the British territory for residence, under any circumstances whatever, without in the first place requiring them to
take the oath of allegiance, and otherwise to give such security for
their conduct as the Government of the country may deem proper
and necessary to require at their hands.

It is easy in fact to foresee the dangerous consequences that may
grow out of the unrestricted immigration of foreigners into the interior of Fraser's River. If the majority of the immigrants be American, there will always be a hankering in their minds after annex-
ation to the United States, and with the aid of their countrymen in
Oregon and California at hand, they will never cordially submit to
British rule, nor possess the loyal feelings of British subjects.

Out of the considerations thus briefly reviewed arises the questions which I beg to submit for your consideration; as to the course
of policy that ought in the present circumstances to be taken, that
is, whether it be advisable to restrain immigration or to allow it to
take its course.

The opinion which I have formed on the subject leads me to
think that, in the event of the diggings proving remunerative, it
will now be found impossible to check the course of immigration,
even by closing Fraser's River, as the miners would then force a
passage into the gold district by way of the Columbia River, and the
valuable trade of the country in that case be driven from its natural
course into a foreign channel and entirely lost to this country.. .

Until the value of the country as a gold producing region be
established on clearer evidence than can now be adduced in its
favor—and the point will no doubt be decided before the close of
the present year—I would simply recommend that a small naval or
military force should be placed at the disposal of the Government,
to enable us to maintain the peace and to enforce obedience to
the law. . .

For the time being, all my efforts will be directed towards maintaining the peace in the gold districts, to supporting the Hudson's
Bay Company, and infusing a British element into the population.[21]

This, then, was the grand decision. To exclude the mounting waves
of humanity from the gold fields was physically impossible; on the
other hand, to let the mainland adjacent to Vancouver Island be swept,
like the valley of the Columbia, into the American orbit was, to Douglas, morally impossible. There remained only the course which he now

resolved upon: to permit the entry of the newcomers, but to bring them from the beginning under British government and institutions. Few were the resources with which to achieve this aim; those which he possessed were mainly intangible; yet, nothing daunted, he set himself to the task. Isolated on the farthest rim of the Empire, supported by a mere handful of soldiers and officials, his chances of success seemed slight; yet, accustomed by all that had brought him to this moment to reckon neither the odds, the cost, nor the dangers, he did not do so now. The history of the year that now followed would be largely the record of his desperate and almost single-handed gamble with the fates.

Delay, he foresaw, would be as fatal as indecisiveness, and at once he responded to the challenge. His first move was to issue a proclamation,[22] announcing to all and sundry in no uncertain terms the policy he proposed to follow. It is worth reproducing in full.

PROCLAMATION

By His Excellency JAMES DOUGLAS, Governor and Commander-in-Chief of the Colony of Vancouver's Island and Dependencies, and Vice-Admiral of the same, &c, &c, &c.

Whereas it is commonly reported that certain boats and other vessels have entered Fraser's River for trade; and whereas there is reason to apprehend that other persons are preparing and fitting out boats and vessels for the same purpose:

Now, therefore, I have issued this my Proclamation, warning all persons that such acts are contrary to law, and infringements upon the rights of the Hudson's Bay Company, who are legally entitled to the trade with Indians in the British Possessions on the north-west coast of America, to the exclusion of all other persons, whether British or Foreign.

And also, that after fourteen days from the date of this my Proclamation, all ships, boats, and vessels, together with the goods laden on board, found in Fraser's River, or in any of the bays, rivers, or creeks of the said British Possessions on the north-west coast of America, not having a licence from the Hudson's Bay Company, and a sufferance from the proper officer of the Customs at Victoria, shall be liable to forfeiture, and will be seized and condemned according to law.

Given under my hand and seal, at Government House, Victoria, this eighth day of May in the year of our Lord One thousand eight hundred and fifty-eight, and in the twenty-first year of Her Majesty's reign.

(signed) JAMES DOUGLAS, Governor
By His Excellency's Command,
Richard Golledge, Secretary.

GOD SAVE THE QUEEN

As we shall see later, Douglas had made in this proclamation a claim greater than could be legally justified. The "Company", indeed, had exclusive trading rights with the Indians on the mainland, but it had no right whatever to exclude from that area those bound there on other pursuits. This would later be emphasized to Douglas by the British Government; but in the meantime he had at least shown that he had no intention of receding from the exercise of what he believed just authority.

Less than a week later, he took action of another sort, appealing to Rear Admiral Baynes, Commander-in-chief of the Pacific Squadron, who was at this time at Callao in Chile, for assistance:

To prevent the entrance of those people into the British territory is, perhaps, altogether impossible with any force that could be collected within a reasonable time; but what may be easily accomplished is—to maintain the authority of the Government, to preserve the peace, to punish offences, and to enforce obedience to the laws, until Her Majesty's Government are in a position to take more decided steps for administering the government of the country.

I therefore take the liberty of making application to you for a sufficient force to aid and assist in maintaining the Queen's authority, until further instructions are received from England.[23]

While awaiting the Admiral's reply, Douglas made use of what naval forces he had. He ordered Captain Prevost of the *Satellite* to anchor his ship off the mouth of the Fraser, and to see that the proclamation of May 8 was enforced. In the meantime, the *Commodore*, which had brought the first party of miners from San Francisco in April, had returned with a fresh load of four hundred. It was now evident

that the reports about the richness of the gold fields were not exaggerated, Douglas reporting to the British Government that

The excitement about the Couteau Gold Mines is on the increase,
and people are pushing from all quarters in that direction.[24]

Some of these fortune hunters were coming overland through the
valleys of the Interior. It was utterly beyond Douglas' power to prevent
this, and he consequently decided that it was best in the circumstances
to facilitate their entry by way of the Fraser, imposing certain conditions which

at once assert the rights of the Crown, protect the interests of
the Hudson's Bay Company, and are intended to draw the whole
trade of the Gold District through Fraser's River to this colony,
which will procure its supplies directly from the mother country.[25]

The core of this new plan was to grant a franchise to an American
steamship company to carry miners and supplies between Victoria and
the rapids of Fraser's River, about 130 miles upstream from its mouth.
The contract was to continue until May 1859, and its terms were
rigidly prescribed. The Company was to carry no goods except those
supplied by the Hudson's Bay Company, and no passengers who had
not paid the Government of Vancouver Island for a mining licence. All
ships were to be commanded and owned by British subjects, and the
HBC was to receive two dollars for each passenger carried.[26]
Eventually, as we shall see, the British government would decide
that this contract was illegal; in the meantime, however, it regularized
the traffic on the river, brought in revenue to the Company, and forced
those making use of the ships to acknowledge tacitly the authority of
the government at Victoria.
Douglas now resolved to see the activity on the Fraser at first hand—
to visit, as it were, the battle front. Setting out in the *Otter*, he was
joined by the *Satellite*, and together the ships ascended the river. They
seized from some miners a quantity of goods which were contraband
under the terms of Douglas' proclamation, found sixteen other miners
without licences, charged them five dollars each for a licence, and let
them go on their way. Douglas and his party soon reached the diggings,

and found that they were indeed rich in gold. One group was making fifty dollars a day, and it was reported that higher up the river the rewards were even greater. On his return to Victoria, Douglas reported on what he had seen in terms which for him were unusually unrestrained:

> The conviction is gradually forcing itself upon my mind that not only Fraser's River, and its tributary streams, but also the whole country situated to the eastward of the Gulf of Georgia, as far north as Johnstone's Straits, is one continued bed of gold of incalculable value and extent.[27]

He also now had some further suggestions to make concerning these startling and unforeseen developments. It was more evident than ever that this onrushing flood of humanity could not be stemmed; he estimated that

> . . . in the course of a few months there may be one hundred thousand people in the country.[28]

The right policy, he believed, was one of imposing some sort of order on what would otherwise be a chaos:

> I think it therefore a measure of obvious necessity that the whole country be immediately thrown open for settlement, and that the land be surveyed, and sold at a fixed rate not to exceed twenty shillings an acre.[29]

Clearly, Douglas was abandoning his early view of the mainland as the private reserve of the HBC; he now went further in this direction, and made the first moves toward setting up some of the machinery of civil government. To be revenue officer for the district of Fort Yale, at a salary of £40 a year, he appointed Richard Hicks, "a respectable Englishman engaged in mining pursuits there".[30]

George Perrier, also a British subject, was appointed a Justice of the Peace at Hill's Bar, and Indians were urged to apply to him for the redress of grievances.

Douglas also in a striking move appointed several Indian magistrates "who are to bring forward, when required, any man of their several tribes who may be charged with offences against the laws of the country"; the Governor described this as "an arrangement which will prevent much evil".[31]

Meanwhile, the tide of immigrants continued to roll on through Victoria across the straits and up the great river. On the first of July, Douglas painted for the Colonial Secretary a vivid picture of the flood on which he was attempting to navigate the ship of state:

> Since I had last the honour of addressing you on the 19th instant, the excitement on the subject of the Fraser's River Gold Mines has been more than ever exhibited in the rush of people from all parts of the coast to this Colony.
>
> The Custom-House books of this place show a return of
>
> 19 steam ships,
> 9 sailing ditto,
> 14 decked boats,
>
> which have entered at the port of Victoria since the 19th of May last, having 6,133 passengers on board, all either bound directly for Fraser's River, or proposing to settle at this place, with the view of entering into business connexions with parties at the mines.
>
> The ascertained number of persons who had actually sailed from the port of San Francisco, with the intention of going into the Fraser's River mines, up to the 15th instant, was 10,573, and there was then no abatement in the demand for passages, every vessel being taken up as soon as advertised to sail for Vancouver's Island.
>
> Those statements give a proximate idea of the number of persons at and on the way to Fraser's River from California and other more distant countries, but do not represent the increase of population derived from the United States territories of Washington and Oregon, through parties of adventurers who have entered the British Possessions by land. We are, therefore, led to the inference that this country and Fraser's River have gained an increase of 10,000 inhabitants within the last six weeks, and the tide of immigration continues to roll onward without any prospect of abatement.

The Governor was, however, still hopeful that he could control this tidal wave, despite the radical change it was producing in the composition of the region:

> About two thirds of the emigrants from California are supposed to be English and French; the other third are German, and native citizens of the United States. There is no congeniality of feeling among the emigrants, and provided there be no generally felt griev-

ance to unite them in one common cause there will, in my opinion, always be a great majority of the population ready to support the measures of government.[32]

In the meantime, he appointed more officials. William Henry Bevis was chosen as Revenue Officer at Fort Langley, and O. J. Travaillot Assistant Commissioner of Crown Lands. The latter made his reports to Douglas in a form which would perhaps disconcert his modern successors in the seat of government at Victoria:

> Conformement à vos désirs j'ai honneur de vous envoyer ci-joint le net produit de quelques rocheurs installés sur la Rivière Fraser. Ayant moi-même pesé jour pour jour la poudre d'or retirée par les mineurs, je puis vous donner ces renseignements comme parfaitment authentiques.[33]

Douglas also organized a police force in the area of the diggings. It consisted of "six men; namely, a serjeant at a dollar and a half, and the remainder at one dollar per diem each, with rations (two shillings) and with clothing."[34] These upholders of law and order were "to carry out the general police business of your district, taking especial care that drinking and gambling and other disorders are as much as possible put down."[35]

Another problem soon forced itself upon the Governor's attention —that of land communication with the Interior. As long as the miners had been content to search for gold along the lower reaches of the Fraser, they experienced no difficulty in moving from place to place. However, once it seemed likely that even richer deposits lay hidden further up the river, a serious difficulty presented itself. Where the Fraser forced its way through the mountain ranges, its current, contracted by narrow rocky gorges, became a seething mass of rapids and whirlpools. Long before, the man whose name it now bore had spoken of it as so dangerous that "I cannot find words to describe our situation at times. We have to pass where no human being should venture."[36] Notwithstanding this, in the summer of 1858 men attempted to make their way up the river; at times they used canoes or rafts, at times they retreated to the shore and followed the paths used by the sure-footed Indians. The goal of their efforts was the "mother lode"; the result was often far different, and those pausing for a moment in their desperate attempts to penetrate the pitiless barrier that guarded the trea-sure-fields often saw washing past them toward the sea the canoes and bodies of those who had gone before them.

Moreover, the native tribes were frequently hostile to these invaders of their age-old hunting grounds, and not all the bodies being carried down the Fraser were the victims of the river. On July 14, something approaching a battle took place between whites and Indians, and there were numerous minor skirmishes.[37]

Some of those in quest of gold took another route. Moving up from the interior of the Oregon Territory, they entered British Columbia (as it would soon be called) south of Lake Okanagan, and, using the old fur brigade trail, moved northward along the shores of the lake to Kamloops. From there, they followed the Thompson River until they reached the upper reaches of the Fraser.

Although this way to the gold fields was safer than that up the can-yon of the Fraser, it had, in Douglas' eyes, an even greater disadvan-tage. Its starting point (or, in the case of returning miners, its ter-minus) lay in American territory, and dependence on it would in-evitably mean that the whole trade of the Interior of British Columbia would be channeled into American hands and eventually subjected to American control. This would in the end defeat the Governor's great aim of retaining the mainland as a possession of the Crown; perceiving this clearly and immediately, he set about finding some way from the coast to the gold fields which would be both safe and entirely within British territory.

One possible solution to the problem at once suggested itself; mak-ing use of the Harrison-Lillooet trail, surveyed in 1846 by A. C. Anderson. In that year, with the signing of the Oregon Treaty, the traditional route of the fur brigades—from Kamloops down Lake Ok-anagan to the upper reaches of the Columbia, and then down that river to Fort Vancouver—had been rendered undesirable, as now pass-ing partly through American territory. The problem then had been to find a new route for the fur brigades from New Caledonia to Fort Langley and the newly built Fort Victoria. Anderson's route was not adopted, however, mainly because it involved too many changes from one mode of transportation to another, and another was eventually chosen which left the Fraser below the rapids and struck eastward into the plains of the Interior. The reports of this pioneer explorer were, however, still readily available, and Douglas, searching for some way out of his dilemma, decided that the trail once rejected for fur might now be used for gold.

Writing to Lord Stanley on July 26, 1858, he explained both the difficulty and his proposed solution:

> The internal communications of the country. . . are, for all practical purposes, nearly inaccessible beyond Fort Yale, in consequence of a range of mountains running north and south, which there interpose an almost insurmountable barrier to the progress of trade . . .
>
> It is therefore evident that the construction of a good road through that mountain barrier, though passable in the first instance only for pack horses, would be of prodigious advantage to the country . . .
>
> Should no instructions militating with that design be in the meantime received from Her Majesty's Government, I will probably make the attempt this summer.

Douglas did not allow Lord Stanley much time to veto his plan. Mail usually took from three to four months to make the round trip from Victoria; yet the Governor, knowing he could not await passively the slow disappearance of "this great gap of time," acted at once. On his orders, Captain J. C. Ainsworth of the *Umatilla*, sailing from Victoria, ascended the Fraser, turned off it into the Harrison River, and successfully navigated it to the northern end of Harrison Lake. The significance of the voyage was emphasized by the presence on board of a special correspondent of the Victoria *Gazette*. The latter on his return pronounced the new route "perfectly navigable".[38]

At once the enthusiastic miners entered into a remarkable agreement with Douglas to construct a road through the area. Five hundred of them deposited $25 each with the HBC as a guarantee that they would complete the work. They were to receive no pay, but Douglas on his part agreed to transport them to the beginning of the proposed road and refund their deposits (in goods supplied by the HBC) when the road was completed. Moreover, once the task was finished, the trail was to remain closed for two weeks to the general public, so that those who had borne the heat of the day could stake their claims first. At a public meeting in Victoria on August 2, signatures of volunteer road-builders were collected; three days later, an advance working-party under Anderson left the capital.

From then on, while Douglas' despatch to Lord Lytton regarding the proposed road made its leisurely progress across the wide oceans to London and return, the actual work of building it proceeded at a breakneck pace. The first party reached the head of Lake Harrison on August 7; this point was henceforth called Port Douglas. On August 9 work was begun, and that day two and a half miles was hacked out of the wilderness. By August 13, ten miles were completed. A shortage of supplies began to cause difficulties, but the resourceful Anderson had them packed in to the miners on mules. By September 3, Little Lillooet Lake[39] was reached, and not long afterwards Anderson Lake and Seton Lake.[40] By the middle of October the trail was almost finished, and on November 30 Douglas was able to write to Lord Lytton, informing him that

> a considerable traffic is now being started by way of Harrison's River, which will eventually become the great commercial thorough-fare of the country.

This prophecy was not in fact to be fulfilled; another great "thorough-fare", also conceived and executed by Douglas—the famous Cari-boo Road—was within a few years to supplant it. Nevertheless, a great step had been taken in binding together the vast area which was now to be called British Columbia, and the Governor no doubt regarded his accomplishment with satisfaction.

Mention should perhaps be made here of a plan conceived by Alfred Waddington to build a road to the gold fields from the head of Bute Inlet. The government was somewhat interested, and preliminary work was done, but a massacre of a party of whites by Indians in May 1864 brought an end to the project. Waddington, who came to Victoria in 1858, eventually became Superintendent of Education for Vancouver

Island, and in recognition of his services to the area, Mount Waddington and Port Waddington at the head of Bute Inlet are named after him.[41]

Douglas' satisfaction was shared, when they were informed of it, by his superiors in London; however, not everything that he had done in this tremendous summer was received there with equal enthusiasm. In particular, his proclamation of May 8, 1858, apparently reserving for the HBC all trade on the mainland, seemed to the Colonial Secretary to be using the powers of government to subserve the interests of a commercial monopoly; thus on July 16 he administered to Douglas one of the few rebukes of the Governor's career. Disallowing the proclamation of May 8, he stated his reasons for this action with some crispness:

> The Company is entitled, under its existing licence, to the exclusive trade with the Indians, and possesses no other right or privilege whatever.
> It is, therefore, contrary to law, and equally contrary to the distinct instructions which I have to convey to you, to exclude any class of persons from the territory; or to prevent the importment of goods into it, on the ground of apprehended interference with this monopoly—still more to make any Government regulation subservient to the Revenues of interests of the Company.[42]

A month later, Lord Lytton repeated even more forcibly the position of his government, as well as informing Douglas of an important new decision:

> I must refer you, in even stronger terms, to the cautions already conveyed to you by my former despatches. The Hudson's Bay Company have hitherto had an exclusive right to trade with Indians in the Fraser's River Territory, but they have had no other right whatever. They have had no right to exclude strangers. They have had no rights of Government, or of occupation of the soil. They have had no right to prevent or interfere with any kind of trading, except with Indians alone. But to render all misconceptions impossible, Her Majesty's Government have determined on revoking the Company's licence (which would itself have expired in next May) as regards British Columbia, being fully authorized to do so by the terms of the licence itself, whenever a new Colony is constituted . . .

The instrument formally revoking the licence will shortly be forwarded to you.[43]

It might seem from these despatches that Douglas was in disfavor
with the Imperial Government. This was not, however, the case. What
was intended by these rather blunt communications was to show Douglas the impossibility of his any longer combining the two offices of
Governor and Chief Factor. As to which of them it was hoped he
would discard, this was made clear in a confidential message which
Lord Lytton enclosed with his despatch of July 16. In it, he stated
that a new colony, that of British Columbia, was to be established,[44]
and that the Home Government was prepared to appoint Douglas as
its first Governor, with a salary of £1000 a year.[45] There was, however, one unalterable condition:

> You will fully understand that unless you are prepared to assure
> me that all connexion between yourself and the Company is ter-
> minated, or in course of speedy termination, you will be relieved by
> the appointment of a successor.
>   . . . It is quite impossible that you should continue to serve
> at once the Crown and the Company, when their respective rights
> and interests may possibly diverge, and when at all events public
> opinion will not allow of such a connexion.[46]

Two weeks later, Lord Lytton outlined for Douglas' benefit some
of the British Government's long-term plans for the new colony:

> You will keep steadily in view that it is the desire of this country
> that Representative Institutions should prevail in British Columbia,
> when, by the growth of a fixed population, materials for those In-
> stitutions shall be known to exist; and to that object you must, from
> the commencement, aim and shape all your policy.
>   It should be remembered that your real strength lies in the con-
> viction of the emigrants that their interests are identical with those
> of the Government, which should be carried on in harmony with
> and by means of the people of the country.[47]

Lytton was clearly in no great doubt as to what Douglas' response
would be to his offer. It was October 4 before the Governor wrote
a letter accepting it, and December 10 before this was received in

London; but already on the 2nd of September, Lord Lytton had sent Douglas his commission. Not all the ability to act promptly and decisively was in Victoria.

A great change in Douglas' career thus impended. As governor of not one but two British colonies, he would soon be assuming a position of more eminence and power than he had so far known. This time, however, one of the ladders by which he had ascended would have to be abandoned. What feelings this aroused in him after forty years in the service of the Company, we can only guess at; reserved as always, he accepted his new honors and their attendant conditions as in times past he had accepted hardships—without undue emotion.

In the meantime, however, while awaiting his formal installation as first Governor of British Columbia, he continued to pursue his aim of dominating rather than of being dominated by events. He preserved law and order in the bizarre city of tents that had sprung up around Fort Victoria, on one occasion subduing a modest riot.[48]

As the summer wore on, he saw tents giving way to wooden houses, and brick buildings, including hotels, beginning to appear. His attention was drawn by the seven-man House of Assembly to the need for such things as jails, hospitals, fire engines, paved streets and bridges.[49] He appointed Victoria's first policemen, in a striking move choosing them all from the ranks of the town's considerable colored population.[50] He promoted social harmony in the community by attending dances given by the British ships in the harbor. He strove to preserve good relations between whites and Indians in the colony. He gave what time he could spare to his wife and family.

By late July, the cause he served had almost miraculously still not suffered shipwreck, as he was able to report to Lord Lytton:

> With the exception of the aid received from Her Majesty's Ship "Satellite", operating on the sea coast, I have had no military force whatever to employ in the interior of Fraser's River, which is now occupied by a population little short of 9,000 white miners, and hundreds of other persons are travelling towards the gold mines, and preparing to join them.
>
> The country, nevertheless, continues quiet, and, notwithstanding

our want of physical force, I have not scrupled in all cases to assert the rights of the Crown, and to enforce the laws of the land for the punishment of offences; and we have, thanks to the Almighty, encountered neither resistance nor opposition in the discharge of those sacred duties.[51]

Amidst all this, he found time to make a second visit to the gold fields in August. Hope and Yale were by this time centres of activity, and he talked at both places with the miners. At the latter place there had been disturbances; Douglas investigated them and took a step which he felt would cure most of the trouble, by issuing a proclamation forbidding the gift or sale of liquor to the natives.

As summer gave way to autumn, he sent the capable J. D. Pemberton to the mainland, where he laid out a townsite at Fort Langley. Town lots measuring 64 ft. by 120 ft. were sold in October at prices ranging from $100 to $725, the terms being 10 percent down and the balance within a month.[52] One of the purchasers was later to achieve much prominence as founder of the Victoria *Daily Colonist*, in whose columns he would unwearyingly attack the Governor. His name had originally been plain Bill Smith, but it had since undergone a metamorphosis into Amor de Cosmos.

Meanwhile the British Government had decided that the new colony would require not only military defenders but experts in engineering, and to this end prepared to send a force of the Royal Engineers to the area. On the first of September Lord Lytton wrote to Douglas, informing him that an advance party of twenty men would shortly be arriving in British Columbia, and that other parties would follow. He was as good as his word; Captain Parsons with twenty men left on the second of September, Captain Grant with twelve more on September 17. Other ships, among them the *Thames City, Briseis,* and *Euphrates* would, Douglas was informed, bring further contingents until a total strength of 150 was reached. Lord Lytton explained to the Governor in some detail the essential functions of this force:

> The superior discipline and intelligence of this force, which afford ground for expecting that they will be far less likely than ordinary soldiers of the line to yield to the temptation to desertion offered

by the gold fields, and their capacity at once to provide for them-selves in a country without habitation, appears to me to render them especially suited for this duty, whilst by their services as pioneers in the work of civilization, in opening up the resources of the country, by the construction of roads and bridges, in laying the foundations of a future city or seaport, and in carrying out the numerous engineering works which in the earlier stages of colonization are so essential to the progress and welfare of the community, they will probably not only be preserved from the idleness which might corrupt the discipline of ordinary soldiers, but establish themselves in the popular good will of the emigrants by the civil benefits it will be in the regular nature of their occupation to confer.[53]

The Colonial Secretary was not, however, of the opinion that the colonies should look to the United Kingdom for protection. He out-lined his views with some succinctness:

From England we send skill and discipline; the raw materials (that is the mere men) a Colony intended for free institutions, and on the borders of so powerful a neighbour as the United States of America, should learn betimes to supply.[54]

Lord Lytton also took the opportunity to point out that there was a happy moral to be drawn from the voluntary and co-operative con-struction of the Harrison-Lillooet road. The same spirit, be believed, might well soon animate the successful operation of other features of civic government such as the observance of the laws and the payment of taxes.[55]

A few days later, the Colonial Secretary wrote to the Governor on quite a different subject. He informed him that a wealthy English phil-anthropist, Miss Angela Burdett Coutts, had donated £15,000 for the endowment of an Anglican bishop for the new colony.[56]

Lord Lytton at this time also wrote to Colonel Moody, who would be commanding the Royal Engineers in British Columbia, giving him some words of advice regarding his new duties:

In the first (place), it is not only the duty, it should be the pride, of a youthful and vigorous community to find means of defence within itself. The consciousness that it is compelled to do so engenders a brave and resolute spirit amongst the immigrators, and serves to bind

man to man against turbulence and crime, by the sense of the common safety. . .

Nothing can be more likely to sap the manhood and virtue of
any young community than the error of confounding the duties of
soldiers with the ordinary functions of a police. Nevertheless, though
soldiers do not constitute a police, there are few societies in which
the authority of the civil power is not more respectfully obeyed where
it is understood that against disorderly force there is always in reserve the unflinching aid of military discipline . . .

But while the Colonists should be taught the necessity of providing against internal disturbance—while they should learn to rally
round the law, and create themselves the machinery for giving that
law its ordinary effect—on the other hand, they must not be left
to suppose that against external aggression Great Britain would not
render them the aid due to the dignity of her Crown, and the safety
of her subjects in every part of Her Majesty's Dominions; for where-
ever England extends her sceptre, there, as against the foreign enemy,
she pledges the defence of her sword . . .

It seems, meanwhile, a good augury of the co-operation of the
Colonists in all measures demanding public spirit that miners themselves are constructing a road, of which seven miles are completed—
that they organized themselves into bands under leaders—thus rec-
ognizing discipline as the element of success in all combined undertakings. Each miner thus employed deposited with the Governor 25
dollars as security for good conduct. I need not add, that a Governor
who could thus at once inspire confidence and animate exertion must
have many high qualities which will ensure your esteem, and add
to the satisfaction with which you will co-operate with his efforts. . .

Whilst I feel assured that the Governor will receive with all
attention the counsel or suggestions which your military and scientific experience so well fit you to offer, I would be distinctly understood when I say that he is, not merely in a civil point of view, the
first magistrate in the State, but that I feel it to be essential for the
public interests that all powers and responsibilities should centre in
him exclusively. Nothing could be more prejudicial to the prosperity
of the Colony than a conflict between the principal officers of Government. . .

I need scarcely add, that it will be among your first cares to
smooth the difficulties of communication by land and water. If you
can at slight cost render the Fraser River navigable to a further extent

than it is at present, you will direct your science to that object. . . .
You will come in contact with Germans, Frenchmen, Americans; with many who may, perhaps, have prejudices against English institutions and the English character. Most of these prejudices will vanish when they who entertain them are brought into familiar acquaintance with that union of energy and prudence, of the devotion to duty, which Englishmen so quietly blend with the attachment to freedom; and the spirit of loyalty, truth, and upright dealing, which signalize the brighter, and, I believe, the larger portion of our national character and race. But if those qualities be common to all classes of our countrymen, at least they become more manifest and attractive when set forth with that courtesy, high breeding, and urbane knowledge of the world which dignify the English gentleman and the British officer; and I anticipate no small advantage towards stamping our native idiosyncracies on a Colony which may comprise so many foreigners, and promoting a high social standard of civilization, from the fact that yourself and your brother officers are amongst its practical founders, and cannot fail by the nature of the civil services you render to be brought into frequent and friendly communications with all classes of settlers . . .[57]

Douglas meanwhile was making his final preparations for severing ties with the HBC. In a letter to the Colonial Secretary he declared, "I place my humble services unhesitatingly at the disposal of Her Majesty's Government", and agreed not only to resign as Chief Factor, but also to sell his shares in the Puget Sound Agricultural Company.

While waiting to assume the governorship of the mainland colony, Douglas made yet another quick trip to the diggings. He found what he described as "a wonderful scene of enterprize and industry," estimated that 3,000 men were working on the river banks, and judged that their average earnings were from $5 to $25 a day. He declared himself

much struck with the healthy, robust appearance of the miners, who were generally living in canvas tents or log huts, exposed to many discomforts, yet all seemingly in good health, pleased with the country, and abundantly supplied with wholesome food.[58]

At Fort Hope he appointed Robert Smith, a native of Scotland, to be justice of the peace and revenue officer, and Robert Ladner to be chief constable. He set up a court, consisting of George Pearkes, Crown solicitor of Vancouver Island, and two assistants, Donald Fraser and Robert Smith, to try one William King on a charge of murder. King was found guilty of manslaughter, and, since the colony had no jails, sentenced to transportation for life.[59] Two licences to sell liquor were also sold at Fort Hope, bringing in a total of $600 toward the cost of government. Douglas also decided to lay out a townsite in the area and sell lots to the general public.

At Fort Yale, he also took steps to lay out a townsite and issued liquor licences. He quickly organized a police force, consisting of one chief constable at $150 a month and five policemen at $100 a month, explaining to Lord Lytton that

This is a very high rate of pay, but no men worth having will serve for less.[60]

Meanwhile, the town of Victoria was also being transformed. Frenzied groups of men were knocking together boats with which to cross to the mainland; buildings were rising on all sides; roads were pushing northward into Saanich; there was now an hourly express between Victoria and Esquimalt.

Inevitably, the burdens of the governor mounted; yet, as there was no one to whom he could delegate authority, he had to bear them as best he could. He saw to the purchase of two fire-engines in San Francisco,[61] considered the needs of the area for roads and bridges, kept a vigilant eye on the native tribes, and meanwhile carried out his duties as chief officer of a commercial enterprise, supervising from Victoria the affairs of a chain of fur trading posts scattered throughout the wildernesses of the mainland.

It is hardly surprising if at times he felt the task almost beyond him. In a despatch written in the fall of 1858, his usual reserve gave way to some extent under the pressures of office, and he spoke of

. . .the labour and responsibilities under which I have been so often ready to sink, having for the last six months discharged unaided the whole functions of two distinct governments.[62]

So, month by month, the struggle raged—the struggle to decide whether the unexpected social convulsion of the gold rush would sweep away the frail framework of law and order that Douglas was almost single-handedly creating, or whether he could successfully channel this sudden outpouring of energy into the forms and institutions he believed it was his duty to uphold.

And, as the months of this extraordinary year wore on, it gradually and amazingly became clear that he might win the battle. His resources lay mainly in his own character, but with the aid of a handful of dedicated assistants and subordinates, they proved sufficient to the task. Those who might have sought to establish their own authority on the river, confronted by one who had no doubt of his, clearly thought twice; when they found that, as they searched feverishly for the precious metal that meant wealth, they were being protected in their lives and property, they responded to the man who had made it possible. On one occasion, though with some reluctance, the motley army of adventurers was even persuaded by Douglas to give three cheers for the Queen.[63]

During the most crucial period of this year of crisis, the Governor, as he himself noted, had been almost alone in bearing the heat of the day. Had he faltered, or abandoned what seemed an unequal struggle, all would doubtless have been lost. Now, one by one, crossing the wide oceans to devote their particular talents and abilities to the creation of a new and distinctive civilization in this distant wilderness, others took their place at his side. The earliest of importance to arrive, perhaps, was Rear Admiral Robert Lambert Baynes, who in obedience to the instructions of the Lords of the Admiralty in London, made the long voyage up the western edge of two continents from Callao to Esquimalt, casting anchor there on Sunday afternoon, October 17, 1858. His ship, the *Ganges*, was for its time a formidable craft. Built in Bombay, it mounted 84 guns, and was at this time the last sailing line-of-battle ship in the British foreign service.[64] It had three decks, was very strongly built, and could hold 800 men; it thus added considerably to the force at the Governor's disposal.

Another substantial addition to the military forces of the colony was soon made in the persons of a contingent of the Royal Engineers. The first advance party, under Captain Parsons, arrived on the 29th of October in the *Panama;* on the 8th of November, a second group, commanded by Captain Grant, arrived at Victoria. Douglas was no doubt relieved that assistance would soon be available for opening up the communications of the mainland colony and other public projects. He also was evidently impressed by the personal character of the engineers, as he suggested to Lord Lytton that arrangements should be made by which members of this and similar forces should be given free grants of land on their retirement, thus "adding a respectable British element to the population and thereby infusing and encouraging sentiments of attachment and loyalty to the Crown".[65] It was decided in the meantime that the headquarters of the Engineers should be at Fort Langley.

Arriving on the same ship as Captain Grant was another figure destined to play an important part in the grand design. This was Mr. Chartres Brew, chosen by the British Government to be Inspector of Police in the mainland colony, at a salary of £500 a year. Born on the last day of 1815 in County Clare, Ireland, he had served fourteen years in the Irish Constabulary and also in the Crimean War. Douglas was well pleased with this choice and soon found use for his services; he also wrote to the Colonial Secretary suggesting that sixty additional members of the Irish Constabulary should be sent out to undertake police duties; he had found, so he informed Lord Lytton, that both successful and unsuccessful gold miners were, though for rather different reasons, unsuitable material for policemen.[66] Brew quickly proved his worth, quelling a disturbance at Yale not long after his arrival, and in later years was to show his capabilities in a variety of positions.[67]

On November 15, 1858 there arrived at Victoria another figure destined to play not only an important and a colorful role in the early development of British Columbia, but also, as we shall see later, to be one of that small band of figures—some of them neglected or misunderstood by historians—responsible for the existence of Canada today, a service for which he received £800 a year. This was Matthew Baillie Begbie, first Chief Justice of the new colony, and described by Professor Sydney Pettit as "Governor Douglas' first lieutenant in the field".[68] Born (like Douglas and Colonel Moody) in the tropics, he had later attended Cambridge. His intellectual interests were manifold, including mathematics, the classics, singing, chess and cards. He was also in his early years an expert oarsman and tennis player. His presence was impressive, and he sported a black mustache waxed into two sharp points. He was not unduly puritanical, but determined from the beginning to uphold the law. His physical stamina was to stand him in good stead in his travels into the interior of the colony, and his unconventionality was perhaps no liability in the unusual circumstances in which he was to carry out his duties.[69]

Other officials were also en route to the new colony to aid Douglas in his duties; the most important of these was perhaps Colonel Moody, commander of the Royal Engineers. He was not, however, to arrive until Christmas Day of this year, and consideration of his background and career may more conveniently be postponed until later in this narrative.

As the year ended, the situation had thus changed greatly from that of six months previously. Then, Douglas had been almost alone, battling to keep his head above a human flood of unexpected origins and dimensions. Now, the framework of government had been maintained on Vancouver Island and established on the mainland, and the course seemed set fair for the future. In October, 1858, Douglas had outlined the main features of what he envisioned for the new colony under his direction, himself admitting that its achievement would be a "herculean task":

> To accomplish that great object of opening up a very inaccessible country for settlement, by the formation of roads and bridges immediately and pressingly wanted; to provide public buildings for the residence of the officers of the Crown; for the use of the judiciary, for offices of record; and, in short, to create a great social organization, with all its civil, judicial and military establishments, in a wilderness of forest and mountain . . .[70] .

So far, but little had yet been accomplished; but as the year drew to its close, at least the materials were now at hand. Money, of course, as well as men, would still be needed, and Douglas in this period appealed constantly to the Home Government on behalf of the colony:

Like a nurseling, it must for a time be fed and clothed; yet I trust it will, before many years, re-imburse the outlay and repay the kind care of the mother country with interest.[71]

By early November, at least one of the many tasks that Douglas had set himself was finished:

I have the satisfaction of announcing that the great work of the season, the route by Harrison's River to a point in Fraser's River, beyond the mountain, about eight miles below the upper fountain, is now completed; and a number of mule trains are upon the road about to engage in the transport of provisions and other supplies for the mining population of "Lytton", and the mining districts beyond that town. It is, in fact, to that route that we must ultimately look for a convenient communication with the interior of the country.[72]

A few days later, Douglas asked if he could appoint William Young to be the Colonial Secretary of British Columbia, a proposal with which Lord Lytton was later to signify his agreement.[73]

The same month, the seal was publicly placed on all that had been done. Not only was Douglas informed that as a mark of trust, approval and gratitude he had been made a Companion of the Bath; but, journeying to the mainland, in the main building of the Company at Fort Langley, Judge Begbie administered to him the oath of office as the first governor of British Columbia. It was a cold wet day, and there was no great crowd of witnesses; yet those that were present—representing the navy, the law and the engineers—gave a certain symbolism to the event. Government had come to the wilderness; more roads would soon be finding their way through the great forests; the laws of England and the local ordinances of the Governor would be enforced; while behind all, ready if need be to come to the aid of the Queen's subjects, would stand the pledged might of Britain and the Royal Navy.

Here, then, perhaps, we should close our account of this amazing year; a year memorable not only in the history of the area but in the career of the man who during it had stood four-square upon the hinge of fate. Much had depended on him in this hour of trial; and much in this crucial time he had supplied. Possible disaster had by skill and resolution been avoided, and as the year drew to its close Douglas and his little cluster of officials on the farthest edge of the Empire well might say, in the words said to have been used by many after the greater world crisis of 1914-1918, "Look! We have come through!"

NOTES

[1] Douglas to Lytton, October 11, 1858. *Papers Relative to the affairs of British Columbia*, Part I, 1859.

[2] Margaret Ormsby, *British Columbia: A History*. Macmillan, 1958, p. 508.

[3] For example, as early as 1852 Chief Trader McLean was buying nuggets from the Indians at Kamloops (J. H. Reid, "The Road to Cariboo", M. A. Thesis, U.B.C., April 1942, p. 3)

[4] Douglas to Labouchère, July 22, 1856.

[5] Douglas to Labouchère, August 20, 1856.

[6] Douglas to Labouchère, October 29, 1856.

[7] Douglas to Labouchère, December 5, 1856.
Capt. Pickett, it is interesting to note, in 1861 declined further service in the army of the United States and enrolled in the forces of the Confederacy. He thus became — or so the unkind might put it — something of a deserter himself.

[8] Labouchère to Douglas, January 2, 1857.

[9] He was later joined by Captain Richards of H.M.S. *Plumper*. The *Satellite*, 1462 tons, carried 21 guns. It was stationed at Esquimalt from 1857 to 1860. The *Plumper* was an auxiliary steam sloop of 484 tons. It arrived at Esquimalt November 9, 1857, and remained there till January 1861. Her second lieutenant, R. C. Mayne, later wrote an interesting book, *Four Years in British Columbia and Vancouver Island*, (London, 1862).

[10] Douglas to Labouchère, May 5, 1857.

[11] Douglas to Labouchère, July 15, 1857.

[12] *Ibid.*

[13] *Ibid.*

[14] Douglas to Labouchère, October 13, 1857.

[15] Douglas to Labouchère, December 29, 1857.

[16] *Ibid.*

[17] Douglas to Labouchère, December 29, 1857.
Under the terms of this proclamation, mining licences (to cost ten shillings a month) had to be obtained from the authorities in Victoria. The licence fee was raised to 21s a month in January 1858.

[18] *Ibid.*

[19] Douglas to Labouchère, April 6, 1858.

[20] *Ibid.*

[21] Douglas to Labouchère, May 8, 1858.

[22] *Papers Relating to British Columbia*, Part I, London, Queen's Printer, 1859.

[23] Douglas to Baynes, May 12, 1858.
Rear Admiral Robert Lambert Baynes was Commander-in-chief of the Pacific Station from 1857 to 1860. His flagship was the *Ganges* of 84 guns (after which Ganges Harbour, Salt Spring Island, is named). Lord Lytton in a despatch to Douglas dated October 16, 1858, informed him that Admiral

Baynes would, he believed, leave Callao for Vancouver Island on August 28, 1858.

24 Douglas to Stanley, May 19, 1858.

25 *Ibid.*

26 As early as June 5, 1858, a public meeting in Victoria saw numerous protests against the HBC monopoly of the river trade. In his despatch to Lord Stanley of June 15, 1858, Douglas enclosed a petition signed by James Yates and "five other persons", asking that the river be freely opened to all vessels. Douglas informed the petitioners that he would do what he could to accede to their demands, though he made it clear that the HBC would probably have to be compensated for this concession.

27 Douglas to Stanley, June 10, 1858.

28 *Ibid.*

29 *Ibid.*

30 Douglas to Stanley, June 15, 1858. Douglas later removed him as "being deficient in nerve for the position he holds" and replaced him by Chartres Brew. (Douglas to Lytton, December 24, 1858, *Papers Relative to the Affairs of British Columbia*, Part II, 1859.)

31 Douglas to Stanley, June 15, 1858.

32 Douglas to Stanley, July 1, 1858.

33 Travaillot to Douglas, June 24, 1858. *Papers Relative to the affairs of British Columbia*, Part I, 1859.

34 *Papers relative to the affairs of British Columbia*, Part I.

35 *Ibid.*

36 *The Letters and Journals of Simon Fraser 1806-1808*, Ed. W. K. Lamb, Macmillan, Toronto, 1960, p. 96.

37 Accounts of these are scattered throughout the issues of the Victoria *Gazette* for July and August. See in particular the issue of August 24, 1858.
One survivor of the fighting that summer was Edward Stout, who had arrived at Fort Yale on May 20, 1858. He died in 1924 at the age of 99. More about him may be found in *Stories of Early British Columbia* by W. W. Walkem, (Vancouver, 1914, pp. 51-62).

38 *Victoria Gazette*, July 28, 1858.

39 Lillooet is an Indian name, and not, as is sometimes stated, a corruption of l'alouette (the lark).

40 Seton Lake was named by A. C. Anderson after a relative, Col. Alexander Seton, who was lost in the sinking of the troopship *Birkenhead* on February 26, 1852. The passage between Seton and Anderson lakes was also at this time named Birkenhead Strait.

41 Much interesting information regarding these roads is to be found in "The Road to Cariboo" by J. Stewart Reid (M. A. Thesis, U.B.C., April 1942).

42 Douglas had already made some changes in his original regulations. In July, traders who took out a licence were allowed to engage in business on the mainland; the following month a tariff of ten per cent ad valorem was imposed on goods shipped to the mainland, and the system of obtaining licences from the HBC was abandoned. After September, American traders were no longer excluded from trading on the river. See Ormsby, *British Columbia: A History*, pp. 152-153.

[43] Lytton to Douglas, August 14, 1858. The revocation of the grant was despatched to Douglas on September 2, 1858.

[44] A bill had been introduced in the House of Commons on July 1, 1858, creating the colony of "New Caledonia". It was to extend from the Rockies to the Pacific Ocean (though it did not at first reach as far north as its present boundary of 60°, which was established on July 28, 1863), and include the Queen Charlotte Islands but not Vancouver Island. To avoid confusion with the French colony of that name, this name was later discarded, and "British Columbia", a name personally selected by Queen Victoria, was substituted for it.

[45] Douglas in his reply (October 4, 1858) suggested a salary of £5000 a year for the combined offices he would hold. Lytton in his reply (December 16, 1858) thought this excessive and suggested £1800.
It is interesting to note that many years later, when Anthony Musgrave succeeded Frederick Seymour as Governor of B.C. in 1869, Douglas wrote to his son-in-law, A. G. Dallas, saying that the governor's salary should be reduced, as it was "out of all proportion to the means of the colony". He went on to say that "this lavish expenditure is unjust and oppressive, and cannot certainly meet the approval of the colonial minister. When made known to him, I feel assured he will put a stop to it". (Douglas to Dallas, June 18, 1869. Sir James Douglas, Correspondence Outward, PABC).

[46] Lytton to Douglas, July 16, 1858 (confidential).

[47] Lytton to Douglas, July 31, 1858.

[48] See Journal of Service of Lt. C. W. Wilson, R.E., entry for July 31, 1858. MS in PABC.
Bishop Cridge, in an interesting article on Victoria's early days in the Colonist for December 22, 1907, tells us that
"Mr. Augustus F. Pemberton, Commissioner of Police, was staying at my house when, after he had gone to bed, a message came from the chief of police that the town was in an uproar, and that the miners were threatening to take the city. Mr. Pemberton immediately repaired to the Governor's and reported. His Excellency's first impulse was to fix on his sword; but he changed his mind and sent a messenger express to order a gun-boat from Esquimalt".
Bishop Cridge in this article says of Pemberton: "Fearless, untiring and vigilant, he suppressed every disorder as it arose."

[49] See Minutes of the House of Assembly of Vancouver Island, 1856-1858, Victoria, King's Printer, 1918. Entries for July 27, August 5, 17, 24, 1858.

[50] See J. W. Pilton, Negro Settlement in British Columbia, 1858-1871, M.A. Thesis, U.B.C., 1951. Also K. Cornwallis, The New El Dorado, London, 1858, p. 274.

[51] Douglas to Lytton, July 26, 1858.

[52] Douglas to Lytton, November 29, 1858. Papers Relating to the affairs of British Columbia, Part II, London, 1859.
Lord Lytton saw fit in this connection to return to the question of the possibility of divergent loyalties in the Governor and Chief Factor. In a despatch dated August 14, 1858, he said: "You will pardon me if I enjoin you, as

imperative, the most diligent care that in the sales of land there should not be the slightest cause to impute a desire to show favour to the servants of the Hudson's Bay Company".

53 Lytton to Douglas, October 16, 1858. *Papers Relative to the Affairs of British Columbia*, Part I, 1859.
54 Lytton to Douglas, October 16, 1858.
55 *Ibid.*
56 Lytton to Douglas, October 19, 1858. Correspondence between Lord Lytton and the Archbishop of Canterbury about this gift may be found in *Papers Relative to the Affairs of British Columbia*, Part I, 1859.
Douglas himself wrote a letter to Miss Coutts some years later, saying, in part: "I deeply sympathize in your solicitude for the welfare and advancement of the native races, and I shall be most happy at all times to give the results of my own experience in the work.
With all their faults the natives are not destitute of those qualities which lend dignity to character; they are generally tractable, and receive with implicit faith the teaching of those whom they respect.
It is nevertheless an arduous undertaking to change the habits, improve the tastes, and reform the character of nations, whether savage or civilized; we may however hope through the blessing of God, and the help of many persons of rank and property, who express a warm desire to forward their Christian instruction, that much good may be done, even though we should fail in accomplishing all that is desired." (Sir James Douglas, Correspondence Outward, Miscellaneous Letters 1859-1863; letter dated August 24, 1861).
57 *Papers Relative to the Affairs of British Columbia*, Part I, 1859, pp. 73-75.
58 Douglas to Lytton, October 12, 1858.
59 *Ibid.*
Douglas wrote to Lord Lytton on November 30, 1858, pointing out that this form of punishment was difficult to enforce, as there was no penal settlement within reach. He wondered if the British Government would be prepared to pay for the removal of criminals to some Australian penal settlement. On August 5, 1859, Lord Lytton demonstrated his capacity for delicate discrimination by replying that Australia was reserved for criminals convicted in the British Isles, and suggested that sentences of hard labor in British Columbia be substituted for transportation.
60 Douglas to Lytton, October 12, 1858.
61 Victoria *Gazette*, July 29, 1858.
62 Douglas to Lytton, October 26, 1858.
63 Douglas to Merivale, private, October 29, 1858. Quoted in Ormsby, *British Columbia: A History*, p. 160.
64 Walbran, *British Columbia Coast Names*, Ottawa, 1909, pp. 198-200. There is a detailed description of the ship in the Victoria *Gazette* for October 26, 1858. Ganges Harbour, Salt Spring Island, was named by Captain Richards of H.M.S. *Plumper* after it.
One resident of Victoria at this time later recalled: "The best thing I heard or saw at Victoria was her band in the summer evenings rousing the shores

and the seas with her masterly playing". (Angus McDonald: "A few items of the west", *Washington Historical Quarterly*, July 1917, p. 226).

[65] Douglas to Lytton, November 8, 1858.

[66] Douglas to Lytton, December 27, 1858.

[67] In 1859 he became Chief Gold Commissioner, in 1863 a Stipendiary Magistrate at New Westminster, and in 1864 a member of the first Legislative Council of British Columbia. When he died in the Cariboo in 1870, it was engraved on his tombstone that he was "a man imperturbable in courage and temper, endowed with a great and varied administrative capacity, a most ready wit, a most pure integrity and a most humane heart."

[68] In "Dear Sir Matthew: a Glimpse of Judge Begbie", *BCHQ*, XI, No. 1, January 1947, p. 1.

[69] An old timer who knew Begbie described him as "six feet four and a half inches in his socks and as straight as a needle. He has a fine education and speaks well in French and German, Italian and Spanish, with a good store of Greek and some Hebrew, but no Gaelic." (Angus McDonald: "A few items of the west", *Washington Historical Quarterly*, July 1917, p. 223. Begbie was the first president of the Victoria Philharmonic Society (*Victoria Gazette*, February 1, 1859). He was also an indefatigable church-goer, and while at New Westminster "he sang in the choir of the cathedral (Church of England), and his voice could be heard drawling out at the end of a verse after every one had ceased singing. He had a chair placed for his use outside of the choir, as the seats would not admit his long legs between the rows". (W. W. Walkem, *Stories of Early British Columbia*, Vancouver, 1914, p. 35).

[70] Douglas to Lytton, October 26, 1858.

[71] Douglas to Lytton, November 4, 1858.

[72] Douglas to Lytton, November 9, 1858.

[73] Douglas to Lytton, November 13, 1858; Lytton to Douglas, March 3, 1859. *Papers Relative to the affairs of British Columbia*, Part II, p. 81.

CHAPTER NINE

Consolidating the Victory

WHEN LATE in 1858 Douglas returned to Victoria after having been sworn in at Fort Langley as the first governor of British Columbia, it is hardly to be doubted that he looked back on the events of the previous six months with some satisfaction. He had witnessed, supervised and facilitated the discovery of a previously unsuspected source of incalculable wealth along the banks of the Fraser River;[1] he had maintained law and order in the area during the turbulent days that followed; he had brought to a distinguished close his career as an officer of the Hudson's Bay Company; and he had received public recognition and approval for his actions from the hands of the British Government.

Despite all this, we can hardly doubt that as he assumed the double duty and honor of the governorships of both British colonies on the Pacific coast, he was keenly aware that many tasks still confronted him. Compared with the tidal wave of humanity that was flooding up from California, through Victoria, and on into the valley of the great river, he and his little band of officials were few indeed; while communications were still tenuous, the force at his disposal small, and England half a world away. So far, this had not resulted in disaster, but the past, he well knew, was no guarantee of the future.

There were, however, signs as 1858 ended that the prospects of his cause were brightening, as from beyond the horizon's rim came men of courage and character to stand beside him in the battle. Arriving in October from South America had come Admiral Baynes in the *Ganges;* its commander was a man of experience, while his formidable vessel with its 84 guns quite dwarfed such craft as the *Beaver*, the *Otter*, and the *Satellite*. The admiral and his ship were to leave Victoria in December after a stay of only two months, yet they were destined to return from time to time, and even when not present were to exercise their influence, as confirming the Colonial Secretary's promise that "wherever England extends her sceptre, there, as against the foreign enemy, she pledges the defense of her sword".[2] From the British Isles had come a variety of figures; one was Matthew Baillie Begbie, appointed the new colony's first Chief Justice; almost single-handed he would uphold the majesty of the law in the gold fields. Chartres Brew of the Irish Constabulary had also arrived; as the colony's first inspector of Police, he would rapidly organize a small but devoted police force in the mining areas. In the last few days of the year Colonel Moody, Commander of the Royal Engineers and Chief Commissioner of Lands and Works, had reached Victoria, full of plans, not all of them practical, for using the men under his command to construct a full-scale civilization in the wilderness.[3]

The history of the next few years in the two colonies would be largely the record of how Douglas and his resolute lieutenants preserved and defended what had already been achieved, while moving steadily forward in the direction of the vision which each of them in his own way had glimpsed. At times, as we shall see, there would be disagreements between the principal figures in this great enterprise, but these were usually either the outcome of individual quirks of character or of the inevitable conflict between what was desirable and what was practical. None doubted that "Men at some time are masters of their fates";[4] what they were now to accomplish would go far to demonstrate it.

As the new year opened, the first of Douglas' lieutenants to take the field was Col. Moody; although he had been in Victoria only since Christmas Day, and the main body of the Royal Engineers was not to arrive until April,[5] he set out early in January for the Fraser River. His purpose was severely practical—to determine the best location for the capital of the new mainland colony; however, since the age of the narrow-minded specialist had not yet arrived, he was fortunately not prevented from either an aesthetic appreciation of the scene that unfolded before his eyes or from philosophic reflections on the astonishing series of events in which he now found himself involved. His comments on his journey, as set down in a letter written shortly afterwards, are therefore of more than ordinary interest.[6]

The gateway to the new colony at once impressed him:

> The entrance to the Frazer is very striking—extending miles to the right & left are low marsh lands (apparently of very rich qualities) & yet from the background of superb mountains—Swiss in outline, dark in woods, grandly towering into the clouds there is a sublimity that deeply impresses you. Everything is large and magnificent, worthy of the entrance to the Queen of England's dominions on the Pacific mainland. I scarcely ever enjoyed a scene so much in my life.

Before long, the Colonel had decided on the best site for the new capital:

> It is the right place in all respects. Commercially for the good of the whole community, politically for imperial interests & military for the protection of & to hold the country against our neighbours at some future day, also for all purposes of convenience to the local government in connection with Vancouver's Island at the same time as with the back country. It is a most important spot.

Some day this "important spot" would be known as New Westminster; at the time, however, it was only a quiet place on the river's bank. Yet already, in the imagination of this remarkable man, a city had taken shape:

> Viewed from the Gulf of Georgia across the meadows on entering the Frazer, the far distant giant mountains forming a dark background—the City would appear throned queen-like and shining in the glory of the midday sun.

Moody next pushed further up the river. Envisioning on the fertile lands near its mouth "horses & cattle lazily fattening in rich meadows in a glowing sunset", he found himself in surroundings very different:

The scenery was very grand all the way, & as "bar" succeeded "bar" with miners all at work at their "rockers" and sluices gathering in the gold dust, it all had a very lively cheerful look. The blue smoke from their log cabins curled up among the trees, & from the brink of the River when fires were on the bank. The trees being chiefly cedar and black spruce contrasted with the dazzling snow. The River was alternatively "rapids" & "still water", reflecting everything—reflecting cottages, blue smoke, trees, mountains & moving figures. A scene full of life. The sun shone splendidly over all . . .

Clearly, this panorama, so different from anything in his experience, had touched the artist in Moody; now, as he watched the miners, drawn from so many corners of the globe, industriously searching for the precious metal, the religious side of this complex man was also stirred:

I was deeply moved that it pleased the Almighty Ruler of the Universe to bring these various nations together under the protection of our Queen, & you will readily believe that I prayed very earnestly to Him to endow me for Jesus' sake with wisdom & prudence & to guide me in the matter before me. I prayed for His blessing on all our ways & for peace. My heart was overflowing with earnest love for all these manly energetic fellows. . .

The "manly energetic fellows" promptly greeted Col. Moody in the fashion they no doubt considered appropriate to his calling:

They gave me a salute, firing off their loaded revolvers over my head. . . Suppose a hand had dropped by accident!

The aesthete and the earnest Christian in Moody were, however, at this point displaced by the soldier:

If it was to try my nerves, they must have forgotten my profession.

Undeterred by this unorthodox welcome and deeming the occasion propitious, the pious Moody (who in September of the same year would become the first president of the Victoria YMCA) promptly invited the miners to a make-shift church service and read prayers over them, though without ascertainable results.[7]

He was already deeply impressed by all he had seen, and as determined as Douglas not to abandon the country to the Americans; indeed, he pictured it as eventually assuming an important place in the "ranged arch of empire":

> I trust & believe they will be mistaken as to their getting the whole country. I hope it will be united some day with Canada as a great nation forming in some federal manner an integral portion of the whole Empire of which it is now a colony.

Moody did not, however, confine himself to long-range speculation. Proceeding to Fort Yale, he was able with the aid (moral rather than physical) of a party of Royal Engineers and the judicial authority of Judge Begbie to bring to a speedy close the somewhat ludicrous affair known as "Ned McGowan's War". McGowan, an American with a long criminal record,[8] had considerable authority among the miners of the area. A controversy between two magistrates, J. P. Whannell of Yale[9] and George Perrier of Hill's Bar,[10] gave him an opportunity to use it. Acting on the orders of Perrier, with a band of twenty followers he went to Yale, seized Whannell in his own courtroom and took him before Perrier, who fined him $50.

McGowan was summoned to appear before Judge Bebgie at Yale to account for his actions. There was a sizable crowd of miners in the courtroom, Moody later reporting that "the only unarmed men were the Judge and myself". Despite this, McGowan meekly pleaded guilty, whereupon Bebgie, in Moody's words, "gave it to McGowan very heavily & stripped bare all their false definitions of right and wrong". McGowan, who had brought his gun with him into the courtroom, left a sizable fine behind him when he left. His feelings, however, were surprisingly not as wounded as might be expected, for when Moody again passed through Yale, McGowan invited him into his cabin and offered him what the Colonel later termed "an excellent glass of champagne", whereupon the two men joined in drinking the Queen's health!

Order was thus restored; the circumstances of the entire affair had been decidedly unusual (Moody later reported that "all the time I was at Yale I slept on three boxes in a passage" and that his orderly and the Judge had had to make do with the floor), but the Colonel was well satisfied with his expedition. He was now convinced that

> . . .among all Her Majesty's colonies there is not a finer one or one with more valuable resources than this, and as a dwelling place for Englishmen few in any way can compare with it.

Moreover, the great principle had been firmly established and upheld that

> . . . .in the Queen's dominions an infringement of the Law was really a serious matter & not a sort of half joke as in California.[11]

On his return to Victoria, Moody reported his conclusions to Douglas. He had already perhaps surprised the Governor, struggling with countless day-to-day problems, by picturing in a letter to him "future great trunk railways into the Interior";[12] he now not merely disturbed but annoyed him by informing him of the site he had chosen for the capital of British Columbia. Douglas had favored Old Fort Langley (later known as Derby), and to this end had had the area surveyed and lots sold at public auction; now Moody informed him that it was too close to the American border, and the Governor felt himself forced to yield to this professional advice. On February 14, 1859 Douglas proclaimed "Queensborough" the capital of British Columbia, in July of the same year announcing that in accordance with the wishes of Queen Victoria it would henceforth be known as New Westminster.

Much encouraged, the Colonel initiated grandiose plans for converting it into an impressive metropolis; the fact that it would for long years yet be only a small settlement and that the funds available for his projects were strictly limited dismayed him not at all; nor, apparently, did the fact that the Engineers could not simultaneously devote their energies to building the new capital and constructing the roads into the Interior that were the colony's prime and pressing need. Inevitably, the initial harmony between the Colonel and the Governor began to exhibit discord, though this did not prevent Douglas from appointing Moody and Judge Begbie to the Executive Council which he formed in the spring of 1859 to assist him in his duties.

Meanwhile, though in a different way, Judge Begbie also advanced the cause of civilization in the colony. In the spring of 1859 he went "on circuit", holding court at Langley, Hope, Yale and Lytton. He was accompanied by Mr. Charles Samuel Nicol, recently appointed High Sheriff of British Columbia, and Mr. Arthur Bushby, who acted as registrar and assize clerk, and who was in due time to become, like Dr. Helmcken, the Governor's son-in-law.

Begbie's report to Douglas, dated April 25, 1859,[13] is a highly interesting document, as in addition to summarizing his judicial activities, he found time to comment on the terrain, resources and inhabitants of the colony. The journey of the first Chief Justice of British Columbia in the cause of duty was, we might note, one which his successors in that high office might well shrink from duplicating:

> The trail between Fort Yale and Quayome, by which we advanced, was at that time I should think utterly impassable for any animal but a man, a goat, or a dog. It might, doubtless, be very much improved. In many places a very painful and dangerous ascent and descent of 20 minutes, in the whole course of which the traveller depends almost as much on his hands as on his feet, brings the path to within a few yards of the projecting precipice through which a few pounds of powder would have made an easy way.

Begbie also noted the change of climate as he advanced into the Interior:

> . . . it was much drier, the springs less frequent, the soil sandier, the undergrowth much less dense, and the spruce, hemlock, Douglas (fir) and cedars which we had carried all the way from the sea all disappeared by degrees, and were replaced by a pine, very similar to the Scotch fir, but with longer spines. . . The whole of the country is tolerably well adapted for stock. It appears rather too dry for arable cultivation.

Begbie had both criticism and praise for the original inhabitants of the area:

> The whites alleged, what is obvious to everybody, that the Indians are extremely averse to work except under the pressure of immediate hunger; and that they are so improvident as rarely to look beyond the wants of the day, and never to consider the wants of a winter beforehand. . . My impression of the Indian population is

that they have far more natural intelligence, honesty and good manners than the lowest class, say the agricultural and mining population
of any European country I ever visited, England included.

The feature of his journey through the Interior that struck the judge
most, however, was the comparatively small demands on his official
services:

It was surprising, with a population so unsettled, so often a great
part of it at least changing, and so little habituated to the presence
of law or justice, to find very few complaints, none of violent
crimes.

Summing up his observations for the Governor, Begbie made five
main points:

1. The ready submission of a foreign population to the declaration
of the will of the executive when expressed clearly and discreetly,
however contrary to their wishes.
2. The great preponderance of the California or Californicized
element of the population, and the paucity of British subjects.
3. The great riches both auriferous and agricultural, of the country.
4. The great want of some fixity of tenure for agricultural purposes.
5. The absence of all means of communication except by foaming
torrents in canoes or over goat tracks on foot, which renders all
productions of the country except such as, like gold, can be carried
with great ease in small weight and compass, practically useless.

All this was soundly reasoned and Douglas in the months and years
ahead would bear it constantly in mind. Few men, however, can have
been more bedevilled by a thousand anxieties than the Governor of
the two colonies in this period. Not only did he have to assess and often
act upon the reports of his more important subordinates such as Judge
Begbie, Colonel Moody, and the Inspector of Police, Mr. Chartres
Brew; he had to supervise the civic affairs of the burgeoning settlement
of Fort Victoria (where Amor de Cosmos was soon attacking him
almost daily in his *British Colonist*), as well as watch carefully the
Americans to the south, whose right to the minor islands in the Gulf of
Georgia he was still resolved to reject.

Nor were these by any means the only matters which forced themselves on his attention as he pointed the prow of the ship of state into the gales of change; there were a hundred others, great and small. His task was to distinguish between the trivial and the essential, and then allocate his own time, the slender resources of the two colonies, and the meagre aid of the mother country, as seemed best. A defeat on a single front—a breakdown of law and order in the gold fields, for example—might lead to total disaster; in such a situation, "the summer soldier and the sunshine patriot" (in Thomas Paine's words) might well have shrunk from the test; but Douglas, now with forty years of fidelity to duty behind him, in the early days of which he had often struggled through snowstorms on the trail, faced into this new hurricane unflinch-ing.

The Fraser River was not, as we noted, the only region of the two colonies to require the unceasing vigilance of Douglas. In Victoria, though there had been some slackening of the feverish pace of 1858, the signs and problems of expansion were still apparent. New buildings, some of them substantial, were rising on all sides; a police barracks, a custom house and post office were constructed, and the paving of the principal streets was begun. Since there were as yet no mayor or aldermen, such matters as the maintenance of law and order and the provision of a wide range of services from hospitals to cemeteries, inevitably, demanded the time and attention of the Governor. He also supervised the construction by J. D. Pemberton of the two lighthouses at Race Rocks and the entrance to Esquimalt Harbor.

It is remarkable in the circumstances that far from being satisfied with the bare minimum of facilities for government at Victoria, he now embarked on an ambitious and dramatic plan to expand them. Thus there came into existence the famous "bird-cages", long to serve as the seat of government for Vancouver Island, and to be destroyed by fire only in 1957. These buildings, though their architectural style was bizarre, were substantial and in their own way impressive. The money to construct them was supplied partly by the HBC and partly by selling lots in what is now the business district of the city, and their total cost was variously estimated as from $40,000 to $100,000, a large sum for those days. As the new structures were on the south side of James Bay, Douglas decided to construct a bridge, several hundred feet long, across the bay, so as to provide easy access to the main part of the town.

When this was disclosed, the House of Assembly[14] became alarmed, fearing that the cost of these projects would soon descend like a heavy weight upon the residents of the area. It proceeded to pass a resolution, which was then submitted to the Governor, expressing opposition to the undertaking.[15] Douglas however pointed out in a message to the House that this body "was not called upon to defray the cost",[16] and refused to change his plans. He noted that he had already provided a wide variety of public services "without any pecuniary aid or assistance whatever from the House of Assembly", and declared that the economic expansion of the area would demand still further government facilities. Among these would be:

A Treasury with fire-proof vault; a Barrack for the military guard; a Land Office; an Office for the Registrar of Deeds and Conveyances; an Office for the Colonial Secretary; a House for the Legislative Assembly; a Supreme Court; an Official Residence for the Governor; and other buildings of inferior importance.[17]

The abashed Assembly raised no further objections; instead, it thanked the Governor for "Your Excellency's courteous and candid reply",[18] and turned to other matters, while the work went steadily forward.

Mention must be made at this point of a minor controversy in which Douglas found himself engaged. This revolved around the question as to what was implied by severing all his ties with the HBC. It was agreed by all that he must have no further voice in the affairs of the Company; but there remained the question of the pension paid to a retired Chief Factor. At this period, the customary payment was 1/85 of the Company's profits for the first six years of his retirement. As Governor, it could be argued, Douglas might be in a position to help the Company to prosper, and therefore to augment his own pension. Douglas, as well as those in charge of HBC affairs, saw no likelihood of this, but the British government was adamant that every tie must be cut.[19] Douglas then tried to sell his interest in the pension, but this, too, came to nothing, as the Company had, after all, no idea as to what its future profits might be. In the end, he received no further payments from the Company.[20]

Douglas was also somewhat reluctant to take no further part in the Company's affairs. As late as March 4, 1859, H. H. Berens, Governor of the HBC,[21] wrote to him, drawing his attention to the fact that A. G. Dallas was now the HBC representative in Victoria, and that Douglas must act accordingly:

> I have therefore to request that you will be good enough to hand over to Mr. Dallas all documents, papers, and accounts connected with the Company's affairs hitherto under your charge.

Douglas replied on May 4 that he had already obeyed this order, and wished the Company well under his son-in-law's "able and attentive management".[22]

Douglas also made an effort in this period to obtain some recompense for his duties as Lieutenant-Governor of the Queen Charlotte Islands. The British Government, however, declined to accede to this request, maintaining that these duties had been only formal.[23]

We have noted previously how from time to time Douglas had been faced with what might be termed an opposition. There had been one in the days of Governor Blanshard, when the independent settlers had banded together to express their dismay at the thought of the Chief Factor succeeding Blanshard in the governorship; later there had been the band of malcontents of which the Rev. Mr. Staines was apparently the guiding force. Neither of these groups (whose membership had not been mutually exclusive) had achieved much immediate success with their agitation, though some of the changes they advocated (such as the creation of an Assembly, and the placing of the posts of Governor and Chief Factor in separate hands) had in time come to pass. Now a new voice of protest would be heard; it was that of Amor De Cosmos, the eccentric idealist who, arriving in Victoria in the summer of 1858, had brought out the first issue of his *British Colonist* on December 11 of the same year.[24] From the very beginning he had focussed the running fire of his editorials on the most visible target in sight—the man who had founded the settlement in 1843 and who for the last decade had guided its destinies. The motives of De Cosmos are hard, perhaps, at the distance of a century to disentangle; some of them likely had their origin in his early experiences in the Maritimes, where the development of parliamentary democracy was considerably more advanced than in Van-couver Island or British Columbia; while some of them were perhaps not dissimilar from those of Cassius, who also found unendurable a world containing a figure greater than himself.

In any case, Douglas was now faced with an opponent who, unlike his predecessors, had a rostrum from which to direct his attacks. The very first issue of De Cosmos' paper plainly suggested what lay ahead. Though fervent in his protestations of loyalty to the Crown and the imperial connection, he proclaimed himself in domestic matters "the sure friend of reform". This involved, he went on to make clear, "such changes as will tend to establish self-government"; he bluntly demanded "a system long established in British America, by which the people will have the sole control over the local affairs of the colony."

The first of the many editorials that would soon be winging their way like envenomed darts from De Cosmos' active pen also contained words which the Governor had not previously been accustomed to see in print:

> He wanted to serve his country with honor, and at the same time preserve the grasping interests of the Hudson's Bay Company inviolate. In trying to serve two masters, he was unsuccessful as a statesman.

It was soon apparent that this was no random outburst, but the first of a series of attacks which De Cosmos was now to launch against the Governor. A week after his first issue, he was demanding "the immediate establishment of self-government";[25] on Christmas Day he evidently felt that the most appropriate compliment of the season would be a scathing attack on Douglas for appointing Dr. Kennedy to be member for Nanaimo, instead of holding a proper election in that district. Early in the new year, the vigor (or, as some might say, the malice), of De Cosmos' attacks increased, as he flatly declared Douglas "unsuited for the office of Chief Magistrate of these colonies";[26] while the following month he clearly lost his sense of fitness and proportion, maintaining that

In fact we honestly believe that the man who will not ask Her Majesty's Government to remove Governor Douglas is a traitor to his country, and unworthy of her protection—and blind to his own interests.[27]

Douglas had not so far in his career been used to such abuse; yet an effective mode of combatting it eluded him. Aware of the possible results of attempting to interfere with the freedom of the press, he sought to achieve the same end by his favorite device of issuing a proclamation. This, made public in March, required that newspapers before being allowed to publish should put up sureties. This did not, however, much hamper De Cosmos. There was evidently in the community some sympathy for him, or at least support for a free press, and at a public meeting held April 4, 1859, arrangements were made to raise the required amount of £800 by public subscription.

Regardless of the attacks of De Cosmos, the Governor had countless duties to attend to in the two colonies under his control, and there was no abatement in his activity. By way of encouraging settlement, he sold land in the country at ten shillings an acre, and gave the purchasers two years to pay. He also reduced the price of mining licences to five dollars a year. To collect the licence fees, as well as to settle petty disputes between the miners, in the summer of 1859 he appointed Gold Commissioners. These officials (who included Peter O'Reilly, whose later career is of considerable interest)[28] were responsible for the registration of mining claims, as well as fulfilling a variety of other functions such as presiding at inquests. Douglas in the midst of a score of other tasks found time to issue them instructions which unconsciously revealed one of his own sources of strength—a tireless attention to detail:

> You will be furnished with a chest for the security of gold and money received by you, and it is desirable that in your temporary absence the same should be given to the care of the sergeant of your party. You will take care that the barracks or tents are not at any time left without a sufficient guard, and you will keep a sentry on the ground at all times, day and night.
> You will settle all disputes between licensed occupiers of the gold fields, visiting the spot in dispute with as little delay as possible.

It is most desirable that every dispute should be instantly investigated and settled, that disputants may not have the temptation to redress their grievances themselves.

Placed at strategic locations throughout the Interior, the Gold Commissioners, by force of character combined with good humor, succeeded in carrying out their duties without serious opposition.[29]

By the summer of 1859, it appeared that the affairs of the two colonies were well in hand. Yet no sooner had a considerable degree of order been established in the gold fields and in Victoria than a serious dispute over the San Juan Islands came dangerously close to the "flash point".

It began when a member of the animal kingdom, not perhaps completely conversant with the delicate international questions involved, initiated a dangerous series of events. A pig belonging to the Hudson's Bay Company invaded the garden of an American settler on the main island, and caused some damage; whereupon the incensed settler, making the characteristic response of his countrymen to vexing situations, promptly shot it. The Company, when apprised of the incident, demanded compensation for the deceased porker. It was clearly a matter to be dealt with at the highest level in the area, and before long the head of the Oregon Military Department, General William S. Harney, was in Victoria discussing the issue with Governor Douglas. From there the Captain went to the scene of the crime and listened to the grievances of his countrymen. Deciding that not merely the settler's garden but the feathers of the American eagle had been disarrayed, he sent orders to Captain Pickett, who was then at Fort Bellingham, to occupy the island. On July 27, 1859, Captain Pickett landed on San Juan with sixty soldiers.

A week later, General Harney wrote a sharp letter to Douglas, explaining that American troops had only landed "to protect the American citizens residing on that island from the insults and indignities which the British authorities of Vancouver Island, and the establishment of the Hudson's Bay Company, have recently offered them . . ."[30]

The Governor was faced with a difficult choice. If he acquiesced in the American move, he might well have surrendered forever any effective power in the Island. A counter blow, however, might be fraught with the gravest consequences. Douglas, undoubtedly a shrewd man but not always a cautious one—long ago, we recall, Sir George Simpson had noted him as "furiously violent when roused"—resolved at first on a prompt and vigorous response. This had, after all, been his reaction to the somewhat different sort of American invasion of Van-couver Island and the adjoining mainland in the summer of the previous year. Audacity and self-confidence then had carried the day; perhaps, he no doubt reasoned, they might well do so again.

Thus on July 29 he wrote two letters in rapid succession to Captain de Courcy, then senior naval officer at Esquimalt. In the first, the Governor's orders were explicit:

> Having received positive information that a body of soldiers belonging to the United States of America have been landed upon the island of San Juan and have usurped an armed occupation of the same, and having reason to believe that it is purposed to augment that body by landing other armed forces, I have to call upon you in the name of the Queen to assist me to prevent this occupation of territory which is regarded as a dependency of this Government, and I beg you will immediately despatch a powerful vessel of war to San Juan, and will instruct the officer in command to prevent the landing of any further armed parties of United States soldiers for the purpose of occupation, and also the erection of fortifications of any descrip-tion by the party already on the island.[31]

Almost immediately afterward, however, it appears that the Governor had second thoughts; at all events, the same day he sent a slightly more cautious letter to de Courcy. In this he explained that he did not wish the proposed naval expedition "to interfere in any way with such persons as may actually be landed upon the Island of San Juan except in the single case mentioned in my aforesaid letter, of throwing up fortifications or erecting military works; the only action that I wish to proceed from the officer commanding the ships you may detach, is to prevent the landing of armed men to take possession of the territory as aforesaid."[32]

Douglas wished to act through the British civilian authorities on the island, the naval force to act only if requested.

In accordance with these instructions, H.M.S. *Tribune* under Captain Hornby was at once despatched to the area, the ship also taking with it Attorney-General Cary. Douglas later referred to this as

the first hurried steps which I adopted, feeling assured that bold and decided measures in the first instance would have the effect of arresting further attempts to occupy the Island, and that as a collision was inevitable in the event of both governments asserting extreme rights of possession, it was better to have to cope with a small detachment than to wait until reinforcements from Washington Territory should make their dislodgement impracticable with our present force.[33]

On the evening of July 31, Douglas received a despatch from Attorney General Cary, reporting that the American forces on the island were too strong to be expelled "without a strong possibility of resistance". This caused the Governor to reconsider his position. He decided to confer with Captains de Courcy and Richards of the Royal Navy as to whether he should proceed with his original plan of forcibly preventing the erection of fortifications on the island by the Americans or the landing of additional troops there. Their advice, to his evident disgust, was to abandon a course of action so unpredictable in its consequences:

. . . . they expressed a very strong opinion of the proposed employment of Her Majesty's forces against the troops of the United States and suggested that milder measures should be first tried, professing however their readiness to receive my instructions, at the same time entering their protest against any forcible demonstration.[34]

Reluctantly, the Governor decided to modify his original plan of action:

Out of respect to the opinion of these officers and especially feeling assured that the measures of government could not be carried into effect with the requisite spirit and vigour unless the officers entrusted with their execution were cordial in their support, I agreed to a modification of the instructions issued to Captain Hornby directing him to prevent the landing of armed parties of United States troops and the erection of military works by the party

Sir Matthew Baillie Begbie, first Chief Justice of British Columbia

Amor de Cosmos, fiery editor of the British Colonist

J. Despard Pemberton, pioneer surveyor of Vancouver Island

17-Mile Bluff, Cariboo Road

Great Bluff on the Thompson River, Cariboo Road

already on the Island, which part of his instructions was revoked and the magistrate was directed not to issue any process against the United States detachment of troops then on San Juan.[35]

In the meantime, consideration was to be given to recalling the Royal Marines from the mainland colony of British Columbia and holding them in readiness for possible hostilities, steps were set on foot to discover whether the American actions had been taken merely on the initiative of local authorities or whether they had the sanction and approval of the federal government in Washington, D.C., and H.M.S. *Pylades* was sent to San Francisco with despatches for the British Government and a request for instructions.

Douglas had till this point felt confident that his Legislative Council was completely in agreement with his policy. However, he now summoned a meeting of this body, which Captain de Courcy and Colonel Hawkins were also asked to attend and to which they expounded their views. After a thorough discussion of the crisis, this body recommended "the withdrawal of all British subjects from the Island of San Juan, under protest against the act of hostility which has rendered such a step necessary."[36]

The reasons given for advocating a policy so different from that which was urged by the Governor were various. One reflected the larger imperial picture—the European balance of power:

> In the present state of European politics it is extremely desirable that the Home Government be as far as possible left unfettered by a war with the United States, over which they have in the inception had no control.[37]

There were in the opinion of the Council several other considerations which indicated a cautious policy. One was that both governments were aware that the ownership of the island was in dispute; another was that the American government was clearly behind the action of its soldiers (a contention which Douglas was later to dispute[38]); moreover, if open hostilities broke out, not only might there be an invasion of Vancouver Island by Americans dispossessed from the San Juan Islands, but it was "also probable that if a collision takes place at San

Juan, insurrectionary and filibustering movements will ensue both in Vancouver Island and British Columbia, the great majority of the inhabitants being either citizens of the United States or embued with their feeling."[39]

In the light of this analysis of the situation, the council concluded that

> It appears that your Excellency could for the moment amply vindicate Her Majesty's sovereignty in San Juan. But we are by no means sure that Your Excellency could maintain that sovereignty for more than a short time. It seems clear that it could not be vindicated without bloodshed—and bloodshed would endanger both these colonies and involve the Imperial Government in a war.[40]

To this report John Work, Donald Fraser, Judge Cameron, Judge Begbie, Captain de Courcy and Colonel Hawkins affixed their names. So too did Roderick Finlayson, with the proviso that he disapproved of withdrawing any British property from the Island. The only objection came from Attorney General Cary, who had it put on record that, "I cannot but dissent from these views".

Such were the considered views of the Governor's advisers. If they stayed his hand, they evidently did not alter his opinions, for the same day that he received this report, he forwarded it to the Colonial Secretary accompanied by comments which indicated that he had had no change of heart:

> I feel assured that not one of the gentlemen who have attached their signatures to that address would hesitate for one moment in hazarding life and property in their country's defence. The difficulty in the present case is that they do not know that San Juan is their country. I therefore profoundly respect their motives, though I still believe that vigorous measures on our part would soon dispose of the question in our favour; a policy of national concession being always mischievous and in the case of these colonies dangerous.[41]

The Governor's next move was one with which he already had some experience. He issued a proclamation, announcing to the world at large in no uncertain terms his views (which he believed to be identical with those of the British Government) as to the ownership of San Juan and the smaller islands in the group:

By James Douglas, C.B., governor and commander-in-chief in the colony of Vancouver's Island and its dependencies, vice-admiral of the same, &c:

The sovereignty of the island of San Juan and of the whole of the Haro Archipelago has always been undeviatingly claimed to be in the crown of Great Britain. Therefore I, James Douglas, do hereby formally and solemnly protest against the occupation of the said island, or any part of the said archipelago, by any person whatsoever, for or on behalf of any power, hereby protesting and declaring that the sovereignty thereof by right now is, and always hath been, in her Majesty Queen Victoria and her predecessors, kings of Great Britain . . . [42]

For the next few days the Governor thought the matter over, and while doing so, the situation was altered (perhaps decisively) by the arrival at Esquimalt on August 5 of Rear Admiral Baynes in the *Ganges*. In the meantime, Douglas had come to a most serious decision:

After mature reflection and with every deference to the opinion of the Council I had called upon the subject of the occupation of the Island of San Juan by a body of American troops, I came to the conclusion that I could not abandon the Island to such an occupation, and I determined to land a body of British troops so that the occupation might at least be a joint one.

For this purpose I addressed a letter of instructions to Captain Hornby of Her Majesty's ship "Tribune", a copy of which I enclose, but I regret to say that Captain Hornby did not deem it advisable to carry out those instructions for the reasons which will be found detailed in his report.

I cannot but regret that circumstance, for I feel satisfied that the absence of a movement of this kind has only increased the confidence of the occupying party, and it places me in a difficult position, for so much time having elapsed, the carrying out of the movement at this period deprives it of most of its force.[43]

What had happened, it seems clear, was that the Admiral, who is said to have believed it ridiculous "to go to war over the shooting of a pig", had ordered Captain Hornby to take no sort of precipitate action, and that the captain had decided to obey his naval rather than his civilian superior.

Douglas, feeling that his knowledge of the area, its inhabitants, and the long San Juan controversy was considerably greater than that of Baynes, attempted to convert the Admiral to his views. In a letter to the naval commander, the Governor declared that his own proposed policy had been based on his "long experience and intimate knowledge of American character" and was, moreover, merely the logical expression of the clearly defined position of the British government.[44] Admiral Baynes, however, was not to be swayed, and the Governor had perforce to refrain from precipitate action. In an address to the Legislative Council and the House of Assembly, he had already expressed himself in a noticeably less belligerent tone; he did, however, state that British Marines and Engineers would be landed on the island if necessary to protect British lives and propery.

This led in turn after a few days to questions being publicly asked by members of the House of Assembly as to just what, in fact, the Governor did intend to do. Dr. Helmcken had some pointed questions to ask regarding the policy of his father-in-law:

> His Excellency sends troops and ships. Why all this expense and show, if for parade? Why were not the troops landed? They should have landed their troops and avoided all degrading negotiations.[45]

James Yates also wanted to know why troops had not been landed, though he declared that he "preferred negotiation to war". J. D. Pemberton recommended the landing of troops, saying he "believed a few soldiers if supported by a man-of-war could land without danger of collision"; he proposed as well the occupation of Lopez Island by British troops. McKay was "favourable to landing troops at all hazard." These varying viewpoints were then summed up in a resolution passed by the seven-man Assembly:

> The House would most urgently impress upon your Excellency to enforce upon Her Majesty's Government the necessity of demanding from the Government of the United States not only the immediate withdrawal of those troops, but also strenuously and at all risks to maintain Her right to the Island in question and also to all other islands in the same Archipelago, now so clandestinely, dishonorably and dishonestly invaded.[46]

De Cosmos, in an editorial on August 17, now commented sarcastically on the way the affair was being handled; he too declared that British troops should have long since been landed on the Island, and that it was "evident that a serious difference of opinion as to our policy exists between the naval and civil authorities".

The crisis was still in this unresolved position when it was taken in hand by the higher levels of the British and American governments. General Winfield Scott, Commander-in-chief of the U.S. Army, was sent to the Oregon Territory in October, and corresponded regarding the situation with Douglas. As a result, a joint occupation of the Island was agreed upon. The following year, General Harney and Captain Pickett, much to their disgust, were removed from the area and the Americans reduced their forces, while British troops did eventually land peacefully on the Island on March 20, 1860. Tension gradually subsided, and for some time afterward no further trouble ensued.[47] As we shall see later, however, there would be another dangerous moment during the American Civil War, and the issue would not be finally settled until 1872, by which time Douglas would long since have retired.

Before passing on to other matters, we should possibly consider some aspects of this affair more closely. We may, perhaps, ask two questions: what policy did Douglas really wish to pursue? What would have been the results of it?

There can hardly be much doubt that from the beginning Douglas favored a "hard line". He had no inner doubts about the ownership of the islands, and he held the firm belief that the Americans lacked both the character and the military forces to thwart his will. As to the psychological factors, a final judgment is of course impossible; but there had been, as Douglas no doubt bore in mind, the evidence of the gold rush of 1858, when a mere handful of Britons had brought into line and subjected to their rule a vastly greater number of Americans. The military balance of power in the event of open warfare is harder to assess. In the immediate area, Douglas undoubtedly held the upper hand; but if escalation had occurred, it is much harder to reckon which government would have been both able and willing to bring the greater force to bear.

What would have resulted from the application of Douglas' intended policy of using prompt and immediate military force can not of course be known; but it seems at least possible that the result might well have been a general war between Britain and America. This was clearly the fear of Admiral Baynes, and also of those other officials who opposed the Governor at the decisive moment. That Douglas himself was quite prepared to face this far-reaching consequence of his policy is apparent from the record. For example, in his letter to Admiral Baynes on August 17, he spoke unequivocally of the possible use of Indian guerrillas in the event of war. There was still much hostility between the Americans and their native tribes; in Douglas' view, this was because "the Americans do not understand the Indian character, and have invariably treated that people in such a manner as to arouse their worst passions". He thus reckoned that in case of war, the Indians could be induced to support Britain — that "it would be a fearful power to use, and one to which I would only resort in the very last extremity".

The comments of some contemporaries on these events may be useful in enabling us to estimate how close the Pacific Northwest came to being embroiled in a general war. To quote Dr. Helmcken:

> I know there would have been a collision and the island would have been captured had Governor Douglas had his own way—but altho he was Vice Admiral, the commanders of H.M. ships were dubious and wanted plain orders. Fortunately or unfortunately the British Admiral just then arrived—so he superseded the authority of Governor Douglas and would not embroil the nations in war on any account—there would be no bloodshed about this matter as far as he was concerned—he would await instructions. Governor Douglas was no little chagrined at this, and subsequently told me if he had had his own way the affair would have been quickly settled, the Island occupied by the British and the diplomacy would have settled the matter—he thought possession of great importance.[48]

Angus McDonald, an old timer who had known Douglas, confirmed that Douglas had thought of using Indians against the Americans.

> Sir James once told me when the row about San Juan was on foot that he, in the event of war, would muster fifty thousand Indian riflemen at Victoria.[49]

Colonel Moody, when referring to the Governor's instructions to the British naval commanders in the area, declared:

> The Governor's letters involved an impractibility—to land, but on no account to come into collision . . . There can be no doubt from Hornby's instructions . . . that a collision was desired.[50]

D. G. Macdonald, at one time a member of the North American Boundary Commission, wrote a few years later:

> In respect to this San Juan affair, let the people of England never forget how nearly we were thrown into all the horrors of war, at a time when the States were not, as now, disunited and helpless, by the intemperate policy of His Excellency Governor Douglas, who is Commander-in-chief of Her Majesty's colony of British Columbia and its dependencies. But for the arrival of Rear-Admiral Sir Robert Baynes, K.C.B. at the eleventh hour, war with America was certain. This I know, having been upon the island when His Excellency's commands were received. The good old Admiral and the captains of his fleet boldly refused to adopt a course which would have created a rupture between England and America . . . To the chivalry and forbearance, therefore, of these wise and valiant men the two kindred nations owe indeed much.[51]

It seems clear, then, that during 1859 Douglas had gone to the very brink of war, with all its incalcuable consequences, and had only been dissuaded at the last moment from stepping over it.[52] Had he done so, the attitude of the British Government is hard to determine, but, regardless of its previous assurances of general support, it is certainly possible that one part of the final outcome might have been the withdrawal of its confidence in Douglas' judgment. It is said that Napoleon, in going over a list of officers submitted for possible advancement, would sometimes scribble in the margin, "Is he lucky?" We may say, that in the San Juan affair, Douglas had been very lucky.

The remainder of 1859 saw no events of comparable importance. Lt. Mayne, R.N., made a journey of exploration into the Interior as far as Kamloops, while Lt. W. S. Palmer, R.E. explored the Harrison and Lillooet rivers and made detailed reports on every aspect of those areas to Douglas.[53] The road by way of the Harrison River to the upper Fraser was being improved, and the Governor was able to report that "about 100 pack mules leave Douglas weekly with freight for Bridge River" and that freight rates had fallen from 37c to 10c a pound.[54] More progress would have been possible, Douglas asserted, if the Royal Marines had not had to be held in readiness to act in connection with the San Juan Islands; if their services had been avail- able, he intimated, he would have put them to work—regardless of any dreams of martial glory they might have cherished—with pick and shovel.[55]

Douglas himself made a tour of the diggings in this period, talking with the miners at some of the main centres of activity. He reported to the Colonial Secretary (the Duke of Newcastle had recently replaced the Earl of Lytton) that at least £14,000 of gold was being exported from British Columbia each month, and that there were about 5,000 white men in the Fraser valley. There were, however, very few women "to refine and soften by their presence the dreariness and asperity of existence".[56]

Another shortage was that of farmers, who in Douglas' view were an essential ingredient in providing a balanced economy for the area:

> The miner is at best a producer, and leaves no traces but those of desolation behind; the merchant is allured by the hope of gain; but the durable prosperity and substantial wealth of states is no doubt derived from the cultivation of the soil. Without the farmer's aid, British Columbia must forever remain a desert, be drained of its wealth, and dependent on other countries for daily food.[57]

Schools had not yet made their appearance in the colony, he reported, but he declared his intention to remedy this defect. There were, how- ever, resident clergy at both New Westminster and Derby, who were giving social cohesion and stability to the residents of those settlements.[58]

Other expeditions in this period, the Governor informed the Duke, were adding to his knowledge of the vast areas entrusted to his rule. Lt. Palmer, R.E., who in May and June had explored the Harrison- Lillooet area, in September and October proceeded eastward from Hope close to the southernmost border of British Columbia, passing south of Lake Okanagan and eventually reaching Fort Colville in American territory.[59] On the north Pacific coast, "a few daring spirits", the remains of a party of miners who had failed to find gold in the Queen Charlotte Islands,[60] ascended the Skeena River, explored the Babine Lake area, and penetrated as far as Fort St. James. Douglas gave it as his opinion that the Skeena River would "soon become a most important outlet for the upper districts of Fraser's River".[61]

We might also note in 1859 the beginning of a development which would eventually have wide repercussions. Already some of the bars near the mouth of the Fraser had been exhausted, and miners were moving farther up the river in search of the "mother lode". Not yet had they stumbled on the fabulous wealth of the Cariboo, but slowly they were approaching it, and on August 23 the Governor reported in a despatch that miners "in the newly discovered diggings at Quesnel's River are making on the average one ounce of gold to the man per diem".[62]

Douglas now gave further proof of the range and force of his mind by forming a picture in it larger than any he had yet envisioned. Once, Vancouver Island had been world enough for him; later, the Fraser River had been added to the regions for whose destiny he was responsible, while the central parts of the colony were slowly beginning to come within the orbit of civilization. Now, however, while the network of roads that Douglas planned for British Columbia was still barely begun, in a great surge of imagination his mind leaped out to embrace all those local projects in a grander vision. Writing to the Duke of Newcastle on October 18, 1859 he touched first on the immediate task he was struggling with:

> The great object of opening roads from the sea coast into the interior of the country, and from New Westminster to Burrard's Inlet and Pitt River, continues to claim a large share of my attention. The labour involved by these works is enormous, but so essential are they as a means of settling and developing the resources of the country, that their importance can hardly be overrated.

Then he conjured up for the Colonial Secretary the shape of a truly tremendous destiny for the scattered colonies in British North America. There was already a pack-road of sorts used by the fur traders that, beginning in the interior of British Columbia, traversed the Rockies and made its way across the great plains to the Red River settlement. This, in the view of Douglas, might be changed from a strand into a rope:

> If the Canadian Government would undertake to open a road from Red River to the borders of Lake Superior, which really presents no very formidable difficulties, the connexion between British Columbia and Canada would be complete, and the whole distance might, I think, be travelled on British soil.

Without waiting for the Duke's reply, Douglas proceeded with his part of this grand design. On December 10, 1859 he issued a procla-mation, putting a charge of 12s a ton on all goods leaving New Westminster for the Interior. The proceeds were to be used to improve the route along the Fraser and Harrison Rivers; and with this new move in the direction of a colony united by its trade routes, spreading out into the Interior but all ultimately converging on the Fraser River, this first year of Douglas' governorship of British Columbia came to an exhausting but triumphant close.

In the first week of 1860, the Governor issued another proclamation. It permitted the pre-emption of land in the Interior, with a maximum of 160 acres for each settler. It was made clear that when the land was eventually surveyed and a legal title granted, the settler would have to pay for his holding, the maximum price envisioned being 10s an acre.[63]

Douglas also granted the Anglican and Methodist Episcopal churches each one acre of free land in Yale, Hope, Derby, Port Douglas and New Westminster. He made it plain, however, in writing to the Colonial Secretary that he had no intention "to advocate the establish-ment of a dominant and endowed church". The Duke agreed to this concession, but vetoed a suggestion by Douglas that in certain rural areas of B.C. churches should be granted a hundred acres of free land as a form of financial support.[65] Douglas did not abandon the idea of giving some assistance to the struggling young churches in the colony, however, and expressed the hope that the Duke would authorize him "to make some other provision calculated to advance and support the cause of religion." [66]

Douglas also gave what stimulus he could to New Westminster. He established an assay office in the capital of the mainland colony, and listened sympathetically when its residents asked that it be incorporated as a town, with its own democratically elected officials. On July 16, 1860 a proclamation granted this wish, and detailed regulations were laid down as to who should have the vote in civic elections.[67] The town, though never as large as Victoria, made slow but steady growth. Two steamers plied between the capitals of the two colonies, and other steamboats of the stern-wheel variety went from New Westminster to Douglas and Yale.

Douglas meanwhile pressed on with his road-building program, and sought for better routes into the Interior than that by way of the Harrison River. Progress, however, was slow; one reason was the shortage of labor, and the other was in his own words that "these routes may, without exaggeration, be severally compared to the passage of the Alps".[68] The Royal Engineers in the meantime considerably improved the navigation of the Harrison River, while a road was pushed eastward from Hope in the direction of the Similkameen by two capable civilian surveyors, Edgar Dewdney and Walter Moberly.[69]

Meanwhile, though some miners had abandoned their hopes of riches and had returned whence they came, others were hastening to take their place. Not all of these were white men, for, as Douglas reported:

> British Columbia is becoming highly attractive to the Chinese, who are arriving in great numbers, about 2,000 having entered Fraser River since the beginning of the year, and many more are expected from California and China.[70]

This despatch also contained a reference to a development whose significance not even the perceptive Douglas yet grasped. This was the persistent northward movement of prospectors in search of the richer deposits which, it was beginning to be rumored, lay farther up the river. Speaking of the miners along the lower Fraser, the Governor reported that:

> The great majority of those hardy wanderers were making their way toward Quesnel River, where it is confidently expected rich hill diggings will be found.

By the summer of the same year, the Governor estimated that there were six hundred white miners working along the Quesnel River, and that their earnings were from $10 to $25 a day.[71] Although these were respectable sums, they did not however suggest the tremendous strikes that would be made in the Cariboo a year later, and for the time being Douglas' attention was devoted to a wide variety of other matters.

One of these was a voyage up the Fraser to Pitt Lake. The practical necessities of the colony's development were his primary motive, but this did not prevent him from noting the sylvan beauty of the waterway:

> The eye never tires of ranging over the varied shades of the fresh green foliage, mingling with the clustering white flowers of the wild apple tree, now in full blossom, and filling the air with delicious fragrance. As our boat, gliding swiftly over the surface of the smooth waters, occasionally swept beneath the overhanging boughs which form a canopy of leaves, impervious to the sun's scorching rays, the effect was enchanting; yet amidst all this wealth and luxuriance of nature, I could not repress the wish that those gorgeous forests might soon be swept away by the efforts of human industry, and give place to cultivated fields and the other accessories of civilization.[72]

Visiting Hope and Yale, the Governor persuaded their residents to agree to a tax on all goods carried from these points into the Interior. As the revenue was to be devoted to the building of roads, the miners readily agreed. Douglas did, however, have to face criticism for this tax from the New Westminster newspaper; this was the *British Columbian*, which loudly maintained that the plan would throttle trade.

Perhaps by way of appeasing critics in the mainland capital, late in the year Douglas proclaimed the "Southern Boundary Act". This put a heavy duty on goods imported into the Interior of B.C. from the corresponding American area. The purpose of this plan was to channel trade through New Westminster, and though it was difficult to patrol the long southern boundary of the colony, the act no doubt benefited the merchants of the Queen City.[73]

Events in Victoria also inevitably made demands on the Governor's attention. In January 1860 an election was held for a new House of Assembly. De Cosmos stood as a candidate, but neglected to retain his

sobriety at a public meeting and in consequence was defeated.[74] Attribut-
ing his ill fortune to the "Establishment", he continued to belabor its most
prominent figure. The new House met on the first of March, and
Douglas favored it with a confident and hopeful address.[75] The following
month he laid the cornerstone of St. John's church, while by summer,
thanks to his efficient subordinate, J. D. Pemberton, work on the two
lighthouses at Fisgard Island and Race Rocks was well advanced. Meanwhile the capable Rev. Cridge continued to supervise the educational
system of the Island, making regular reports to the Governor.[76]

A figure destined at a considerably later date to share the spotlight
with Dean Cridge in the most serious religious controversy ever to shake
Victoria had also arrived in the island colony. This was Bishop Hills,
whose appointment had been made possible by the generosity of Miss
Angela Burdett Coutts. The bishop was at once enamored of his new
home, and within a week of his arrival in January 1860 had written a
letter describing it in glowing terms:

> Victoria must be, I think, the most lovely and beautifully situated
> place in the world. I never saw anything before like it. In the
> summer it must be exquisite. I was agreeably struck with it altogether;
> there is every sort of scenery. Sublime mountains, placid sea, noble
> forest trees, undulating park-like glades, interspersed with venerable
> oaks, inland lakes, and rivers abounding with fish . . . On the
> whole I was surprised to see the size and rapid growth of the town . . .
> It will be a large city ere a few years are over.[77]

A question in which both the Bishop and the Governor were to be
involved was also a matter of public controversy at this time: that
of state assistance to religion. Douglas had even in his Fort
Vancouver days done what he could to advance the cause of Christianity, and when Governor of Vancouver Island supervised the construction
of churches and the provision of clergy for both Victoria and Nanaimo.
Some members of the public, however, believed that all such matters
should be the responsibility of private citizens, and that the state should
take no part in them whatever. Prominent among the supporters of this
view was Amor De Cosmos, and in his editorial columns he vigorously
assailed the policy of the Governor.

For example, when the Rev. Mr. Cridge's five-year term as Colonial Chaplain expired in 1859 and it was proposed to renew it, De Cosmos bitterly attacked this suggestion. Declaring that the issue was whether "religion shall be supported by governmental aid" and whether "one sect of Christians shall receive support and the other none", he laid down the dictum in an editorial in the *Colonist* for September 14, 1859 that there should be no state aid to religion as "the spirit of the age is opposed to it". The following spring, a week after the cornerstone of St. John's Anglican church had been laid by the Governor, De Cosmos spoke scathingly of "the church monopoly" and remarked that, "the followers of the lowly Jesus are certainly well treated in this Ultima Thule".[78] This controversy was to continue until the summer of 1861, when upon Bishop Hills' sturdy refusal to accept any further government aid to the Anglican Church, it was finally resolved to the satisfaction of all parties.

The question of maintaining good relations with the native tribes at all times engaged the Governor's attention. That the traditional occupations of their ancestors had not yet been abandoned was shown in July 1860 when a band of Cowichans massacred a group of Bella Bella Indians on Salt Spring Island.[79] There were only about seventy white settlers on the island at this time, and they naturally felt much alarm.[80].

A few months later, when on a tour of the settlements on the mainland, the Governor held frank conversations with the natives of the area. At Cayoosh, he made it clear to them that land would be set aside exclusively for their needs, that they would have clearly defined hunting and fishing rights, and that they were as free to look for gold as anyone else. In a despatch to the Duke of Newcastle, Douglas summed up the policy he planned to pursue:

> In short, I strove to make them conscious that they were recognized members of the commonwealth, and that by good conduct they would acquire a certain status and become respectable members of society.[81]

Later in the same month, the Governor spoke to the Indians of the "Shimilkomeen", and assured them that they would not be herded onto reservations, as was being done by the Americans in the areas south of the line.[82]

1861 seemed likely to become another year of steady progress. Victoria had recovered from the brief depression of 1859 and had much of the heady atmosphere of a "boom town". As one observer recalled:

> The average Victorian's sense of bliss apparently consists of the largest possible number of drinks in the shortest possible time, varied with cigars and billiards ad lib. The number of billiard-tables is simply astonishing to English eyes; there are at least eighty to a town of five or six thousand inhabitants, and they seem to be kept well going day and night.[83]

At a more responsible level, the Governor was able to organize a Volunteer Rifle Corps among the colored residents of Victoria, and also envisioned a substantial reserve militia drawn from the population at large, to be called upon in case of a sudden emergency.[84]

Such a crisis seemed perhaps to have arrived in April, when the outbreak of the American Civil War caused much excitement; on occasion, partisans of one side or the other made their feelings public in the streets of Victoria, as "the Confederate flag was hoisted in Langley St. after a battle and the North cut it down and vice versa".[85] As we shall see later, Douglas was before long to envision a drastic intervention in this conflict, but for the moment he acquiesced in his orders from the British Government to maintain a strict neutrality.

Meanwhile, De Cosmos continued to belabor the Governor in his columns. On January 24, 1861, for example, he described Douglas' council as "a weazened contrivance . . . which has kept its doors so closed to the refreshing and invigorating popular breeze, that it has become asthmatic", and on July 16 of the same year he attacked the Governor for providing money for the building of churches at Port Douglas and Cayoosh.

1861 also saw an event in the Governor's own household which must have disconcerted him considerably. In August his daughter Alice, then 17, suddenly eloped with Charles Good, son of the Rev. Henry Good. The impulsive couple were married at Port Townsend, U.S.A., by an American Justice of the Peace, aboard the British schooner *Explorer*. Douglas, whatever his private feelings, knew he could not prevent the match; but as a precaution he insisted when the couple returned on a second ceremony in Victoria. This did not, however, stop the circulation of satirical comments on the affair, among which we might note a poem which ended with the lines:

> Back then they came, and in the church,
> both Pa and Ma consenting,
> The pair were wed, all nice things said,
> but some were left lamenting.[86]

All these matters, however, were dwarfed by a development which, slowly gathering for some time, now forced itself inescapably upon the attention of the Governor, and to which he would respond with an achievement which would set the crown of success upon his long career. The development was the discovery of gold deposits on the Upper Fraser far richer than any yet found along its lower reaches, and the response and achievement of the Governor was to be the building of the fabulous "Cariboo Road".

The first big strike was made by four men—"Doc" Keithley, John Rose,[87] Sandy MacDonald and George Weaver—in a remote valley in the Cariboo; one autumn day in 1860 they stumbled on a stream which for only a few hours' work gave results beyond their fondest imaginings. Although they attempted to keep their discovery secret, word soon leaked out, and before long, first in hundreds, then in thousands, adventurers began converging on the Cariboo. All through the winter of 1860-1861 they arrived at Keithley and Antler Creeks,[88] and when the snow melted in the spring many of the newcomers made discoveries that seemed almost unbelievable. Later, Williams Creek[89] and Lightning Creek would be added to the sources of good fortune for the lucky, and as rumors of the rich new finds were confirmed, more thousands began making their way to the Cariboo from the four quarters of the earth. Some of these—the "Overlanders"—even essayed the long journey from the prairies across the Rocky Mountains; their hardships were countless, their casualties numerous, but to those who had caught in their mind's eye the gleam of El Dorado, there could be no turning back.[90]

From about May 1861 there was no further doubt that a great new gold field had been found, far richer than anything yet discovered or even imagined. Writing to the Colonial Secretary on May 2, 1861, Douglas reported that

> the confirmed impression is . . . that a gold field of extraordinary richness has been now discovered, and I sincerely trust that those impressions may be fully realized.

Not content to rely on the reports of others, the Governor now resolved on a personal investigation. Crossing to the mainland, at New Westminster he noted that the mainland capital was spreading toward Burrard Inlet (Vancouver was not yet thought of); at Hope and Yale he heard with satisfaction that prospective farmers were beginning to clear land; the road from Hope toward the Similkameen was also going forward. Then, setting out from Yale on horseback, he made his way up the Fraser Valley. As he advanced, he talked with miners returning from the new gold fields with bulging pokes of gold dust and tales of sudden wealth. In his despatch to the Colonial Secretary report-ing this journey, we find, intermingled, descriptions of the scenery, reports of the new discoveries, and reflections on their possible tremendous implications:

> Entering the passes of the Fraser beyond Yale we pursued our route over the new road amidst scenery of the grandest description. Mountains rising to the skies on both sides of the narrow pass, and immediately beneath the Fraser frantically tearing its way in foam-ing whirls convey a faint idea of the scene. Neither are softer features wanting, every spot of the earth being prolific of vegetation, and the mountains' sides covered with the most beautiful flowers . . . The new road on Fraser River from Spuzzum to Quayome runs along the face of frightful precipices, but is, nevertheless, perfectly safe for horse and mule travel . . . We are daily receiving the most extra-ordinary accounts of the almost fabulous wealth of the Antler Creek and Cariboo diggings . . . Every successive discovery indeed tends to confirm the impression that the gold fields which have been struck at Rock Creek and Quesnel River or Cariboo, are but two points in

a range of auriferous mountains containing incalculable wealth . . . a theory which, if correct, opens a magnificent vista of future greatness for the colony.[91]

By the time Douglas had reached the most northerly point of his journeys, the Bonaparte Valley, he was in no doubt as to the richness of the new discoveries. On his return to Victoria, he wrote that:

It would in fact appear that Cariboo is at least equal, in point of auriferous wealth, to the best parts of California.[92]

As he had by this time heard of two men who made $525 in a single day, of two others who arrived at New Westminster with $10,000 worth of gold dust, the product of five weeks' work,[93] while he was personally to meet many men who had made this latter sum during the summer,[94] the evidence was now undeniable.

As a first step toward meeting the conditions which he perceived would soon exist, Douglas established the "Gold Escort", which made its first trip from the new diggings in August 1861. However, despite the fact that the Escort consisted of uniformed, heavily-armed men, the Governor felt himself unable to guarantee unconditionally that gold entrusted to its care would arrive safely at the coast, and most miners in consequence preferred to bring their own winnings to the Assay Office at New Westminster.

Many men at this point would have been content to await the outcome of the new gold rush, and in the meantime to let the miners find their way to and from the gold fields by way of the Harrison-Lillooet Road or the old HBC trail through the Okanagan valley. Such an attitude, if we consider Douglas' position, could surely have been justified. He was half a world away from the mother country, whose aid had seldom been on the scale he had desired; he was responsible for the governance of two colonies, each with a wide variety of problems; he was already engaged in an ambitious program of road-building, part of which was intended to link British Columbia with the distant settlements on the Red River; he had limited resources of men, money and materials; moreover, he was now nearly sixty. Yet, in spite of all these obstacles, each sufficient to daunt a lesser man, he now resolved on a project more difficult, daring and ambitious than any he had so far attempted in his long career. This was the construction of a road up the valley of the Fraser, across the Thompson River, and northward into the Cariboo. In a despatch to the Duke of Newcastle, Douglas announced his decision in terms as unwavering as the vision that informed it:

> To provide for the wants of that population becomes one of the paramount duties of government. I therefore propose to push on rapidly with the formation of roads during the coming winter, in order to have the great thoroughfares leading to the remotest mines, now upwards of 500 miles from the sea coast, so improved as to render travel easy, and to reduce the cost of transport, thereby securing the whole trade of the colony from Fraser's River and defeating all attempts at competition from Oregon.[95]

One of the obstacles to Douglas' great plan was readily apparent, but he had already decided on a solution to it:

> The only insuperable difficulty which I experience is the want of funds. The revenues of the colony will doubtless, in the course of the year, furnish the means, but cannot supply the funds that are immediately wanted to carry on these works. I propose, as soon as those roads are finished, and the cost of transport reduced, to impose an additional road tax as a further means of revenue . . .
> I have in these circumstances come to the resolution of meeting the contingency, and raising the necessary funds, by effecting a loan of £15,000 or £20,000 in this country, which will probably be a sufficient sum to meet the demands upon the treasury on account of these works, until I receive the loan which your Grace gave me hopes of effecting for the colony in England.[96]

Douglas was clearly aware that his decision might startle the Colonial Secretary as much as the actual discovery of the gold fields. He hastened to disarm in advance, if possible, the objections of his superior:

> In taking this decided step, I feel that I am assuming an unusual degree of responsibility; but I trust the urgency of the case will justify the means, and plead my apology with Her Majesty's Government, especially as it is so clearly for the honor and advantage of Her Majesty's service; and the neglect of the measures, which by a stern

necessity are thus forced upon me, might prove in the highest degree disastrous to the best interests of the colony.

Accustomed to exact obedience within my own official sphere, I know the importance of the rule; but this is one of those exceptional cases which can hardly serve as a precedent—and as I have always paid implicit attention to instructions, and in no case involved Her Majesty's Government in any dilemma, I trust your Grace will con, tinue to place that degree of confidence in my prudence and dis, cretion which heretofore it has always been my good fortune to experience.[97]

This, then, was the second of the two great decisions on which his fame would some day rest. The first had been that of 1858, when he had decided in the face of the first great wave of gold miners from California that he would maintain at all costs the supremacy of the Crown and the rule of British law along the Fraser. Now he had made another: to bind this great new source of wealth and centre of economic activity to the older settlements at the coast by a link that, however precarious at first, would strengthen with the years. Such a link, he foresaw, would provide an artery along which the life-blood of commerce could flow, and create out of all the great area that stretched from the Rockies to the Pacific a single economic and political organism. It would also (though this knowledge was of course concealed from him in the as yet unturned pages of history) crown a lifetime of service with an imperishable achievement:

Death closes all; but something ere the end,
Some work of noble note, may yet be done.

So on the other side of the world wrote Lord Tennyson. The next two years would show how, in pursuit of his vision and undaunted by the most formidable obstacles that nature could provide, Douglas would make these words come true.

NOTES

[1] The Colonial Secretary, the Earl of Lytton, writing to Douglas, described the gold fields as "resources which have so strangely been concealed for ages, which are now so suddenly brought to light, and which may be destined to effect, at no very distant period, a marked and permanent change in the

commerce and navigation of the known world." (Lytton to Douglas, August 14, 1858. *Papers Relative to the Affairs of British Columbia*, Part I, 1859, p. 49.)

2 Lytton to Moody, October 29, 1858. *Papers Relative to the Affairs of British Columbia*, Part I, 1859, p. 73. As we shall see later, Admiral Baynes was also during the San Juan crisis of 1859 to restrain Douglas from embroiling the Pacific northwest in a general war.

3 Moody's salary was to be £1550 per annum. He was later responsible for reserving Stanley Park, Vancouver, as a permanent place of recreation for the public. Port Moody is named after him, but Moodyville, on the north side of Burrard Inlet, is named after Sewell Moody, who established a saw mill at that place.

4 Shakespeare, *Julius Caesar*, I.ii.

5 They arrived at Esquimalt in the *Thames City* on April 12, 1859.

6 Moody to Arthur Blackwood, February 1, 1859. Blackwood was a personal friend of Moody, and also a senior official of the Colonial Office. Moody's account of his journey and report on the "Ned McGowan affair" (from which all of the following excerpts are taken) is to be found in *BCHQ*, XV, 1951, pp. 91-107.

7 It is noteworthy, however, that, incredible as it may seem, many miners, even at the height of the Cariboo gold rush, refused to work their claims on Sunday.

8 He had, it seems hardly necessary to add, been a judge in his own country.

9 It later transpired that Whannell was a deserter from the Victoria Yeomanry Cavalry (an Australian force) and had left that country hurriedly in 1856 with some one else's wife.

10 Perrier was dismissed by Moody on Douglas' orders, partly as a result of this affair. See Douglas to Lytton, January 8, 1859, *Papers Relative to the Affairs of British Columbia*, Part II, p. 56, where Perrier is described by Douglas as having acted in the affair "either under the influence of fear or fraud". Douglas had previously removed from office Richard Hicks, Assistant Gold Commissioner at Fort Yale, describing him as "weak rather than corrupt" and "deficient in nerve for the position he holds". (Douglas to Lytton, December 24, 1858 and January 8, 1859) Douglas placed "nerve" high in his list of virtues. On July 13, 1868 he wrote to his daughter Jane: "I am sorry for Governor Seymour, as he is really a nice fellow, exceedingly clever, but irresolute. With more nerve he would be perfect as a colonial ruler." (Sir James Douglas, Correspondence Outward, Provincial Archives, Victoria)

11 An account of this affair is given in *Four Years in British Columbia and Vancouver Island* by R. C. Mayne, (London, John Murray, 1862, pp. 58-70). Lt. Mayne, R.N., played a useful part in maintaining communications between Col. Moody, H.M.S. *Plumper*, and officials of the HBC. Some have seen "Ned McGowan's War" as part of the long "struggle for the border". Certainly there was always the danger that the large American colony on the banks of the Fraser might appeal for aid to the American government and that British Columbia might go the same way as Oregon.

¹² Moody to Douglas, January 28, 1859. *Papers Relative to the Affairs of British Columbia*, Part II, 1859.

¹³ This report (from which all the following excerpts are taken) may be found in *Papers Relative to the Affairs of British Columbia*, Part III, 1860, pp. 17-24.

¹⁴ Its members were Yates, McKay, J. D. Pemberton, Skinner, Kennedy and Muir, with J. S. Helmcken as the Speaker. Muir was seldom present and Kennedy died in April 1859.

¹⁵ *Colonist*, May 7, 1859.

¹⁶ *Gazette*, May 12, 1859.

¹⁷ *Loc. cit.*

¹⁸ *Gazette*, May 19, 1859.

¹⁹ Lord Carnarvon to H. H. Berens, Jan. 7, 1859. PABC.

²⁰ It is not clear whether Douglas disposed of all his interests in the subsidiaries of the HBC. On July 31, 1858, Lord Lytton, the Colonial Secretary, wrote to Douglas: "I think it right to state, as it was omitted on the last occasion, that besides relinquishing directly or indirectly all connexion with the Hudson's Bay Company, it will be indispensable to apply that condition equally to any interest you may possess in the Puget Sound Company". (*Papers Relative to the Affairs of British Columbia*, Part I, 1859). On the other hand, two letters in the Provincial Archives suggest that Douglas' disposal of his holdings was, at the very least, leisurely. On April 5, 1862 he wrote to H. H. Berens: "Having an opportunity of disposing of my interest in the Puget's Sound Company, I beg in the first place to offer it for your acceptance, at an advance of 100 per cent on the amount of capital, as may be ascertained by the books of the Company, which I have paid into the concern. I beg that your decision may be signified to me by an early opportunity, that I may dispose of my said interests should this offer be declined". On February 19, 1868 he wrote to W. Armit, Secretary of the Puget Sound Agricultural Company, mentioning that he had recently disposed of five shares in the company and had received £50 for them. (Sir James Douglas, Correspondence Outward).

²¹ Henry Hulse Berens was Deputy Governor of the HBC from 1856 to 1858 and Governor from 1858 to 1863. Berens Island in Victoria Harbor is named after him.

²² Although Dallas had married Douglas' daughter Jane in 1858, relations between the two men did not always go smoothly. There was evidently some quarrel between them, for in the Provincial Archives there is a letter from Douglas to Dallas, dated December 3, 1860, which is both short and sharp:
"I have received and perused your letter of the 16th of November. The statements it contains are so inaccurate and unjust as respects myself, that I decline entering upon any discussion with you on the subject". (Sir James Douglas, Correspondence Outward, Miscellaneous Letters).

²³ Carnarvon to Berens, Jan. 7, 1859; also Thomas Fraser (Secretary of the HBC) to Douglas, Jan. 14, 1859. PABC.

²⁴ De Cosmos was born in Windsor, Nova Scotia, on August 25, 1825. In

1851 he crossed the continent from Halifax via New York to Utah and then California. After a career there as a photographer, he came to Victoria in 1858. He became a member of the Vancouver Island legislature in 1863, and resigned as editor of the *Colonist* later in the same year. He was premier of B.C. from 1872 to 1874, and a federal M.P. from 1874 to 1882. He was adjudged insane in 1897 and died later the same year. He never married. A writer in the *Victoria Daily Times* of January 19, 1906 gives an interesting portrait of him: "A tallish, handsome man, pale complexion, dark hair combed back, regular features set off by a sufficient, shapely nose, addicted to a frock coat, top hat, and big handled stick hung on the forearm . . . such was the man to the eye. He was wide-minded, yet methodical, laborious, and a master of details . . . Few ascribed to him humor, but in reality Mr. De Cosmos had a pretty good, though perhaps limited sense of it."
See also *British Columbia and Confederation*, ed. W. G. Shelton, Morriss Printers, Victoria, 1967; Roland Wild, *Amor De Cosmos*, Ryerson Press, 1958; Margaret Ross, Amor De Cosmos; a British Columbia Reformer, M. A. Thesis, U.B.C., April 1931.

25 *Colonist*, December 18, 1858.

26 *Colonist*, January 8, 1859.

27 *Colonist*, February 12, 1859.
De Cosmos eventually died insane, and traces of mental instability were present throughout his career. Failure to recognize Douglas' great services to the two colonies was not, however, confined to De Cosmos. D. G. Macdonald, a member of the North American Boundary Commission, declared, "It is painfully apparent to all under his rule that Governor Douglas is but poorly fitted to regulate the affairs of a civilized community. His public conduct is, indeed, universally and emphatically condemned by all except those who bask, or hope to bask, in the sunshine of office." (*British Columbia and Vancouver's Island*, London, Longman Green, 1862, p. 271).

28 O'Reilly was born at Ince, Lancashire, England in 1828 (*Colonist*, Sept. 4, 1905). He was educated in Ireland, and came to B.C. in 1859. He served for many years as stipendiary magistrate and Gold Commissioner in the Cariboo. In 1863 he married Caroline Agnes Trutch, a sister of Sir Joseph Trutch, the first Lieutenant-Governor of B.C. His wife died in England in 1899, and he himself in Victoria on Sept. 3, 1905, aged 77. Their three children, Frank, Kathleen and Jack, died in Victoria in 1941, 1945, and 1946 respectively. Kathleen never married, but was at one time courted by Capt. Robert Falcon Scott, who later perished after reaching the South Pole.

29 Not all of Douglas' appointees were able to relate to their environment. William Bevis, Revenue Officer at Langley since June 1858, wrote to Douglas on Jan. 1, 1859: "I would also most respectfully inform Your Excellency that the constant firing of pistols and guns is getting dangerous, particularly during the night-time. The practice of gambling is becoming very glaring, and to endeavour to prevent the same would, I fear, be useless."

Douglas did not permit his subordinates to have both public duties and private interests. When one magistrate, Thomas Elwyn, invested money in a valuable mining claim, the Governor made him resign.

30 *Colonist*, August 24, 1859.
31 Vancouver Island Miscellaneous Letter-Book No. 2, pp. 184-185.
32 Vancouver Island Miscellaneous Letter-Book No. 2, pp. 186-187.
33 Douglas to Lytton, August 1, 1859.
34 *Ibid.*
35 *Ibid.*
36 *Ibid.*
37 The formal conclusions of the council were enclosed in a despatch which Douglas sent to Lord Lytton on August 1, 1859.
38 Douglas to Lytton, August 17, 1859.
39 Douglas to Lytton, August 1, 1859.
40 *Ibid.*
41 *Ibid.*
42 Sage, *Douglas*, p. 268.
43 Douglas to Lytton, August 8, 1859.
44 Douglas to Baynes, August 17, 1859. Vancouver Island Miscellaneous Letter-Book, No. 2, pp. 216-220.
45 *Colonist*, Aug. 17, 1859. These are perhaps not verbatim quotations, but the recollections of the reporter.
46 *Ibid.*
47 Indeed, a certain atmosphere of gaiety soon enveloped the Island. Many social events were held there by the occupying forces, and the steamer "Diane" brought guests from Victoria for the dances, which often lasted till dawn. (J. R. Anderson Notes and Comments, MS in PABC, p. 248.)
48 J. S. Helmcken, Reminiscences, IV. p. 19.
49 Angus McDonald, "A few items of the west", *Washington Historical Quarterly*, July 1917, p. 225.
As early as October 31, 1851, we might note, Douglas had told Lord Grey that the Indians of Vancouver Island would "form a valuable auxiliary force in the event of war with any foreign power." (See chapter 7).
50 Moody to Sir John Burgoyne, August 8 and 12, 1859. Quoted in Sage, *Douglas*, p. 274.
51 D. G. Macdonald, *British Columbia and Vancouver's Island*, London, Longman Green, 1862, p. 258.
52 "The ability to get to the verge without getting into the war is the necessary art"—John Foster Dulles, *Life* magazine, Jan. 11, 1956.
53 His report is given in full in *Papers Relative to the Affairs of British Columbia*, Part III, 1860, pp. 40-49.
54 Douglas to Newcastle, July 4, 1859.
55 Douglas to Lytton, August 23, 1859. *Papers Relative to the affairs of British Columbia*, Part III, 1860.
56 Douglas to Newcastle, October 18, 1859.
57 *Ibid.*
58 Douglas thought, however, "that there should be but little opening for the

introduction of any foreign clergy". (Douglas to Lytton, Nov. 6, 1858). It is obvious that in this context "foreign" meant American.

[59] His report is given in *Papers Relative to the affairs of British Columbia*, Part III, 1860, pp. 79-89.

[60] They had some reason to expect success. In the spring of 1859 a nugget of pure gold weighing over 14 ounces was found there (Douglas to Lytton, March 25, 1859).

[61] Douglas to Newcastle, November 21, 1859.

[62] The Quesnel River was named by Simon Fraser during his descent of the Fraser River in 1808 after one of his lieutenants, Maurice Quesnel, who was then 22.

[63] See Douglas to Newcastle, Jan. 12, 1860. This despatch and the proclamation of Jan. 4, 1860 are given in *Papers Relative to the Affairs of British Columbia*, Part III, 1860, pp. 90-91.

[64] Douglas to Newcastle, Feb. 17, 1860.

[65] Newcastle to Douglas, May 19, 1860. See *Papers Relative to the affairs of British Columbia*, Part IV, 1862, p. 66.

[66] Douglas to Newcastle, August 4, 1860.

[67] See *Papers Relative to the Affairs of British Columbia*, Part IV, 1862, pp. 16-20.

[68] Douglas to Newcastle, April 23, 1860.
Douglas had not, of course, ever seen the Alps.

[69] Born in Devon and trained in engineering, Dewdney had come to Victoria in 1859. He contracted to build the road for £76 a mile, payable £1000 in cash and the remainder in bonds bearing 6% interest and redeemable in December of 1860, 1861 and 1862. The actual location of the road was determined by a party of Royal Engineers under Sergeant McColl. (Howay and Scholefield, *British Columbia from the earliest times to the present*, Vancouver, 1914, Vol. II, p. 94.)
Dewdney became a member of the Legislative Council of B.C. in 1869 and was later a federal M.P. He was appointed Commissioner of Indian Affairs of the Northwest in 1879 and Lieutenant-Governor of the Northwest Territories on Dec. 3, 1881. He was Lieutenant-Governor of B.C. from 1892 to 1897, and died in 1916.

[70] Douglas to Newcastle, April 23, 1860.

[71] Douglas to Newcastle, July 6, 1860.

[72] Douglas to Newcastle, May 31, 1860.

[73] The HBC monopoly of trade with the Indians had ended on May 30, 1859.

[74] Helmcken, Reminiscences, IV, pp. 45-46.

[75] *Colonist*, March 3, 1860.

[76] See Donald Maclaurin, The History of Education in the Crown Colonies of Vancouver Island and British Columbia and in the Province of British Columbia, Ph.D. Thesis, U. of Washington, 1936.

[77] *Colonist*, January 13, 1929.
A more grudging tribute by another observer might be noted here: "There is a charm in the whole aspect of this English Siberia which truly fascinates

the senses". (D. G. Macdonald, *British Columbia and Vancouver's Island"*, London, Longman Green, 1862, p. 332.)

[78] The cornerstone was laid on April 13, 1860. De Cosmos' editorial was that of April 19, 1860.

[79] See Walbran, *British Columbia Coast Names*, pp. 117 and 199. Also *Colonist*, July 12, 1860.

[80] The first house on Salt Spring Island had been built in the summer of 1859 for Thomas Lineker (Walbran, *op. Cit.*, p. 200).

[81] Douglas to Newcastle, October 9, 1860.

[82] Douglas to Newcastle, October 25, 1860.

[83] R. Byron Johnson, *Very Far West Indeed*, London, 1872, p. 45.

[84] Douglas to Newcastle, Feb. 19 and August 8, 1861.

[85] J. S. Helmcken, Reminiscences, IV, p. 57.

[86] J. R. Anderson, Notes and Comments, p. 286.
The marriage, despite its romantic beginnings and double tying of the knot, was a failure, ending (after three children) in a divorce. Douglas' comment is said to have been, "Had she trusted her father more, and put less faith in Good, how different, and how much more happy, would her lot in life have been". Alice lived on till 1913. (See *BCHQ*, Vol. XXI, pp. 174-175); also Douglas' letter to his daughter Martha of Sept. 15, 1873, where he says, "All is gloom and darkness. Very dearly has she paid for the one false step she made in youth . . . " (MS in PABC).

[87] Rose did not long enjoy his luck. About 1863 he left Barkerville with a companion on a prospecting trip and was never seen again.

[88] When Philip Henry Nind, Gold Commissioner for the area, visited this district early in 1861 he found several hundred miners living in holes in the snow. He also reported that acts of violence in the area were very few, giving as the reasons that, "it was patent to all who were old residents that English law, if transgressed, was not to be evaded with the same impunity as California law; no one therefore cared to risk the loss of what might be a fortune to him; besides this, there was an absence of every kind of intoxicating liquor." (Nind's report, dated March 27, 1861, is in *Papers Relative to the affairs of British Columbia*, Part IV.)

[89] Named after William (Dutch Bill) Dietz, one of the first to "strike it rich".

[90] For a vivid account of the Overlanders, see Bruce Hutchison's *The Fraser* (Clarke, Irwin & Co., Toronto, 1950), pp. 89-106.

[91] Douglas to Newcastle, June 4, 1861.

[92] Douglas to Newcastle, September 16, 1861.

[93] *Ibid.*

[94] Douglas to Newcastle, October 24, 1861.

[95] *Ibid.*

[96] *Ibid.*

[97] *Ibid.*

CHAPTER TEN

Completing the Task

I HAVE BEEN for a long period among the Rocky Mountains, but have never seen anything equal to this country, for I cannot find words to describe our situation at times. We had to pass where no human being should venture. Yet in those places there is a regular footpath impressed, or rather indented, by frequent travelling upon the very rocks.[1]

So wrote Simon Fraser during his desperate voyage in 1808 down the river that was some day to bear his name. Over half a century later, a young officer in the Royal Navy, detailed to examine and report on the possibility of a route through the upper reaches of the river, confirmed these impressions:

Before and behind, peak after peak rose 1000 or more feet above us, although we were probably 600 or 800 feet above the river, each more rugged, bold and grand than the other; while beneath, the river, white with foam, whirled along, gurgling and eddying, its wild reverberations continued in endless echoes. Grand as the scene was, watching it, my brain grew dizzy, and I was glad to turn away and continue my journey, fearful lest, if I looked longer, that strange desire which creeps over you to spring into the boiling torrent should become too strong for further resistance.[2]

Such was the country through which the determined Douglas drove a road. Men, money and materials were in short supply; the only thing not lacking was the will. With this, however, joined to his vision of a great highroad of commerce down the centre of the mainland colony, he was able in little more than two years to achieve what seems almost a miracle: a wagon road, eighteen feet wide and four hundred miles long, joining the rich new gold fields of the Cariboo to the older settlements at the coast.

This was to be the crowning accomplishment of his long years of public service; yet in essaying to give an account of it, at once we are faced with a difficulty. If the building of the Cariboo Road had engaged the whole of Douglas' energies in this period, to describe this great feat—however inadequately—would at least be a straightforward task. Yet this was, of course, merely one, albeit the most important, of a score of matters which demanded his attention and judgment. He was governor not of one, but of two colonies; many interests beside those of gold miners had to be considered; relations between the white inhabitants and the native tribes needed vigilant supervision; while the powerful neighboring country was being rent by a desperate civil war. Victoria was to become a city in 1862, and other communities were growing; the many demands of a more urbanized form of society had to be satisfied. Moreover, Douglas had to fulfil his many duties not only under the distant but demanding eye of the authorities in London, but under the critical daily scrutiny of an independent press, as represented by Amor De Cosmos in Victoria and John Robson in New Westminster. Any narrative must perforce be consecutive; it must always therefore fall short in describing events that are varied, complex and simultaneous; especially, perhaps, in this case. Only the imagination of the reader can remedy these deficiencies.

It had been, as we saw, in October 1861 that Douglas had outlined his great new project to the Colonial Secretary. The actual work of construction did not begin, however, until the following spring, and in the meantime the Governor was busy with a score of tasks. Some of these were in preparation for the building of the road, but others had little connection with it.

He was, for example, in this period faced with an embarrassing number of black sheep in high places. John D'Ewes, the acting post-master of Victoria, absconded, and was to commit suicide in Germany some months later; Douglas was also forced to dismiss the acting harbormaster of Victoria, Jeremiah Nagle, because of "discovering irregularities in his accounts". In their place he appointed to the two positions thus left vacant Mr. Henry Wootton, "a gentleman who has been for some time serving as clerk of the writs in the Supreme Court". Douglas gave a few more details of him in a despatch to the Duke of Newcastle:

> Mr. Wootton is a certificated master in the mercantile marine, and has earned for himself a high character for integrity and ability since he has been in the colony, and I believe will prove himself a very capable and trustworthy person in the position in which I have placed him.[3]

This was not, however, the end of such troubles for Douglas. In December he was forced to suspend from office Mr. George Gordon, the Colonial Treasurer; it appeared that he had defaulted to the sum of about £600, and he was charged with embezzlement.[4]

The Colonial Secretary eventually became disturbed by these repeated scandals, and asked Douglas some sharp questions about them. He defended himself as best he could, pointing out that there was no pool of trained civil servants to draw officials from, and that conditions in the gold colony were in other ways highly unusual. ("But what has been my position? I will venture to say it is without a parallel".)[5] Gordon, he noted, had been a member of the House of Assembly, had a wife and seven children, and was a graduate of Cambridge.

> Could I under the circumstances have desired more satisfactory evidence of character and respectability—or, as to the point I mainly sought, honesty? I must contend that I am more entitled to the sympathy than to the reprehension of Her Majesty's Government.[6]

Troubles with dishonest subordinates did not, however, deflect Douglas from the pursuit of his larger vision. In the spring of 1861 he had received permission from the British Government to borrow £50,000 toward the building of the great new wagon road to the north. In October, as we saw, he spoke of borrowing a further £15,000 or £20,000. Later, he had hopes of floating a loan of £100,000. The authorities in London, however, considered this too large a sum, and granted him permission to borrow only a further £50,000.

Considering that the public debt of British Columbia was at this time £4750,[7] these were large sums by comparison; Douglas correctly calculated, however, that the road would soon be crowded with miners travelling to and from the diggings, and that by charging tolls for men and supplies the outlay would be rapidly recovered. He thus felt, or at least expressed, no uneasiness about the magnitude of the project he was about to undertake, and preliminary surveys of various sections of the road were begun.

The winter of 1861-62 was unusually severe, and the actual work did not begin till spring. It was while he was waiting for the snows to melt in the canyons that Douglas now put forward for the benefit of his superiors some suggestions which must have caused considerable astonishment in the Colonial Office.

He had barely managed to retain control of Vancouver Island and later British Columbia during the upheaval of 1858; he had only the most modest forces at his disposal; and was unable, as events had shown, to place implicit trust in all his subordinates; he had just committed himself to a major engineeering project, difficult, dangerous and expensive. Yet despite all this, he now found time to outline to the British Government a proposal which, if implemented, would have embroiled the entire Pacific Northwest in a general war.

Douglas had not yet forgotten what he felt to be the humiliations of 1859 over the San Juan Islands. Now, he believed, while the American republic was convulsed by a great civil war, might well be the time to revenge them. Whether he felt this revenge as a personal or a national one would involve a knowledge not only of his conscious thoughts but of the deeper layers of feeling underlying them; and this of course is impossible. All we have is the record; beyond that there can be only speculation.

We may note, however, a statement of political philosophy which he had expressed some years before, and which there is no reason to think he ever subsequently abandoned:

> When the Legions were recalled from Britain, and other remote possessions, the Roman Empire fell rapidly into decay; with a territory nearly as extensive, our dominion would suffer from the same course.

There is danger in receding; strength, power and safety are to be found only in a bold advance.[8]

Douglas evidently believed that the moment had arrived to apply these principles, and in a despatch to the Colonial Secretary, dated December 28, 1861, he outlined the steps which he believed should be taken in the evest of hostilities between England and America over the "Trent Affair". This referred to an incident in which an American boarding party removed two representatives of the Confederacy from a British ship, in violation of international law. Douglas felt that "complications may grow out of so rash and insolent an act", (as indeed on the other side of the world so did the Prince Consort, one of his last acts before his death being to use his influence to moderate the crisis); he therefore unfolded his plan:

> In such circumstances, I conceive that our only chance of success will be found in assuming the offensive, and taking possession of Puget Sound with Her Majesty's ships, reinforced by such bodies of local auxiliaries as can, in the emergency, be raised, whenever hostilities are actually declared, and by that means effectually preventing the departure of any hostile armament against the British Colonies, and at one blow cutting off the enemy's supplies by sea, destroying his foreign trade, and entirely crippling his resources, before any organization of the inhabitants into military bodies can have effect.
>
> There is little real difficulty in that operation, as the coast is entirely unprovided with defensive works, and the Fleet may occupy Puget Sound without molestation.
>
> The small number of regular troops disposable for such service would necessarily confine our operations to the line of coast; but should Her Majesty's Government decide, as lately mooted, on sending out one or two regiments of Queen's troops, there is no reason why we should not push overland from Puget Sound and establish advanced posts on the Columbia River, maintaining it as a permanent frontier.
>
> A small naval force entering the Columbia River at the same time would secure possession and render the occupation complete— there is not much to fear from the scattered population of settlers, as they would be but too glad to remain quiet and follow their peaceful avocations under any government capable of protecting them from the savages.

With Puget Sound and the line of the Columbia in our hands, we should hold the only navigable outlets of the country, command its trade, and soon compel it to submit to Her Majesty's rule.

Douglas then obligingly drew up for the benefit of the Duke a balance sheet of the military forces available on both sides in the north-west. He himself had at his disposal the steam frigate *Topaze*, the survey ship *Hecate* and the two gunboats *Forward* and *Grappler*; also about two hundred men of the Royal Marines and Royal Engineers. The United States, on the other hand, he believed, had no naval forces and very few soldiers, most of them having been withdrawn from the area for service in the Civil War.

Douglas concluded this remarkable despatch by attempting to set the minds of his superiors at rest regarding any flaws they might detect in his reasoning:

This may appear a hazardous operation to persons unacquainted with the real state of these countries, but I am firmly persuaded of its practicability . . .

The British Government, however, was understandably disinclined to implement this vision of their zealous subordinate, and told him so; the proposal inevitably languished, and Douglas redirected his attention to the Great North Road.

For the moment, the country was held fast in the grip of the worst winter in many years, and the actual start of construction was delayed. While waiting for warmer weather, he received news of the death of the Prince Consort, and immediately asked the people of the colony to wear mourning, a request which at once met with what he oddly termed "a warm response". He also asked that condolences be sent to the widowed Queen.

Meanwhile, regardless of the weather, the indefatigable Judge Begbie was on circuit in the Interior, and sent back to the Governor a report containing much useful information regarding roads, soils and crops. Douglas, forwarding a copy of this report to the Colonial Secretary, declared himself "deeply obliged to Mr. Begbie for this useful contribution to our local information."

Finally, the grip of winter was broken by advancing spring, and Douglas was able to report that

The Fraser River burst its frozen barriers a few days ago, sweep-ing before it the vast fields of ice which for nearly 12 weeks have rendered navigation impossible and completely interrupted the com-munications by water with Yale and Douglas. The river steamboats are again at work, the wants of the country are being rapidly supplied, trade is active and the population generally full of hope and enterprise.[9]

Something of all this clearly communicated itself to the Governor, for even though almost none of his proposed new road existed outside his own imagination, even though he knew that before it did he would have to drive his way through a score of obstacles, physical, economic and human, he now painted for the Colonial Secretary a picture not merely of what he himself intended to do, but how it could later be incorporated into an even larger and more daring project that other hands than his would have to finish. As for his own plan of action, the course was set:

These important works are . . . to be commenced and vigorously prosecuted, the Chief Commissioner of Lands and Works having been authorized to give out contracts for two separate lines of carriage roads intersecting the best farming districts in the Colony.[10]

As to the significance of what he planned to do, to him it had already expanded to embrace much more than British Columbia. His road, he declared, would be

. . . part of an overland communication with Canada by a route possessing the peculiar advantages of being secure from the Indian aggression, remote from the United States frontier, and traversing a country exclusively British, and which from its position, character and general resources can hardly fail, in the ordinary course of events, to become the seat of a large population.[11]

Indeed, he predicted, there would be eventually a road "the whole way to the Red River Settlement"; drawing on his knowledge of the fur trading routes of the great plains, he even gave a detailed account of the best way across them, noting that there would have to be a pass through the Rockies between Edmonton and "Tête Jaune Cache". All this, he estimated, would make it possible to travel from Victoria to the Red River Valley in 25 days.

Finally, his mind catching fire from the heat of its own enthusiasm, and forgetting that he was supposed to be giving a factual account of day-to-day occurrences to his superiors, the role of harassed colonial governor dropped from him, and he stood forward as the inspired prophet of "the ranged arch of empire":

> I will not hazard an opinion on the character of the route from Red River to Lake Superior. I may however observe that it represents to the best of my opinion no serious difficulties—nothing comparable for example to the obstacles successively encountered in pushing roads through the mountains of B.C. I may also observe that when that section is completed, the overland route from Canada to B.C. will be opened to the world, and I believe the effort will cost so little, and tend so much to the public advantage, that when the task is accomplished, it will be a matter of surprise that the attempt was not sooner made, and I sincerely trust that the glory of this great national achievement will be remembered as one of the trophies of Your Grace's Administration.[12]

The road to the gold fields now began in earnest. Although the grand conception was a unity in Douglas' mind, the work itself was parcelled out. Some sections of the road were constructed by the Royal Engineers, and others by means of agreements with civilian contractors. The Engineers, for example, were responsible for the section between Yale and Boston Bar and another from Cook's Ferry (later known as Spence's Bridge) along the Thompson River.

Most of the rest was the work of a remarkable group of civilian contractors. Among these was Thomas Spence, who signed a contract in April 1862 with the government of the colony (in the person of Col. Moody, the Commissioner of Lands and Works) to build a section between Boston Bar and Lytton for £17,600; by late October of the same year this project was completed.[13]

The contract for the section between Chapman's Bar and Boston Bar was signed by J. W. Trutch, later to become the first lieutenant-governor of the province of British Columbia. The government of the colony advanced £15,000 toward the project, and Trutch himself was required to put in £9000 of his own funds. In return, however, he was granted the right to collect tolls for the next five years. The rate was to be a farthing a pound for all goods, and a shilling for each animal.[14]

Later in 1862, the government signed a contract with Trutch and Spence for the construction of the section between Pike's Riffle (on the opposite side of the Fraser from Spuzzum) and Chapman's Bar, at a cost of £9,400.[15] By the spring of 1863, this, too, would be completed.

There would then be two long stretches of the highway fit for use; one on the west bank of the Fraser from Yale to Spuzzum and one from the other side of the Fraser from Spuzzum northward along the eastern bank of the river to Lytton. There would remain what was perhaps the greatest challenge of all: to link these two sections of the road by means of a bridge across the river.

This challenge was to be successfully met, but in the meantime, work was begun on the more northerly part of the road. On August 18, 1862 a contract was signed by the Department of Lands and Works and perhaps the most remarkable of the road-builders, Gustavus Blin Wright. He agreed to build a wagon road from a point across the river from Lillooet along the east bank of the river to Alexandria. As in the case of most other sections of the road, he was granted the right to charge tolls for the following five years; the rate was to be ½d. per lb. on all goods, and one shilling for each animal. Work on this section of the road also went ahead rapidly, although it was to be the fall of 1863 before it was completed.

Some difficulty was encountered in constructing another section of the road—that from Lytton along the Thompson River and up the Bonaparte Valley to join the Lillooet-Alexandria Road. The contractors —Charles Oppenheimer, Thomas Lewis, and Walter Moberly—ran out of money, and the government was forced to intervene. Lewis withdrew, and another contractor, William Hood, contributed his talents. With the use of Chinese labor, this project, too, was to be completed by late in 1863.

In the meantime, an enterprising figure destined to make a valuable addition to the success of the Cariboo Road had entered the picture. Francis Jones Barnard received a contract from the government to deliver the mail along the route. A little earlier, he had begun in a modest way by carrying letters in a pack on his back; later, he would organize a whole fleet of efficient stagecoaches to carry both mail and passengers; in this period, however, he delivered the mail on horseback, and was soon a familiar figure along the highway.

Other matters not directly connected with road-building also from time to time engaged the Governor's attention. He succeeded in getting the permission of his superiors for the formation of local militia to be used in emergencies; 500 rifles were promised by the British Government to equip it. Anxious to attract population to the colonies over which he presided, he had what might be called "tourist literature" printed and forwarded to the Colonial Secretary for distribution in the British Isles. He defended Chief Justice Cameron of Vancouver Island against the attacks made upon him by Captain E. E. Langford, now in England, declaring that, "so far as I am aware Mr. Cameron performs his duties with much ability, and his decisions give general satisfaction."[16] He also praised J. D. Pemberton, the Surveyor-General of Vancouver Island, whom Langford had accused of not being impartial in his regulations and decisions.

It was in this year that the island colony finally adopted a decimal system of currency, which considerably simplified accounting.[17] There was still a noticeable shortage of actual cash in circulation, and Douglas outlined a plan for minting $10 and $20 gold pieces, forwarding samples (made of silver) to London.[18]

Stirrings of political unrest now became more vocal. In Victoria, Amor De Cosmos continued to carry on a persistent guerilla warfare against the Governor in his columns, not hesitating to declare on one occasion that:

> Sooner or later the administration of Gov. Douglas will break down—will end—and a new administration will be inaugurated in its place. The elements of dissolution abound. Its glaring blunders, its sins of omission and commission, and above all its scandalous

disregard of moral and legal right, preclude the possibility of its ever becoming popular or successful, but, on the contrary, holds out the uninviting prospect of being continually and justly execrated.[19]

Nor must we dismiss such statements as the mere ravings of a malcontent. True, De Cosmos was largely blind to the great achievements of the Governor, but on the other hand he did from time to time put his finger firmly on some issues which before long would have to be resolved. In an age when the tide of democracy was steadily rising throughout the western world, Vancouver Island was by no means in the forefront of this trend. Despite the existence of the seven-man Assembly, the Governor, appointed by and responsible to the British Government, was the real power in the colony; one of his privileges was that of vetoing any act of the people's representatives. Not many years would elapse before this conception of government would be swept away; thus, despite the unbalanced nature of many of De Cosmos' charges, he had at least perceived with clarity "the shape of things to come".

In this he was not alone. There was now a newspaper in the mainland capital, the *British Columbian* and its editor, John Robson,[20] also kept up a running fire of criticism of the Governor and his paternalistic view of government. In his first issue, for example, (February 13, 1861) he declared that the central aim of his paper would be to promote "responsible government, liberal institutions, the redress of all our grievances, and the moral and intellectual improvement of the people".

Nor did Robson's language fall far short of De Cosmos' in intemperance. He referred to the Governor as "the arch-enemy of British Columbia",[21] and declared that under "our present abominable system" Douglas seemed "fully determined to hold on to the despotic and outrageous power he possesses, with that nervous tenacity with which a miser clutches his gold when death approaches".[22] He urged his readers to demand changes in the form of government, and also attacked the Governor's policy of giving financial aid to churches of his own choosing.

As in the similar case of the *Colonist*, Douglas made some efforts at retaliation; he had the *Government Gazette*, which had previously been published in the *British Columbian*, put out instead by the Royal

Engineers, thus depriving Robson of a steady source of revenue.[23] This move did not, however, have any permanent effect on either Robson's newspaper or his temper, and Douglas for the balance of his term of office had to endure a steady drum-fire of criticism from the principal organ in each of the colonies which he governed.

Nor were the critics of the Governor content with mere editorial expostulations. Robson, for example, was active in political affairs. In September 1861 he was a delegate to a convention at Hope, when a memorial to the Colonial Secretary, outlining various purported griev- ances, was drawn up. This harmless gathering seems to have alarmed the Governor considerably; even the word "convention" apparently carried with it strong emotional overtones, for soon Douglas was writing to the Colonial Secretary that

> The term is associated with revolution and holds out a menace— the subject has an undoubted right to petition his sovereign, but the term "convention" seems something more, it means coercion.
>
> I have no desire to accuse the authors of this memorial of enter- taining any malevolent designs, the majority of them being known as quiet well-meaning tradesmen, sincerely attached, I believe, to the institutions of the colony; but at the same time I am not disposed to overlook the fact that they may become for seditious purposes the dupes of artful men. I have therefore charged the magistrates to keep an eye over their movements and not to interfere with their proceed- ings so long as they commit no violation of the law.[24]

At this point in his despatch, however, the Governor seems to have felt the incongruity of seeing the members of the "Convention" as so many Dantons and Robespierres, merely because they maintained that rights taken for granted in England should be extended to Britons beyond the seas:

> I fully and cordially admit the proposition that liberty is the Englishman's birthright, and that the desire for representative institutions is common to all H.M. subjects—I have no wish to say anything to the contrary or to advocate any system of government which deprives the meanest of H.M. subjects of their just rights and privileges.

It seems likely that in considering the question of an extension of democracy in the colony, a variety of influences were at work at this time in the Governor's mind. On the one hand, he was beyond much doubt by nature autocratic; yet he was also proud that his spiritual homeland was successfully placing the powers of government on an ever broadening popular foundation, and aware that this development must in time include the colonies. In the immediate context, however, he knew that the great majority of those under his control were but recently Americans, and unlikely either to have discarded all traces of loyalty to the United States or to have embraced the authority of British officials and institutions with any very fanatical fervor. In the circum-stances, then, he no doubt sincerely deemed it best if the reins of government remained firmly in his own hands, and he so informed the Duke:

> For my own part, I would not take the responsibility of recom-mending any immediate change in the form of government as now established until there is a permanent population attached to the British throne and constitutions and capable of appreciating the civil and religious liberty derived from that constitution, blessings which I venture to assert are now enjoyed in the fullest sense of the term by the people of B.C.[25]

The Governor's disapproval of his activities did not, however, dis-hearten Robson, who continued to promote his chosen cause with zeal. In July 1862, for example, he announced there would be a public meeting in order that a petition demanding representative government could be sent to both Douglas and the British Government. Robson also poured out his grievances into the ear of a wandering politician from eastern Canada, Malcolm Cameron, who faithfully passed them on, when he was next in London, to the Colonial Secretary.

There is some evidence that these representations were not entirely ignored; certainly some time during this period the British Government decided that a more democratic form of government must be established in the mainland colony; also that when Douglas' term of office expired it would not be extended, and that men more attuned to the burgeoning century would succeed him.

One member, however, of this band of Britons who were essaying to transplant some of the values of their race into the wilderness of the Far West still had many years of service before him in the colony. This was Judge Begbie, who continued throughout this period to travel the roads and trails of the Interior, usually on horseback, dispensing the law as he understood it to the miners and settlers of the region. Nor was this his only service to the colony; he also took intelligent note of the economic possibilities of each district and likely routes for new roads, reporting his conclusions in careful detail to the Governor.

Fortunately for the colony and for posterity, he was well endowed with the qualifications necessary for these tasks. Born into a family noted for producing soldiers and clergymen, he was deeply educated, widely travelled, physically strong and morally incorruptible. This rare combination of qualities was exactly what was needed in the circum-stances, so novel and so challenging, in which he now found himself and in which he was to labor for so many years. His education stood him in good stead in the preparation of reports, as well no doubt as giving him a certain aura of authority among the miners; his zest for travel, which in earlier days had carried him as far afield as Turkey, had every opportunity for indulgence amid the varied scenes of the newest colony of the Crown; his powers of endurance were to be often tested in rugged terrain or severe conditions; while his incorruptibility was essential in a time and place that saw fortunes made almost daily and their source displayed before his very eyes.

Some recollections of Begbie's formidable manner with malefactors have come down to us. For example, when sentencing a man to eighteen months for robbing a church poor-box, he thundered:

> When you come out, never shake an honest man by the hand—never look an honest man in the face! Go to the other side of the world where you are not known. Should you be so unwise as to stay in this country, and should your form again throw its shadow in this court-house, charged with crime, and you are found guilty, and I am sitting on this bench, I will send you to a place where you will speak to your fellow man no more, at least while there incarcerated. Go down! Warder, take him out of my sight![26]

Again, when sentencing an American miner to three years for

stabbing another, he took the occasion to touch on several related subjects:

> Prisoner, I am glad to see that your case has drawn together, in this temporary court of justice, so many of your compatriots. I am given to understand that the mining class of the western states look upon liberty as a condition of life which gives them the right to defy the laws of their country, and to govern it according to their wishes by the might of the Bowie knife and Colt's revolver. You, prisoner, are a good representative of that class, and I am told that there are many more of your kidney within the sound of my voice . . .
> We have a law which prohibits the use of bowie knives, pistols and other offensive weapons, and in those countries over which the British flag flies there is no necessity for carrying or using offensive weapons, and let me tell those who are in court that in the course of my duty I will punish most severely all those who, coming into this British colony, make use of such deadly weapons. Prisoner, the jury have very properly found you guilty of this wanton and cowardly attack. You will spend three years in a place of confinement to be determined on, and in giving you this sentence I feel that I have been very lenient with you.[27]

So throughout this period (and until long after Douglas had retired into private life) up and down the hills and valleys of the Interior in solitary dignity the judge would ride. Usually he slept in a tent which in the daytime served as his chambers. Always when holding court (which was sometimes on horseback) he wore his robes, as a reminder that though but a single individual he embodied and represented the whole power and majesty of government. Douglas was well aware of his worth, declaring that

> Able, active, energetic and highly talented, Mr. Begbie is a most valuable public servant. I feel greatly indebted to him for the zealous discharge of his official duties and for many services beyond the strict line of official duty.[28]

In the fulfilment of his duties, he was supported by a small but conscientious group of lesser officials. There were county court magistrates for lesser cases, and the gold commissioners who settled disputes over mining claims. Enforcing the decisions of Begbie and his magistrates were the unsung heroes of this period—the underpaid constables, who while thousands about them were reaping fortunes for a season's work, served for a mere £25 a month, a sum barely sufficient to support themselves. Some of them, indeed, — the adventurous younger sons of well-to-do English families — were dependent on remittances from home; on such uncertain foundations was raised the structure of empire.

Begbie was not, of course, beyond criticism; he had an ingrained distrust of lawyers not trained in the United Kingdom, and until finally overruled by Douglas did his best to prevent them from practising in his court; his knowledge of the law was not profound, and he had frequently to fall back on justice; he stood in no great awe of juries and sometimes told them so. Yet despite his occasional shortcomings (which like those of Douglas were from time to time the subject of acidulous editorials by Robson), he upheld according to his lights the rule of law in a vast region which might otherwise have subsided into anarchy. We should reflect that had this occurred, out of it in turn might have come rule by vigilantes, who indeed might have called to their aid the support of the adjoining country from which most of them had come. It is fair to say, then, that though as the supreme authority in the colony the final tribute for what was accomplished in these triumphant years must be paid to Douglas, the name next to his in the gratitude of posterity should be that of Matthew Baillie Begbie.[29]

So, as the months of 1862 passed, Douglas' vision steadily became reality. Parts of the road had to be blasted from the sides of rocky gorges; parts were built out on trestles over the raging flood itself. At times, the barriers raised by nature appeared insurmountable; but always, clinging tenaciously where all but the boldest might have halted or turned back, the road inched forward, drawn by the rich gold fields ahead, driven by the unrelenting will behind.

In the autumn the Governor made a personal inspection of what had been accomplished, and was more than satisfied with what he saw. As he reported to the Duke of Newcastle on October 27:

I cannot speak too favorably of the newly formed roads. In

smoothness and solidity they surpass expectation—Jackass Mountain, the Cleft, the Great Slides, the Rocky Bridges, and other passes of ominous fame, so notorious in the history of the country, have lost their former terrors.

Nor was this the only good news that Douglas had to report. Settlers were already taking up land along the new road; there had been only one serious crime in some months, and at the assizes at Van Winkle and Lightning Creek there were only two cases on the calendar, "which most strikingly illustrates the quiet and orderly behavior of the large mining population assembled there". The tolls being collected were bringing in a good revenue (Douglas estimated it at £6000 a year); steamboats were beginning to appear on the upper reaches of the great river, and there had been an important new discovery at Williams Creek. Douglas, viewing these numerous omens of good fortune, had no hesitation in declaring that "the resources of British Columbia are almost of boundless extent".

Meanwhile, political changes were occurring in both colonies. Douglas, and more importantly the British Government, had come to realize that a move in the direction of a more democratic form of government for British Columbia could not be longer delayed. After studying a "memorial" presented to him in the summer of 1862 by some citizens of the mainland capital, urging that a form of government such as existed in the British colonies to the eastward should be set up in British Columbia, Douglas outlined to the Colonial Secretary on July 28, 1862, his candid conclusions on the issue:

> The Memorial is, I am persuaded, the work of a party; yet so fondly are we attached to the name of liberty, that I feel assured that were it a matter of choice, every Englishman in the Colony, without stopping to inquire about its effect on the country . . . would at once give his suffrage in behalf of Representative Government. The concession of some form of popular government will therefore I believe give general satisfaction to the people of the country, and may probably be considered a political necessity.[30]

Douglas ventured the suggestion that an Assembly should be estab-lished in which one third of the members would be nominated by the

Crown and the remainder elected by the people, with the Governor having a veto over all their acts. By way of confining the suffrage to the more responsible elements in the mainland colony, he suggested that the possession of £100 worth of property be the prerequisite for the suffrage, and £500 worth for membership in the proposed Assembly.

A less important political change had meanwhile taken place in the capital of Vancouver Island. Victoria, which only four years before had been a small trading post of the Hudson's Bay Company, had been transformed by the gold rush of 1858 into a town; now, after the passage of appropriate legislation by the Vancouver Island House of Assembly, it became a city, and in August 1862 the first election was held for mayor and councillors. Douglas, however, retained the right to veto any laws or regulations which the city fathers might enact.

So, on these notes of change, the year drew to its end. All in all, the portents seemed distinctly favorable, yet the new year of 1863—it was to be, though he did not as yet know it, the last full year of Douglas' long term of service to the Crown—had not long begun when it became clear that it would be a "time of troubles" for the sixty-year-old Governor.

Much of the difficulty that now ensued may perhaps be traced to the thousands of miles of land and ocean which separated Douglas from his superiors in London. He knew at first hand the nature of the task he had essayed; they knew it only from his reports and what descriptions they could gather from other sources. To him, the road was a project which, though at first expensive, would soon return the investment many-fold; to them, all that was evident was his incessant and sometimes almost peremptory demands for funds or for permission to float substantial loans in the two colonies. Inevitably, a slight coolness developed; they were determined that some halt should be called to what seemed an unceasing outflow of money; he was determined that nothing should stand in the way of completing what was not only by now a part of himself, but which he believed was a project on which the whole future of British North America might depend. So, as explosions of dynamite reverberated in the chasms of the Fraser, despatches made the long journeys across the seas; in the end, the strong-willed governor was to see his dream triumphant.

In January, tenders were called for a section of the road from Alexandria north toward the mouth of the Quesnel River and from there to Van Winkle in the gold fields. In February, a contract was signed to build a suspension bridge across the Fraser at Spuzzum. A group headed by Joseph Trutch had assumed this responsibility, and work began at once. All spring and summer it went forward, and fall saw the completion of what was perhaps the most remarkable feat of engineering ever attempted in British Columbia until very recent times. Nearly three hundred feet in length, it was so well built that when tested by a heavily laden wagon, it showed almost no deflection. This, it had been agreed, would be a toll bridge, and in honor of the Princess of Wales was named the Alexandra Bridge. For seven years those cross-ing the river were to be charged one-sixth of a penny (one-third of a cent) a pound for goods, 25 cents for oxen, horses and mules, and 12½ cents for sheep, pigs, colts or calves. Passenger vehicles drawn by a single horse would be charged 50 cents, those drawn by a pair of horses one dollar, and those drawn by four or more horses two dollars. Vehicles regularly transporting farm produce in the district would be allowed to use the bridge free of charge.

All these projects of the Governor, however, required at least some immediate cash, and often Douglas found himself uncertain where to turn. On January 10, 1863 he reported that he was "much pressed for funds"; yet he was informed that henceforth the colony of British Columbia must bear half of the cost of the Royal Engineers. To Douglas this seemed a cruel blow for "a young colony struggling against most extraordinary difficulties", but knowing that it was now too late to turn back without involving himself in disgrace and the colony in bankruptcy, he pressed resolutely forward.

Meanwhile, his critics gave him no peace. Captain Langford was still attempting to cause trouble in London over what he alleged were the shortcomings of Judge Cameron. Douglas was forced in the midst of many other more pressing problems to devote time and energy to convincing the Duke of Newcastle that "Mr. Langford is a person wholly unworthy of credence", whereas, in his opinion, the Judge was "a man of good business habits, of liberal education, some legal know-ledge, and, what was equal to all, possessed of a more than ordinary amount of discretion and common sense."[31] He hazarded a guess that Langford had hoped to be chosen from the ranks of Vancouver Island's magistrates to be the colony's first judge, and had viewed Cameron's appointment "with much jealousy and heart-burning".

Similar motives, he believed, were behind the similar agitation of James Cooper. In this case, Douglas suggested, he was piqued at being told by the Governor that he ought not to be both a member of his council and also a retail liquor vendor. In contrast, the judge's "high integrity, his firmness, discretion, and sound common sense, coupled with the most even temper and amiable manners, have been a source of much satisfaction to me".

In April, Douglas sent J. D. Pemberton on the long voyage to London to procure dredging equipment for Victoria Harbor, and the same month found himself engaged in a complex controversy over whether the Crown or the Hudson's Bay Company owned various parts of the Victoria area. It is noteworthy that although Douglas had been for so many years a servant of the Company, and indeed owed his eminence to the start in life and subsequent promotions it had given him, he did not hesitate to defend what he believed to be the rights of the Crown. The Company, he declared, had done much too well out of their operations on Vancouver Island:

> They are left in undisturbed possession of large sums of money which the sale of portions of that property has brought them; not one farthing being deducted for the benefit of the Colony, or even to pay for the expense of surveying and selling, which has been mainly borne by the Colony and by the Imperial Government.
> All their actual outlay in connection with their tenure of Van-couver Island has been generously repaid by Her Majesty's Govern-ment, And what does Her Majesty's Government take by the agree-ment? A few acres of comparatively valueless land on the sea coast, and a few town lots that would have been sold long ago had anybody considered them worth buying.[32]

Taking up the question as to whether some of the sales of land purportedly made by the HBC before January 1, 1862 were bona fide, Douglas stated his own beliefs forthrightly:

> At the present I can only say that if the case be otherwise, and the Company feel hurt at such a suspicion being cast upon them, it has been brought about by their own proceedings. Had the sales of land been in all cases genuine, and beyond question, I cannot understand why so much delay should have occurred in declaring what was sold, or why so much secrecy should have been observed, so that the Surveyor-General could never at any time obtain the slightest information upon the subject.[33]

Douglas was also by this time having his difficulties with Colonel Moody. Not only did the Governor feel that the Engineers were no longer giving good value for the amount of money they were costing, but a personal coolness was developing between Douglas and the Colonel. Douglas had asked for some statistics about the affairs of the Engineers, but had been rebuffed, and was forced to inform his superiors that "I regret that I cannot testify to Col. Moody's cheerful cooperation in the matter."[34]

When the Governor did succeed in accumulating enough data to estimate the cost of the Engineers and to compare it with the value of the work they had accomplished, he was noticeably disturbed; here was a steady draining away of money which in his opinion it was time to stop:

> The system of combining civil with military duties has not been attended with the success anticipated, but the results now given me are so startling, and the drain upon the funds of the Colony so great while I am struggling to raise means to devote to the work of opening the communications—a work (with) which the very vitality of the colony is concerned—that I feel bound to bring the matter to the immediate attention of Your Grace.[35]

Moreover, the Engineers had initiated projects other than engineering ones to a degree which was becoming burdensome to the colony:

> ... the number of children in the detachment having been more than trebled since it left England, and the number is increasing every day.

To lessen the costs to the public of this epidemic of philoprogenitiveness, the Governor suggested that some of the Engineers should be discharged from the service and encouraged to settle in the colony, perhaps on land supplied free by the government.

Hardly had Douglas offered his opinion on this question than he found himself faced with a very different sort of problem. Several murders of whites by Indians had occurred in the Gulf Islands, and Douglas was forced to resort to his unwavering policy in such cases. The gunboat *Forward* destroyed an Indian village which had refused to surrender some culprits, and soon afterward an expedition under Commander Hardinge of H.M.S. *Cameleon* captured three men and one woman wanted in connection with the murders. After a speedy trial the woman was given life imprisonment but the three men

were publicly hanged in front of the Victoria Gaol on Saturday the 23rd instant at 7 o'clock in the morning.[36]

Douglas felt no uneasiness about the executions, declaring that

these prompt and vigorous measures were necessary to repress an apparently increasing mania amongst certain tribes of Indians to become great and noted by the commission of crime.[37]

By June it was possible to travel from Yale to Cook's Ferry[38] by coach, and shortly afterward the road from Lillooet to Alexandria was opened. Douglas now re-activated the Gold Escort, and some miners, but not all, made use of its services.

Political matters again took the spotlight in July. Not only was the northern boundary of British Columbia extended to 60°, but Douglas was informed that he must now take appropriate steps toward the introduction of a measure of democracy into that colony's affairs. Accordingly, he divided the colony into five electoral districts, elections were held, and thus the Legislative Council of British Columbia came into being. The majority of its members were still appointed by the Crown,[39] but a considerable step had nevertheless been taken in the direction of full responsible government.

In August, Douglas found himself again engaged in the controversy over the HBC claims to land in the Victoria area. The British Government was anxious that an amicable settlement should be reached, but

Douglas felt and asserted that in such matters there were higher virtues than amicability:

It has ever been my desire to act with the Company's officers in the settlement of all these matters in the most frank and cordial manner, but consistently with the duty I owe Her Majesty's Government, and with the interests of the public. I could not refrain from pointing out to your Grace what appeared to me a most remarkable and unnecessary delay on the part of the Hudson's Bay Company in revealing what extent of land would revert to the Crown under the Indenture before mentioned of the 3rd February, 1862 . . .

I desire most sincerely, and that speedily, to see the Hudson's Bay Company confirmed in all that they have a legal and equitable right to under the concessions made by Her Majesty's Government, but I do not desire in a settlement of that right to see the public necessities disregarded, and land yielded up to the Company that is actually possessed and occupied for public purposes.[40]

In all this, he declared, he was only "performing a simple act of duty to the public which it would be culpable to neglect".[41]

This dispute subsided for a time, and later in August manifestations of democracy appeared in Vancouver Island as elections were held for a new House of Assembly. Such well-known figures as W. A. G. Young and Amor De Cosmos were chosen by the voters to represent them, as were a notable quartet of medical men: Dr. Powell, Dr. Trimble, Dr. Tolmie and Dr. Helmcken.

As spring gave way to summer, the Governor continued to struggle with the problems of completing his great project. Having received the necessary permission from the British Government, he passed an act authorizing the raising of a further loan of £50,000; part of the proceeds was to be used to redeem previous bond issues, and the new bonds would be repaid in twenty years.

The Royal Engineers were once again of service, being called in to finish a seven-mile stretch of the road where much dynamiting was necessary, and Douglas reported that:

These great road works being accomplished, the Government has faithfully done its duty to the country, and the development of its valuable resources may safely be left to the energy and enterprise of the people, governed by wise and wholesome laws.[42]

There were, in fact, as the summer advanced, many encouraging signs. Receipts from tolls, Douglas calculated, were 83 percent ahead of the corresponding period of 1862, and he also estimated that the miners on Williams Creek alone had made a million dollars during the previous winter.[43] Peter O'Reilly, one of the colony's efficient gold commissioners, had personally reported good news to the Governor:

> Mr. Commissioner O'Reilly, visiting from Williams Lake on 29th April, remarks that the Lillooet Road was then completed to the north end of Lake La Hache, a distance of 128 miles, and that the works had sustained no injuries from the effect of the weather that were not repairable at a very trifling cost. He also observed on his way from Lillooet large tracts of land that were fenced in, and at all the wayside houses great preparations for embarking largely in farming operations and moreover in the district of Bridge Creek and Williams Lake he states that 500 acres of land were actually under crops of various kinds . . . Mr. O'Reilly fully confirms the previous reports of successful mining in winter at Cariboo. He adds "Labour is in great demand at rates varying from $10 to $12 per diem".[44]

Other matters with but little connection with the road or the gold rush continued to engage the Governor's attention. There was a considerable amount of smuggling of liquor to Indians on the remoter coasts, and Douglas did his best to stop it. He noted that:

> The vile spirit that is sold to the Indians is the origin of nearly all the trouble we have with them, and for years past my anxious attention has been given to intercept the trade.[45]

H.M.S. Devastation under Commander Pike succeeded in capturing three vessels engaged in this trade, and a considerable amount of liquor was seized.

Douglas also noted that the Rev. Duncan, a church of England missionary, was doing good work among the Indians at Metlakatla. The Governor declared that in his view Mr. Duncan had "done much to prove that the permanent elevation of the aboriginal races is not altogether a hopeless attempt".[46]

Douglas' superiors in London, however, apparently failed to appreciate the tireless labors of the Governor, or to extend him much sympathy. They felt that a halt must be called to the financial help they were granting him, and finally told him so. Specifically, the Colonial Secretary drew his attention to the fact that early in the year he had requested Douglas to return £6900 in specie which had previously been sent to the colony. Douglas in his reply explained why he had delayed in complying. To have done so at the time, he asserted,

> . . . would have brought the progress of the Colony to a standstill, would have depopulated the country, would have given the people cause to cry out in bitterness against their rulers, and in fine would have created such a mass of evil that would I conceive when brought about by me, have caused H.M. Government justly to have regarded me unfit for the responsible position in which they have been pleased to place me.[47]

Douglas was not only disheartened but exasperated by this demand. He felt that those in distant London had no real understanding of the true value of the work to which, amid trying and novel circumstances, he was devoting all his energies, and whose success or failure might be finally determined by small weights in the great scale. Discarding the deference which he usually displayed in his communications, he spoke out "clear and bold":

> If I have not made these matters clear to your Grace in the despatches I have had the honor to address you, if I have not sufficiently explained the unprecedented circumstances of the colony —the distance of the gold fields from the port of entry, the impracticable character of the country, the famine prices of provisions at the mines, checking industry, killing enterprise, retarding immigration, and if I have not represented in fully strong terms the imperative necessity for the salvation of the country at any cost to establish communication with the mines, then indeed I have signally failed in my endeavor. I have felt it my solemn duty never to pause for the moment in the great work of rendering the country accessible, notwithstanding I have been surrounded and occasionally almost overwhelmed by difficulties and impediments, financial and otherwise.[48]

Having said his piece, he agreed to transmit to the Imperial authorities the balance which was due to them, which he carefully calculated at £5053.3.8.[49]

As the year moved into summer, the various sections of the great road neared completion. Great sums had been expended—Douglas reckoned them at £91,952 in 1862, which included reconnaissance work on two possible new roads into the Interior, from Bentinck Arm and Bute Inlet[50]—but revenues, too, were increasing; gradually and amazingly, it became clear that Douglas was winning through to victory.

Something of this is reflected in his despatches. The notes of urgency, sometimes almost of desperation, grow fewer; with success virtually assured, he was able already to consider the structure which would someday be raised on the foundation he had laid. In response to an enquiry regarding sending settlers out from England, he expressed his preference for married men with small families, but was also prepared to welcome "100 young women of good character who have been employed in the mills but who have had some experience of domestic service or seem capable of undertaking it."[51]

Also in July, he acknowledged the receipt of further instructions regarding the new Legislative Council of British Columbia. When Capt. Gosset, the Colonial Secretary and Treasurer of the mainland colony, went on leave to England and showed no signs of returning, he suggested that the British Government should choose Chartres Brew to succeed him as Colonial Secretary, and Charles Good to succeed him as Treasurer. The former, he declared, was

... possessed of discretion, of an even temper, and of mild unassuming manners, joined to good business habits and sound common sense; qualities which are essential.[52]

Mr. Good, on the other hand, was also well qualified, being an Oxford graduate, Douglas' former private secretary, and "a gentleman of high integrity and good address". Douglas neglected to add that young Mr. Good had some time previously eloped with his daughter and was now his son-in-law.

The Royal Engineers, it had now been decided by the British Government, were to be withdrawn from B.C., and Douglas suggested as

Colonel Moody's successor in the post of Commissioner of Lands and Works either Captain Henry Reynolds Luard or Joseph Trutch, both of whom he regarded highly.

The road to the gold fields, however, still held the first claim on his energies; steadily the work went forward, and with autumn at last came success, undisputed and irrevocable. The Lillooet-Alexandria section of the road was completed, and soon afterward so was the section from Lytton to Clinton, where the Cariboo Road joined the road up the Harrison River through Lillooet. The most northerly section of the great road, from Alexandria northward to Quesnel and then eastward to the heart of the gold fields at Richfield and Barkerville, was still under construction, and was not to be finished until some months after Douglas' term of office had expired. A good trail did, however, by this time exist between the gold fields and the nearest point on the Fraser, and horses if not yet stagecoaches were able to make use of it. Thus it was no doubt with some elation that the Governor reported to the Colonial Secretary:

> The whole journey from New Westminster to Alexandria may be performed in 8 days by a connecting line of steamers and stages running constantly between those two places. From Soda Creek below Alexandria a river steamer plies on Fraser River to Quesnelle, and a good horse road formed this season connects the latter place with Richfield 63 miles thus completing the chain of communication between the coast and the centre of the Cariboo district. These works have been necessarily expensive but they are of incalculable value to the colony which in fact could not have attained any degree of prosperity without the facilities they offer.[53]

Douglas also reported other signs of progress. The Gold Escort was operating efficiently, there had been very little crime, and machinery of some complexity was being brought in from the coast by the miners. He also enclosed for the Duke's inspection samples of wheat, oats, barley and corn that had been successfully raised in the Interior.

As the year waned, signs of impending change multiplied. The Royal Engineers, who had done so much at the very moment when it was most needed, began either returning to the British Isles or taking their discharges and settling down in their new home. On November 11, Col. Moody himself sailed from New Westminster, and two days later the Governor, forgetting past differences, testified to his abilities and services:

> The mild conciliatory and gentlemanly bearing of Col. Moody have always been conspicuous, and I believe he quits the colony leaving many friends behind him.[54]

Nearly five years before, when they had set sail for the Far West of the New World, Lord Lytton, then the Colonial Secretary, had addressed a detachment of the Engineers in these terms:

> The enterprise before you is indeed glorious. Ages hence, industry and commerce will crowd the roads that you will have made. Travellers from all nations will halt on the bridges you will have first flung over solitary rivers, and gaze on gardens and cornfields that you will have first carved from the wilderness.[55]

The noble lord was a literary man (his *Last Days of Pompeii* was for long a best-seller), and his language was poetic, but he expressed a sober truth.

Douglas himself now knew that his term of office was not to be renewed. This came as neither a surprise nor a disappointment, as he was content to have it so. He had accomplished, as he knew himself, more than most men, and was ready, having laid the foundations of British Columbia's greatness, to see others rear the structure of its future prosperity.

Indeed, there were already signs that his own achievements would soon be incorporated into an even larger design. In a private letter to the Duke of Newcastle, he had saluted the already discernible future for which he had prepared the way:

> I was surprised and delighted to hear of your Grace's success in starting the overland telegraph and road company; a boon that both colonies will prize, and have to thank your Grace for. It is truly a glorious undertaking, worthy of the age and country, and should your Grace ever take a whirl over the Rocky Mountains I am sure you will appreciate the scenery and the roads too, especially those about which I have given your Grace so much trouble. After seeing the country

COMPLETING THE TASK / 243

I think Your Grace will say that I have done right in making them.[56]

In the same letter, he had expressed some uneasiness lest the fact that he had not served out his full six-year term as Governor of British Columbia might cause unfavorable comment:

I confess that I do not clearly perceive how my premature removal from office one year previous to the expiry of the term for which I was originally appointed can be managed without leaving an impression derogatory to the character of my administration . . . Probably the difficulty may be got over by granting me a leave of absence for 1864.

For all that, he was content to abide the verdict of history. He was "nearly worn out with the toil and incessant cares of my present position" and admitted "old age is creeping upon me";[57] it was time, he realized, to relinquish the helm to younger pilots. As a sign that his superiors, whatever their occasional doubts and remonstrances, thought highly of his great achievements, he was now awarded a knighthood, and the one-time fur-trapper's assistant could henceforth style himself Sir James Douglas, K.C.B.

De Cosmos had meanwhile given up direction of the *Colonist*, stating in his last editorial (October 6, 1863) that "nothing but delicate health, arising from over-application to the duties of a laborious profession, has induced me to retire",[58] and its new editors on October 13 expressed the general public approval of the Queen's mark of favor accorded to Douglas:

His services to his country as Governor of these colonies will not be forgotten for many years to come, and we believe that nothing will be remembered of his administration of the government that will tend to tarnish the name of Douglas. Her Majesty in conferring the honor of knighthood upon our Governor has paid him a well-deserved compliment, which the colony will thoroughly appreciate.

Early in 1864 the man who once had held almost unlimited power in the colony gave formal recognition to a new era, as he journeyed to the mainland and opened the first session of the Legislative Council of British Columbia at Sapperton, site of the Royal Engineers' first encampment. The past was saluting the future, but so clearly had each seen its place in the chain of history that the change was without friction or acrimony.

So the days of his long term of office were accomplished. January passed, and February came and went; then it was March. Still he labored at his desk; his official despatches, though he knew them to be the last he would ever pen, showed the same attention to detail, the same tireless desire to establish the just society. Finally, the last line of the last page was written, the last official acts performed, and there remained only the formalities of farewell. He had fought the good fight, he had finished his course, he had kept the faith. Now there were only the shadows of retirement and old age.

NOTES

[1] *The letters and journals of Simon Fraser 1806-1808.* ed. W. K. Lamb, Macmillan, Toronto, 1960, p. 96.

[2] R. C. Mayne, *Four Years in British Columbia and Vancouver Island,* London, 1862, p. 105.

[3] Douglas to Newcastle, October 25, 1861.
Henry Wootton's son, Edward Ernest Wootton, had a distinguished legal career. He was called to the bar in 1888, married Frances Amelia Smith in 1893, and died at the age of 78 in 1944. Their son is Judge R. A. B. Wootton of Victoria.

[4] Douglas to Newcastle, Dec. 28, 1861.
Gordon was eventually acquitted of embezzlement, but immediately confined in the debtor's prison (*Colonist,* Dec. 27, 1861). From here he escaped by means of a "false key" (*Colonist,* May 19, 1862). De Cosmos, in an editorial on August 6, 1862 complained of "the vice of embezzlement and corruption which seem almost chronic in certain other quarters, and have well nigh exhausted our patience".

[5] Douglas to Newcastle, May 17, 1862.

[6] *Ibid.*
Douglas was also for a time deprived of the services of the capable Philip Henry Nind, the Assistant Gold Commissioner in the Cariboo area, who was granted a leave of absence to return to England to secure medical treatment for a paralysis of the right side of his face. (Douglas to Newcastle, Dec. 29, 1861).

[7] Douglas to Newcastle, November 14, 1861.

[8] Douglas to Simpson, April 4, 1845. Quoted in J. S. Galbraith, *The Hudson's Bay Company as an Imperial Factor 1821-1869,* U. of Toronto, 1957, p. 216.

[9] Douglas to Newcastle, April 15, 1862.

[10] *Ibid.*

11 *Ibid.*
12 *Ibid.*
On May 22, 1868, Douglas wrote to his son James: "I had everything ready to make a beginning, a large body of engineers, tools, laborers, the means of transport and all the other appliances requisite for the grand enterprise. I know almost every inch of the road and with God's blessing would have brought it to a rapid and successful close." (Sir James Douglas, Correspondence Outward, PABC).
13 The Road to Cariboo, J. H. Reid, M.A. Thesis, U.B.C., April 1942, p. 47.
14 *Ibid.*, p. 48.
15 *Ibid.*, pp. 48-49.
16 Douglas to Newcastle, August 23, 1862.
17 The change took place on Dec. 12, 1862. See Peter Palmer, A Fiscal History of British Columbia in the Colonial Period, PhD Thesis, Stanford, July 1932, p. 178.
British Columbia did not adopt decimal currency until Jan. 1, 1866. (Palmer, *Op. Cit.*, p. 76).
18 Douglas to Newcastle, May 10, 1862. On November 14, 1861 Douglas had reported, "that at this moment there is an amount of gold dust in the hands of miners from Cariboo, residing at Victoria, exceeding one quarter of a million sterling, and so great is the present dearth of coin that it brings a premium of five percent and over when procurable, which is not generally the case, as men may be seen hawking bars of gold about the streets of Victoria, who cannot raise coin enough to defray their current expenses."
19 *Colonist*, Feb. 3, 1862.
20 Robson was born in Perth, Upper Canada (now Ontario) on March 1, 1824. He emigrated to B.C. in 1859, and became editor of the *British Columbian* in 1861. In 1869 he moved to Victoria and commenced a newspaper there which did not prosper. In the famous debate of 1870 in the "bird-cages", he supported confederation, but also demanded responsible government. He represented Nanaimo in the B.C. legislature between 1871 and 1875. He resumed publication of the *British Columbian* in New Westminster between 1880 and 1883, became a member of the B.C. legislature again in 1882, provincial minister of finance and agriculture in 1883 and premier in 1889. He died suddenly in London on June 29, 1892. A memorial service was held in Westminster Abbey, and Queen Victoria sent a wreath. His body was returned to Victoria and buried in Ross Bay Cemetery.
21 *British Columbian*, May 16, 1861.
22 *British Columbian*, May 9, 1861.
23 *British Columbia and Confederation*, ed. W. G. Shelton, Morriss Printers, Victoria, 1967, p. 102. This volume of essays gives an interesting picture of the period immediately preceding B.C.'s entry into Confederation. Considerable attention is paid to the careers of Robson and De Cosmos.
24 Douglas to Newcastle, October 8, 1861.
25 *Ibid.*

26 W. W. Walkem, *Stories of Early British Columbia*, Vancouver, 1914, p. 33.

27 Walkem, *Op. Cit.*, pp. 33-34.
Judge Begbie, it is interesting to note, refused permission to Walkem's brother, Charles Walkem, to plead before him, as he had not received his legal training in the British Isles. Douglas, however, eventually overruled him on this matter, and appropriate legislation was enacted to uphold the rights of lawyers trained in Eastern Canada.

28 Sage, *Douglas*, p. 301.
Begbie remained a striking figure even in retirement and old age. He walked about Victoria, followed by several Gordon setters, and appeared at parties dressed in black velvet knee breeches and buckled shoes. A life-long bachelor, he was knighted in 1871 and died June 11, 1894.

29 Begbie frequently secured samples of the crops of the areas he passed through. On one occasion, someone came across him carrying some specimens of oats and asked him if he had been sowing or reaping them. The judge promptly replied: "Neither, my friend. The man who comes to this country to sow his wild oats will find so many difficulties besetting him that he will quickly abandon the project".

30 In a private letter of the Colonial Secretary, dated October 31, 1862, Douglas expressed his views more unreservedly:
"I will take this opportunity of assuring your Grace that a more contented or prosperous community than exists in British Columbia is nowhere to be found. A petty Californian-Canadian clique about New Westminster, the authors of all the clamour about "responsible government", form the only exception. That party is composed of men utterly ignorant of the wants and condition of the country; who never have done anything, and never will do anything for it, but complain; and who are, not unjustly, the objects of its derision . . . These gentlemen are not in reality dangerous; they are more formidable with the pen than with the sword. Small as is the police force, it is sufficient to deal with them; and the enclosed address from the firemen— a numerous and influential body—shows that there is no want of good and true men at New Westminster." (Sir James Douglas, Correspondence Outward, Miscellaneous Letters, 1859-1863).

31 Douglas to Newcastle, Feb. 14, 1863.
Despite Douglas' poor opinion of Langford on this occasion, when Langford had left the colony for England in 1861, he had taken with him the following testimonial from the Governor:
"His Excellency the Governor having learnt that you are about to leave the Colony and proceed to England, has desired me to acquaint you that he has much pleasure in stating that during several years past you have been employed as a Justice of the Peace for Vancouver's Island, and that you have discharged the duties of that office in a proper and satisfactory manner. His Excellency requests me to add that you have his best wishes for your success and happiness." (Douglas to Langford, Jan. 11, 1861. Sir James Douglas, Correspondence Outward, Miscellaneous Letters).

32 Douglas to Newcastle, April 20, 1863.

33 *Ibid.*

[34] Douglas to Newcastle, April 22, 1863.

[35] *Ibid.*

[36] Douglas to Newcastle, May 30, 1863.

[37] Douglas to Newcastle, July 4, 1863.

[38] Thomas Spence later built a bridge at this point, which then became known as Spence's Bridge.

[39] Douglas, as we saw, had suggested that a majority should be popularly elected; he was thus, in this respect at least, more progressive than the Imperial Government.

[40] Douglas to Newcastle, August 11, 1863.

[41] Douglas to Newcastle, May 14, 1863.

[42] *Ibid.*

[43] Douglas to Newcastle, May 18, 1863.

[44] *Ibid.*

[45] Douglas to Newcastle, May 21, 1863.

[46] Douglas to Newcastle, May 29, 1863.

[47] Douglas to Newcastle, June 3, 1863.

[48] *Ibid.* I have slightly amended the above passage, as the copy of the despatch in the Provincial Archives is evidently defective in one place. Its actual words are "at any course to communication to the mines".

[49] *Ibid.*

[50] Douglas to Newcastle, June 15, 1863.

[51] Douglas to Newcastle, July 14, 1863.

[52] Douglas to Newcastle, Sept. 2, 1863.

[53] Douglas to Newcastle, Sept. 14, 1863.

[54] Douglas to Newcastle, Nov. 13, 1863. Moody retained for several years some land he had bought in the Fraser Valley, but never returned to B.C. He died at Bournemouth in 1887.

[55] Quoted in *BCHQ*, Vol. XV, Jan-Apr. 1951, p. 99.

[56] Douglas to Newcastle (private), May 13, 1863. Sir James Douglas, Correspondence Outward, Miscellaneous Letters 1859-1863.

[57] Douglas to Doughty, June 23, 1863. Sir James Douglas, Correspondence Outward, Miscellaneous Letters, 1859-1863.

[58] De Cosmos died on July 4, 1897.

CHAPTER ELEVEN

The Sundown
Splendid and Serene

How STRANGE (he must have thought, as he sat in the place of honor amid the great assemblage that had come to pay public tribute to him) it all seemed! Ever since he had come to North America over forty years before, he had held posts of steadily increasing power and responsibility. For thirteen years now, he had been Governor of Vancouver Island, and for nearly six, Governor of British Columbia; but soon he would be only a private citizen. It would be a strange feeling when it came.

Well, at least his last great struggle—against nature, against the blindness of his superiors—had been successful. The stagecoaches could already get as far as Alexandria, and soon they would be able to go all the way from Yale to the heart of the gold fields. Not many had thought it could be done—a wagon road, eighteen feet wide and four hundred miles long, built through the magnificently mountainous terrain of a colony almost uninhabited but a few years before; but he had known that it had to be done.

It had been a near thing, though. In the end, the men, materials and money had been scraped together, but there had been times when it had seemed almost hopeless to continue. Still, it had looked impossible, too, in 1858, when twenty thousand miners had arrived in Fort Victoria, and he had had only a ship or two and a few officials to control them—to preserve Vancouver Island and New Caledonia for the Crown.

How had he come through safely? A bold front, certainly, had helped; he had found that with the Indians long before, and perhaps the miners were in their own way another kind of primitive people. Everyone, it might be, responded to a leader.

He must take care, though, not to think he had done it all himself. The Navy, the Marines, the Engineers—he could have done nothing without them. Some of them, he was glad to see, had decided to take their discharges and settle down here; well, they would make the very best sort of settlers. No republicans there.

Perhaps the greater part of the credit for stability was really owing to Judge Begbie. A distinguished man, certainly, in every way—he would be speaking in a few minutes; he hoped he would say nothing too fulsome—who had upheld the law in the gold fields almost single-handed. Without him, and the handful of poor devils of constables who had enforced the law while other men were making fortunes all about them, it might all have ended in failure. Well, it had not, and he hoped that those who came after them would remember Matthew Begbie.

So here they all were in the Victoria Theatre: Dr. Helmcken, his son-in-law, whom he could depend on to look after Cecilia—Dr. Tolmie, Judge Cameron, Mr. Cary, Mayor Harris—"only an humble tradesman", he liked to call himself—Southgate, Franklin, Ring, A. C. Anderson who had found the routes into the Interior—how long ago that seemed. They had all helped.

P. M. Backus was here, too; he was to speak for the Americans in Victoria. There were still plenty of them, of course, but they were gradually, he believed, forgetting their old loyalties and acquiring new ones. When the process had gone on long enough, perhaps the result would be a new kind of man, neither British nor American but with the good qualities of both. Already there was talk that all the British colonies in North America would some day be joined in a great confederation; perhaps he would live to see it. He himself believed he would; would people see then that his roads had helped join the new country together? What should he say to them though now, he wondered? He might never speak to all the leading members of the Vancouver Island community again. What should be his last message to them?

Perhaps he should simply tell them the plain truth—that he could have done nothing without their assistance. All of them, great and small, had contributed something; he would put in a special word, he decided, for the members of the House of Assembly. They had helped to carry the colony over from the old days when he had ruled alone to the days that were coming when everyone would have a voice in government. It was a new way of doing things—when he was younger, almost unheard of—but it was coming in everywhere, and though it was, he realized, a little uncongenial to his temper, he did not fear it. It would come in any case, whether he feared it or not. New times, new ideas, new men.

They were clapping now, and his old friend Alfred Waddington was introducing him. His heart felt full, but of what emotion he could scarcely say. In a moment he would have to rise and address them. Well, he would simply say . . . one does what one can, and he would tell them so.[1]

*   *   *

It was the tenth of March that the farewell banquet had taken place; for a few days more, the old Governor was to be glimpsed in the streets of Victoria; then on the 14th came the final scene. To the strains of "For he's a jolly good fellow" he went on board the *Enterprise* at the HBC wharf. The guns crashed out a salute, the people cheered, and slowly the ship moved out of the harbor and across the straits to New Westminster. Here he would still have a few more weeks of office in the mainland colony, but on Vancouver Island his thirteen years as Governor were over.

Douglas' second official farewell was made at New Westminster early in April. The leading organ of the mainland colony, John Robson's *British Columbian*, did its sullen best to throw cold water on the proceedings, declaring that "upon principle and out of self-respect we are opposed to any public demonstration being given to Governor Douglas".[2] The reason it advanced was that "some of his more recent acts more than ever convince us of his settled, determined hostility to the best interests of this colony". Not many, apparently, agreed with the attitude, and the banquet duly took place, Attorney General Crease presiding. Only 79 guests were present—it would seem that the invitations were sent out by the Governor himself, and that its purported purpose was to celebrate the birthday of a member of the Royal family—but there was no sign of hostility to the principal guest. This, indeed, was reserved for his critics, for when a toast was proposed to "The Press", a storm of hisses drowned out the speaker. Douglas, by contrast, was the subject of an address to the Colonial Secretary, the Duke of Newcastle, in which his character and achievements were accorded high praise.

> During the period His Excellency has been in office, he has assiduously devoted his remarkable talents to the good of the country; ever unmindful of self, he has been accessible to all, and we firmly believe that no man could have had a higher appreciation of the sacred trust vested in him, and none could have more faithfully and nobly discharged it than he has.
>
> The great road system which Governor Douglas has introduced into the Colony is an imperishable monument of his judgment and foresight. It has already rendered his name dear to every miner, and future colonists will wonder how so much could have been accomplished with such small means. The colony already feels the benefit resulting from his unwavering policy in this respect, and year by year will the wisdom of that policy become more manifest.
>
> During the term of office the laws have ever been rigidly, faithfully and impartially administered; the poorest man has always felt that in a just cause he would not have to seek redress in vain, and the country has in consequence enjoyed a remarkable exemption from crime and disturbance.
>
> Under these circumstances we cannot resist thus spontaneously and heartily laying before your Grace our appreciation of the services of a noble and wise man.[3]

Douglas was much moved by this tribute, as his reply makes evident:

> Envy and malevolence may be endured, but your kindness overwhelms me; it deprives me of the power of utterance; it excites emotions too powerful for control . . . A pyramid of gold and gems

would have been less acceptable to me than this simple record. I ask for no prouder monument, and for no other memorial, when I die and go hence, than the testimony here offered, that I have done my duty . . . Assure the people of British Columbia that they have my heartfelt thanks for this gratifying expression of their opinion; assure them that I shall ever rejoice to hear of their prosperity and of the progress of all that relates to the moral and material interests of this colony.[4]

A few days later, Douglas returned to the Island capital, where he put his affairs in order and continued to perform a few minor official duties. Then, on Saturday the 14th of May, he once more left Victoria, this time for an extended holiday in Europe. Leaving his family behind, he embarked at Esquimalt on the *Sierra Nevada,* and was soon moving down the western coast of the continent.

We are fortunate indeed to possess a detailed account by Douglas himself of his daily life during the next twelve months. Released at last from the cares of office and its multifarious duties, he was free to give all his attention to the varied scenes which now passed before his eyes, while in recording his reactions to them he could discard the studied formality of his public utterances. We are thus given a valuable insight into Douglas' character, for by noting what themes and judgments recur with some regularity in his diary we are able to gain a deeper understanding of his complex and closely guarded personality. Certainly we are shown in these pages a remarkably active and wide-ranging mind. Not only was Douglas much interested in statistics of all sorts— not many of us, surely, while travelling by sea, give much thought to the fuel consumption of the vessel or the design of its engines—but the poetic and artistic side of life, it is clear, appealed equally strongly to him. It is obvious, also, that behind his impassive public exterior there had been at all times a sensitive and affectionate family man, who, once off history's spot-lighted stage, could feel and express deep emotions without embarrassment.

The diary begins with his reactions to what would be his home till he reached Panama, and his efforts to adjust to his new surroundings. It is clear that they were scarcely commodious:

My cabin is 6 1/6 feet long, 5 5/6 feet wide, 6 4/6 feet high and has three sleeping bunks piled one above the other and a washstand for three human beings under a tropical sun—there is exactly 25 inches in height between the beds—scant breathing room this.

However, it evidently transpired that Douglas was to enjoy these spartan surroundings in solitary grandeur, and soon "tea and toast with champagne banished grief and restored hilarity". After retiring at ten and finding the lamp too dim to read by, he fell asleep; he was apparently not yet accustomed to the conditions of the voyage, however, for he "awoke several times during the night, lost the coverings, and after long gropings in the dark for the sheets, discovered them gathered napkin fashion about my neck".

The next morning, after washing in salt water ("two towels like pocket handkerchiefs") he "made a capital breakfast on excellent beef chops". It was Sunday; he had "thoughts of home and of the dear ones there" and reflected "what a blessing the Sabbath is to toiling harassed man. It brings rest, joy and peace of mind; man should be grateful for so merciful an institution". He noted, however, without comment, that there was "no service on board".

The ship moved steadily down the coast, and soon a melancholy sight reminded Douglas of his years of office, and the policy he had followed toward the Indian tribes—so different from that almost invariably employed by the Americans:

> The flourishing settlements once existing here have been nearly all deserted, the settlers having been attacked one after another, their running stock slaughtered and their habitations destroyed by the native tribes. The settlers are said to have provoked their hostility by many acts of atrocious cruelty, on the occasion of a native festive meeting in Humbolt Bay—the assemblage was held on a small island not over a quarter of a mile distant from the principal town or settlement. In the midst of their rejoicing six of the settlers attacked the throng of unarmed savages and slaughtered about 80 of them, chiefly women and children. Forty of the former had been living for months as domestics in the families of the townspeople, who heard their piercing shrieks but did not suspect the cause until the tragedy was over and it was too late to prevent it. No measures were taken to

punish the outrage—the Sheriffs and Justices are elective and depen-dent on the people, and would not take proceedings against them on behalf of the natives. But a fearful retribution was in reserve—the authors of the crime were discovered by the natives and were success-ively waylaid and shot by the friends of the slaughtered victims of savage cupidity and an unrelenting war was immediately waged by the tribe upon the settlements and it has led to the almost general depopulation of the district.

These sobering reflections, however, were soon displaced by more cheerful ones, as the ship arrived at San Francisco. Douglas hired a carriage and drove around the town; later he visited "Santa Clara College", where he was much impressed by "the neat walks, the shady coolness, the rich green verdure, the glowing flowers bending in graceful festoons and filling the air with fragrance". A few days later he had his hair cut by "a very amusing fellow", and found that by a coincidence the barber "had been to Victoria and thought he might have made a heap of money had he remained there".

At San Francisco Douglas transferred to the *Golden City* which he described as "a beautiful side wheel steamer, 4500 tons burthen, 350 feet long". Before many days had passed, he saw in the evening sky the Southern Cross, and early in June he reached Panama.

He now crossed the isthmus by train, passing through "deep swamps covered with jungle, full of reptiles and venomous insects". He was informed that the building of this railway had cost "10,000 deaths, making a grave for every 15 feet of road".

Soon he was in the West Indies. Stopping briefly in Jamaica, he visited a cotton plantation and set down a brief outline of the history and geography of the island.

Facts and figures plainly fascinated him, for he made calculations of the length of the various phases of his long journey. Victoria to San Francisco he reckoned at 800 miles, San Francisco to Panama as 3520 more, the railway trip at 48 miles, and the final voyage to Southampton as 4897 miles, making a total of 9265 miles. He also carefully wrote down details of the *Shannon*, the ship that was to take him from the West Indies to England, noting the power of its engines, their cost, the amount of coal they required, and the speed that the vessel attained. Finally on June 27 he reached Southampton, travelled up to London, and engaged a room at the Clarendon Hotel. He was already captivated by the English countryside, which he had not seen for over forty years:

> The country charming—every inch cultivated like a garden— bright green fields—sunny slopes—graceful undulations, shady groves —beautiful trees—towns and villages—farm houses, noble seats embowered in trees laid out with an astonishing degree of good taste form an assemblage of objects that fill the mind with delight; to me it was enchanting and as we flew over the ground in a comfortable first class car I could not take my eyes off it for a moment. I gazed in fact till both eye and head ached. Let who will boast of the tropics, to me there is no country half so beautiful as old England in June.

Soon, like any other tourist, he was "seeing the sights". He drove through Hyde Park, saw the Crystal Palace, the Houses of Parliament and Westminster Abbey. The latter, however, evoked thoughts of human mortality, as he saw how "a diminutive marble slab is all that remains of Warren Hastings". Such thoughts apparently came easily to Douglas, for even Madame Tussaud's wax-works gave him only a "melancholy impression—vain and fleeting is human greatness—oh the vanity of life".

The British Museum, however, he considered "a wonderful place". He also was shown over the Bank of England and visited the zoo.

Late in June he left for Scotland, where he saw the castle where King Duncan died and also "the waste where Macbeth met the weird sisters who gave him so many fatal promises".

His daughter Jane, who had married Alexander Grant Dallas,[5] was by now living in Scotland, and Douglas hastened to pay them a visit. The scene is put vividly before our eyes:

> On enquiring at the door of the house, she recognized my voice, and I heard her exclaim Oh my own dear papa she rushed to the door and threw herself into my arms . . . Overcome by my emotions, I could hardly speak either to her or Dallas, but made up for my silence by a hearty and prolonged shake of the hand. I cannot express

the joy I felt on this happy occasion. The dear children are charming . . .

For the next two weeks father and daughter, we may be sure, told each other all their news, though Douglas found time to visit the battlefield of Culloden ("What melancholy associations are connected with this spot!"). Then they were forced to say good-bye:

> Bade my daughter Jane and her dear children farewell and it is impossible to repress the painful feeling that it may be for the last time, that we may never meet again on this side of eternity. I kept these sad feelings strictly confined to my own breast, and talked to Jane cheerfully about our next meeting and that possibly we might meet again in the autumn and spend the winter months near to each other either in London or in the south of Europe . . .

Late in August Douglas visited the graves of Wordsworth and Coleridge near Windermere in the Lake District,[6] and then went on to Oxford, with which he was much impressed. He also paid homage to another distinctive feature of English life by taking part in a game of croquet.

Interestingly enough, Douglas was soon afforded a glimpse into two very different conceptions of human history and destiny, at this moment locked in a death struggle in the minds of at least the educated members of the British public. He listened with attention to a sermon in which the role of the Jews in the divine plan of the universe was exhaustively explained, and which "concluded with the words of prophecy that the conversion of the Jews must precede the spread of Christianity among the heathen". Soon afterwards, he attended a meeting of the British Association for the Advancement of Science, and heard a learned speaker demonstrate convincingly that "man must have co-existed with some of the great fossil mammalia". On the former occasion, Douglas contented himself with simply recording the event, but on the latter he permitted himself the observation that:

> No one can be more sensible than I am of the benefits to be derived from the extension of Science. It was by efforts such as theirs that the foundations of new discoveries were laid. In this way clouds of error and prejudice were dispersed, and they arrived step

by step at the grand and brilliant results of all toil and investigation, the unobscured light of knowledge and of truth.

A more personal item of news now reached Douglas, as he received word that his daughter Jane had given birth to a child. At once he wrote to Lady Douglas to tell her of her new grandchild.

Then, late in September, he crossed the Channel to France; travelling to Paris, he engaged a room at the Hotel de Louvre, and was much taken by his surroundings, which were

. . . beautifully furnished—4 large mirrors each 9x4½ feet with gilt frames in sitting room and 2 in the bed room, crimson and gold paper—and window curtains of the same colour—handsome centre and corner inlaid tables—crimson sofas and chairs with carpet to match—one must of course pay for all this splendour.

Soon, like any other sightseer, he was strolling down the Champs Elysées, and deciding that "Paris is really a splendid city". Douglas was of course completely bilingual, and was able to converse readily with citizens of all classes.

Then, journeying southward early in October, he entered Switzerland and stayed a few days in Geneva. There he recorded how

. . . the fog lifted this morning a little after sunrise and I had a glorious view of Mount Blanc.

He felt himself forced to record, however, that the Alps

. . . do not appear so grand or massive as the Rocky Mountains.

The scenery was, however, undeniably very striking:

The lofty chain of the Jura meets the horizon forming the distant background, and adds by its wild and rugged aspect to the charm of the green and smiling country beneath.

Nor was this the only aesthetic experience that Douglas allowed himself. Hearing that there was a celebrated organ in a nearby Gothic cathedral, he attended a recital and was deeply impressed by the varied effects created by the instrument:

. . . the tempest, the tolling of the alarm bell, the rushing sound of the wind—the Gloria in Excelsis—the duet of voices—dying away with delicious softness in the distance—are all exquisite—worth going a hundred miles to hear.

After visiting Berne, Zurich, Lucerne and Basle, Douglas journeyed down the Rhine; it had, he decided

> . . . all the wildness of the Fraser between Langley and Harrison River, the resemblance being very striking save that no high land is seen on either side of the Rhine . . .

Soon afterward, he was able to perform a characteristic act of courtesy. Coming across an Englishwoman and her daughter, stranded by a temporary lack of funds, he lent them money to permit them to return to England.

Douglas also attended the service in Cologne Cathedral, but the sturdy old Scot decided that the mass "resembles a magnificent pageant more than the solemn worship of God."

He was not, however, insensitive to art in what he considered its right setting, and we next see the old fur trader standing rapt before the Rembrandts at the Hague. One wonders if perhaps he felt specially attuned to the Dutch master, whose subjects seem to emerge for a moment from an obscure background into the light, yet carry a suggestion that they are destined to recede once more into the great mystery whence they came. Douglas, too, with his uncertain origins and sudden emergence onto history's stage, may at times have felt life in some such terms.

In November, after visiting Rotterdam and Amsterdam, he was in Antwerp. Here, too, he visited the galleries, where the work of Rubens and Van Dyck was displayed. He seems to have been in an out-going mood; certainly he found time to note the "women not so pretty as the Dutch girls of Rotterdam".

In Belgium his experiences were varied. He attended a sitting of the Belgian parliament, visited the museum, and went to the opera and ballet. Later, re-entering France, at Reims he was shown over a winery where choice champagnes were made. Late in November he was once more back in Paris.

After a visit to Versailles ("which has not its equal in any other country—it is truly fairy land—realizing the fancies of the poets' dreams"), he toured southwestern France. The prominent position of the Catholic church in French life engaged his attention, and he decided that "the celibacy enjoined by the church is not favourable to morals".

The year now drew to its close. Only a few months before he had stood on the bridge of the ship of state and directed its affairs; now far from home and friends, the old man sat alone on Christmas Day and read the gospels:

> How touching and beautiful is the answer of Mary to the Angel Gabriel. "Behold the handmaid of the Lord; be it unto me according to thy word". It breathes the profoundest hope and joy.[7]

Between Christmas and New Year he visited Bayonne, recording "pleasant temperature—not unlike Victoria at this time of the year".

Most of January was spent in Spain; but apart from the pictures in the Prado (which he thought better than the Louvre) and the Cathedral of Seville, he was not impressed:

> Spain is not the fairy land I thought it was. How one's youthful dreams are dispelled with advancing years and growing experience.

Not only did Douglas think it "a sadly misgoverned country" which "has never enjoyed a tolerable government", but he was not impressed by the high dignitaries of either church or state. The queen, he saw reason to believe, was "superstitious and immoral"; every time she had a baby, he was informed, "the bishops come to the palace with the arm of one saint and the leg of another, to promote a safe and easy delivery". Douglas also found "the officials corrupt and unprincipled" and that "many of the clergy lead immoral lives". Moreover, he recorded, "I have seen no land equal to the rich bottoms of Vancouver Island".

Returning to France considerably disillusioned, he soon went to Italy. Here, after visiting Genoa, Naples, Leghorn and Elba, he inspected the ruins of Pompeii:

> It is wonderful to see this city of the dead peering out from its covering after lying buried in the dust for more than 17 hundred years. How touching are the appearance of the skeletons—their

attitudes, the compression of the limbs and fingers indicate the agony of suffering and despair.

After drawing up a careful statistical table of densities of population in various countries, as well as the depth of the ocean in several parts of the globe, he went on to Rome (the stagecoaches were rolling triumphant into Barkerville), where he was once more greatly impressed by the art galleries. He made several purchases of copies of the great masterpieces, and also soon afterward bought a bracelet and three brooches for Lady Douglas.

Vienna ("an atmosphere of tobacco smoke and onions") next saw this indefatigible tourist, and soon afterward so did Salzburg, Munich, Ulm and Baden Baden.

On his return to Paris, he once more found that tragedy had struck his family. His daughter Cecilia had died in Victoria, leaving five children to be cared for by the sorrowing Dr. Helmcken. Declaring that "we were not worthy of her", he went on to write:

> She was the joy of my eyes, the light of my life; her ear was ever open to the calls of distress; the poor and afflicted never appealed to her in vain; they will miss her sympathizing heart and helping hand.

News soon came of another, less personal tragedy—the assassination of President Lincoln. The old man's spirits seem to have become subdued; certainly the entries in the diary are now perfunctory and few. On the second of May, his *wanderjahre* over, he set sail on the *Atrato*, and in due course was back in Victoria.

He still had a dozen years to enjoy his retirement. They were years which we do not know in detail, but of which we can form a fairly good picture. He supervised his business affairs—he owned land and houses in various parts of the Victoria area—presided like other Victorian papas over his family, and corresponded with relatives beyond the seas. The Queen had granted him a pension of £500 a year, and he managed his investments prudently, with occasional periods of anxiety when the business cycle turned down.[8] He followed both domestic politics and the maneuverings of the great powers, and, like most old men, recalled the days of his youth ("the northern passes, where I have made my bed on 20 feet of snow"⁹) and from time to time discerned dark days ahead. In a letter to his daughter Jane (Mrs. A. G. Dallas) on May 17, 1867, he gives some details of his mode of life:

My property here is not so valuable as it was, but still, thank God, my income is ample, far exceeding my present expenditure. I live in very good style, not seeing much company nor indulging in wasteful extravagance, but I have everything comfortable about the house, and the grounds are beautifully kept. In addition to my income here, my pension and property in the English funds yield me an income of nearly £1200 a year, so you see I have every reason to be thankful to God, for his goodness and mercy have followed me all the days of my life.

In another letter, dated July 18, 1869, and addressed to "my dearest child" (no doubt Jane), he informs her that

My delight is to be in motion, either driving or riding about, inspecting this thing or visiting that; property, you know, has its duties as well as its pleasures; and I strive to combine the two.

Those with causes to forward often sought his support, but he usually declined to participate in their efforts, declaring that

. . . the little influence I once possessed from my official position as a public servant is forever gone; and I must from principle decline all connection with companies or enterprises of a private character.¹⁰

From time to time during the remainder of his life he was in the public eye, at least of the residents of Victoria. When a cable was laid from San Juan Island to Cadboro Bay, he was recorded as among those present.¹¹ When a later Governor, Frederick Seymour, died suddenly in 1869, he was one of the pallbearers. He followed the debates over the desirability of a Confederation of all the British North American colonies, and appears to have acquiesced in British Columbia's entry into it. On March 22, 1870, writing to his son-in-law, A. G. Dallas, Douglas declared:

Confederation with Canada is now one of the ruling manias; and my impression is that it will not be long delayed.

By October 11 of the same year, however, he had reconsidered sufficiently to declare:

There is however a better feeling among all classes in view of confederation with Canada & the public works (overland railway & graving dock) to follow in the train of that event".[12]

He also took intelligent note of events beyond the seas, declaring, for example, in a flash of prescience in a letter to his daughter Jane that "Bismarck has commenced a new era, and his conquests end not, I fear, with Austria".[13]

Now that activity was no longer the substance of his life, his physique began to show a change. His old friend, John Tod, noted in 1868 that

. . . although he is very stout, and always in good health, yet old age has evidently wrought a perceptible change in his once powerful mind, which seems now entirely absorbed in itself.[14]

A year later, Tod noted that

. . . his clothes hang loose upon him, his head is white as the snow, his step is infirm and dim with age.[15]

One piece of good news was received by the Douglas family in this period. The Supreme Court of Canada decided that the first marriage of William Connolly, Lady Douglas' father, had been valid and his later marriage to Julia Woolrich null and void. Not only did this mean a modest legacy for Lady Douglas, but ended doubts as to her legitimacy, which had long been a topic of gossip in some circles and no doubt a factor in her decision to take almost no part in the social life of Victoria.[16]

Sometimes he seems to have yearned for the old days. During the early years of his retirement he wrote to Dallas:

The whole machine is in a strange incomprehensible muddle, wanting only a firm and experienced hand to bring it into good working order.[17]

Slowly the years crept up on him. In the spring of 1870 John Tod noted that:

Friend Douglas has of late become very unsteady of step, shaky of hand, and dim of eye, but as he gets older, seems more and more engrossed with the affairs of this world, notwithstanding his ample means . . .[18]

His wife, too, was moving into the shadows:

> Lady Douglas is now a great invalid, and seldom leaves the house except for a walk in the garden.[19]

He began to live more and more in his children. He hoped that his son James, born in 1851, would some day succeed him as head of the family, and he was sent to England for his education. Douglas had high hopes for his son, but preferred to make decisions for him, informing A. G. Dallas that:

> I have reproved him for his many boyish projects of going to sea in the merchant marine, becoming a farmer &c, which would be altogether inconsistent with my plans.[20]

Douglas also cautioned his son, as he was later to warn his daughter, against unwise emotional entanglements:

> I see you are carrying on a correspondence with a young lady and fancy you are in love with her. You must be very careful in such things. You are too young for any serious attachment and too honourable to trifle with a young lady's affections.
> It will be time enough for you, in 8 or 10 years hence, to think of marrying, when you have finished your education, and made your mark in the world and have wherewith to support a wife in comfort.
> Remember this counsel and be wise.[21]

In the meantime, Douglas favored his son with much moral advice:

> There is no royal road to learning; it is impossible for anyone to get on, and make his mark in the world, without plenty of hard work. You have a great deal yet to learn. I wish you to write a better hand and a less slovenly letter; you must study composition to express your ideas neatly and clearly . . . You must be careful and methodical in money matters, keeping a correct account of your expenses. If you do so, Mr. Dallas proposes to increase your weekly allowance to 2/- a week, and I approve of this increase, strictly however on that condition.[22]

On one occasion, however, Douglas opened the vials of his wrath upon his son:

> I understand you have sold the gold chain your mother gave

you as a parting token of her love; an act of such utter heartlessness that I could never have believed you capable of it had not you yourself told me of it. You have also sold the watch you got from me, and this you did in a disreputable manner—at a pawn-broker's shop— altogether unworthy of any member of my family . . .

Well for all this you will be the sufferer, for neither watch nor gold chain will you ever get from me. The next you wear will be earned by the sweat of your own brow—which will teach you to set a proper value on such things . . .

I pray God that there may be extenuating circumstances to soften the irrepressible feeling of aversion with which I now regard you— and which prompt me at this moment to write Mr. Dallas to put you to learn some handicraft trade, that I may have no further torment with you.

I commend you to God's holy keeping, poor Mamma is in deep grief, nobody here besides Mamma has heard of your folly, nor shall I make it known even to your sisters.[23]

Less than a month later, however, the old man was describing for the benefit of his son a picnic he had enjoyed saying that:

A ride in the woods is delightful just now, the syringa and spiraeae being in flower & lighting up the masses of dark foliage with their splendid array of white and pink blossom—and mingling their delicate perfumes with the grateful fragrance of the pine trees, so that we had altogether a most enjoyable day.[24]

He did, nevertheless, return once again to the subject of the lost mementoes, drawing for James the moral lesson it exemplified:

We are all poor frail creatures when left to ourselves; our sufficiency is of the Lord; we must look to him for strength and guidance in the hour of trial. His power is sufficient for us; His strength delights in weakness when He dwells supreme in our hearts, we have nothing to fear, neither powers, nor principalities nor any of the agents of darkness can ever prevail against the good soldier of Christ. Fully armed in the panoply of His Lord, he wars against the temptations of the world, the flesh and the Devil and never basely yields to sin.[25]

James was, it is apparent, a disappointment to his father, who could make little of him. A certain invisible barrier seems to have separated the two such different personalities; one catches the old man's awareness of this in some of his letters:

> You might tell me in few words, how you spend the hours when not in school, what you are reading, and what books most interest your mind—you might also give your opinion on the aims and merits of the works you have read. Tell me also about friends and companions, and many other personal matters which would be of interest to me.[26]

James' health was never good, and after his return to Victoria in 1870 it slowly deteriorated.[27] In a letter to A. G. Dallas, dated March 22, 1870, Douglas conceded that his high hopes for his son were probably destined not to be fulfilled:

> I fear from his constitutional infirmities and continued debility that he has not many years to live.

This proved to be an accurate prediction, as James did not long survive his father, dying in 1883.

Four of Douglas' daughters', however, were destined for a fairly long life: Jane (who married A. G. Dallas); Agnes (who became Mrs. Arthur Bushby); Alice (who had eloped so romantically with Charles Good, but whose marriage eventually foundered); and Martha (later Mrs. Dennis Harris), who was to live on till 1933. On these their father lavished affection, but was at the same time careful to supervise the most minute aspects of their social and intellectual development.

Alice, like James, caused her father much concern. As he noted in a letter to her sister (Mrs. Dallas), dated November 13, 1869:

> Alice is a strange girl, very nice and ladylike, but she has taken an inconceivable dislike to Good, so much so that she can hardly bear to see him. I have pointed out the folly and wickedness of ceasing according to her marriage vows to love and obey her husband, and I hope through the blessing of God that she will be brought to a better state of mind.

The old man's hopes were destined to be disappointed, as he admitted a few months later. Alice had taken her three children to England, and Douglas sadly noted, "She hates her husband with a bitter hatred which amounts to insanity."[28]

Money matters appear to have been partly responsible for the break-down of this marriage. Douglas states several times that Good was deeply in debt, and calls him on one occasion "an incurable idiot".[29]

We are fortunate in possessing a sizable collection of letters from Douglas to his daughter Martha. In 1872, when she was 18, he sent her to England for two years to complete her education, declaring that "it will take that time to get rid of the cobwebs of colonial training and give you a proper finish".[30] While she was away, Douglas wrote her a few lines almost daily; then, when he had composed a full-sized letter, committed it to the post.

Nearly a century has passed since Douglas wrote these letters, but in them he still comes vividly before us. We are given, indeed, a full-scale portrait of an upper middle class Victorian papa. The deep religious convictions, the constant exhortations to self-improvement, the frequent sentimentality, the occasional hypocrisy, the strict division between the innocent and the not-so-innocent pleasures: all these are present in unambiguous and unabashed abundance.

They appear, indeed, from the very beginning of this remarkable series of letters, where Douglas describes for his absent daughter the distress her departure had occasioned:

> I hurried up from the garden gate, where I bade you adieu, to comfort Mama, and found her in a burst of incontrollable grief— I caught her in my arms, but her heart was full—she rushed wildly into your room, and casting herself upon the bed lay sobbing and calling upon her child.[31]

Douglas also recorded that he had driven down to the waterfront and watched the ship move past:

> We watched you till out of sight, and returned with sad hearts to our deserted home.[32]

In his account of the next morning, we are shown two typical aspects of this now vanished age:

> Not a dry eye at morning prayers. We all sobbed out our griefs aloud . . .[33]

Douglas' deep religious faith finds expression in numerous passages:

May the God of your Fathers, the blessed Saviour of mankind, have you in his holy keeping . . . Worldly enjoyments soon lose their power to please, but the love of God delights the heart forever . . . Mamma who is in excellent health sends her love. She hopes that your communion with God is growing more and more intimate. Open your heart freely to us on that subject; for we desire most ardently that you should love your Blessed Saviour, and serve him with the noblest faculties of your mind and soul. This is the great object of life, the wise course, and the chief end of man . . . O that I could live more devotedly and enjoy a closer walk with God![34]

Douglas was not, however, sympathetic to the movement in the Anglican church of Victoria toward a more elaborate form of ceremony. This was eventually to cause a very serious rift in the religious life of the city, and result in Douglas himself, with other prominent citizens, leaving the Anglican church and becoming members of the Reformed Episcopal Church. Foreshadowings of this occur here and there in his letters to his daughter:

Archdeacon Reece preached in the evening at Christ Church; his sermon gave great offence to the congregation, as he advocated ritualism. The Dean said a few words in dismissing the congregation, protesting against the doctrine, which has no warrant in Scripture.[35]

Actually the Dean's "few words" had caused a sensation, and marked the beginning of an open conflict within the Anglican church of Victoria, which was eventually to split that body in two.[36] Douglas, however, seems not to have realized at this time how serious the division would become, though on January 10, 1874, he noted that

. . . our good worthy Dean is taking a course I do not exactly approve, in opposition to the Bishop, which may give rise to serious misunderstandings in the Church, and be a cause of grief to the congregation.

On March 24 of the same year, he explained more explicitly to his daughter the point at issue:

The worthy Dean, who is a sound churchman, has conscientious objections to ritualism, and he imagines the Bishop has a leaning that way, and is seeking to introduce its forms in the churches here.

Alexandra Suspension Bridge, built in 1863 — a remarkable feat of engineering for the times

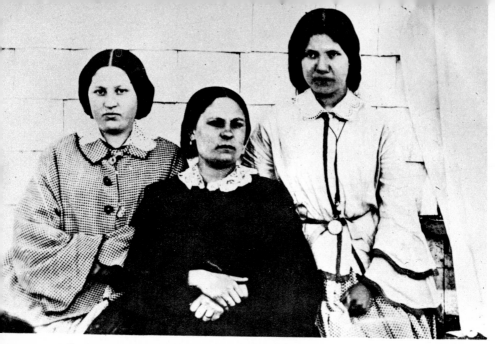

Lady Douglas and two daughters of the thirteen children born to the Douglases

Residence of Sir James Douglas

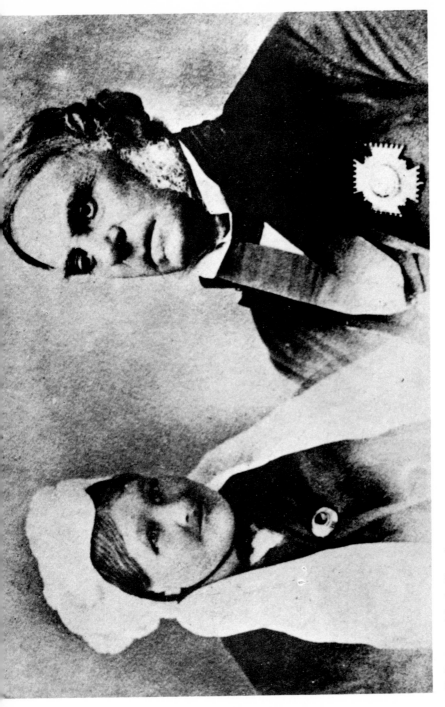

Sir James and Lady Douglas

Funeral of Sir James Douglas, August 7, 1877, from the Reformed Episcopal Church in Victoria

This is the whole and sole cause of the difficulty in our church; we all deplore but cannot remove it.

Closely allied with religion in Douglas' character (perhaps here the work of Wordsworth was an influence; we recall how Douglas had made a pilgrimage to his grave) was the love of nature. The changing seasons are regularly described to his absent daughter:

> You would be delighted with a morning peep of the varied and highly tinted foliage at James Bay. The splendour of its rich and gorgeous hues, reflecting the bright rays of the morning sun, are beautiful beyond description . . . The air is fragrant with the sweets exhaled by the wild rose, now blooming in countless abundance. It is indeed delightful to wander about, amidst the beauty and wild luxuriance of nature—so far surpassing in grace the utmost efforts of art . . . The sweet little robin is pouring out his heart in melody, making the welkin ring with his morning song of praise and thanks-giving. Would that we were equally grateful to the Author of all good![37]

The sentimentality of the old man was also given free rein in his letters. He told his daughter that he had put a large apple on her bed-room table ("It makes me fancy you are here; though a mere delusion, it alleviates the pain of absence");[38] on other occasions he wrote, "I will pick a few violets to send with this letter as a memento of home" and "I enclose a few violets which I have just picked in the flower border".[39] When new streets were made through some of his property, he named them Jane, Alice, Martha and Bushby—"a monument, you see, in honour of my dear little daughters".[40]

All this, however, is interspersed with moral maxims that can hardly have added much to Martha's enjoyment of life in England:

> Shun extravagance; it is the sure road to poverty and ruin . . . Arithmetic must not be neglected; no art is more necessary or useful in the daily affairs of life . . . You speak in Amy's letter of "resting your weary *legs*—would it not be nicer to say "weary *limbs*"? . . . I wish you to be in all respects lady-like, both in speech and manner. A lady never uses slang phrases, which are essentially vulgar, and to me unbearable.[41]

He even returned one of her letters to her with comments and corrections:

First, I wish to observe that it is somewhat of a scrawl, carelessly written, and not so neatly worded as it should be . . . In order to improve your style, study the writings of good authors. Read a page attentively, and after mastering the sense, write it out in your own words, without looking at the book. By comparing the two, you will observe the beauties and defects of each . . . I enclose a part of your last letter, pruned of redundancies, as a study. Observe how it is improved by the process.[42]

That there was a persistent melancholy strain in Douglas is evident here and there in these letters:

The trees are loaded with fruit, and everything is lovely, but we missed the old familiar faces, whom we shall meet no more on earth. So passes away the glory of the world.[43]

Various details of his life in retirement find mention in these letters. He sold a house that he owned on Yates Street for $11,000 to a Mr. Pritchard,[44] and later another property on the same street for $5000;[45] also one on Johnson Street for $4500.[46] He drove out to Saanich with his son James to see the new city waterworks being built, and later noted that:

The foundation stone of the dam at Beaver Lake for the water reservoir was laid yesterday with imposing ceremonies.[47]

He followed affairs of the day, noting that "Christ Church will be finished in a few weeks more and looks remarkably well".[48] The following year he attended the consecration (on October 23, 1873) of the Metchosin church, noting that:

Metchosin looked its best, the beautiful slopes, the richly tinted foliage, the bright clear sky, the warm sunshine, the glassy smooth sea, and the grand mountains in the distance, formed a combination of indescribable beauty. I felt an exhilaration of mind, which led me to wander away through the woods toward the white cliffs bordering the sea, from whence I contemplated its placid waters with delight.[49]

He also noted changes in the city he had founded as a stockaded trading post. New buildings were rising where once the now dismantled palisades had stood:

The new Post Office, a pretensious building, faced with freestone from Nanaimo, is finished externally, and is a great ornament to Government Street, on which it is situated. The Custom House is to be erected near the water at the lower end of Fort Street. It will be finished in the coming year.[50]

The old pioneers, however, were passing from the scene:

Mr. McKenzie of Craigflower died yesterday of heart disease—aggravated by a fall from his carriage . . . He died in peace after receiving the communion, and was perfectly resigned to the will of God. May we be found so also when our turn comes.[51]

Larger issues of the day continued to engage his attention. He sorrowed over the final loss of San Juan Island ("Well, there is no help for it now, we have lost the stakes and must just take it easy . . . The Island of San Juan is gone at last! I cannot trust myself to speak about it and will be silent").[52] Railways were always of interest to Douglas, and he looked forward to the construction of the C.P.R., proud that Esquimalt had been chosen for its terminus.[53] When the first sod was turned for the Vancouver Island portion of the railway, he recorded it with satisfaction.[54] The discovery of a large body of iron ore on Texada Island confirmed his belief that British Columbia had untold mineral resources.[55]

He still regarded Amor De Cosmos, who had become both an M.P. and Premier of B.C., with a suspicious eye, and declared "it is suspected De Cosmos is betraying the country".[56] He did not, however, permit his daughters any such sentiments; when Martha evidently expressed some, he at once reprimanded her:

You are rather hard upon poor De Cosmos. Young ladies must not be so decided in their politics; they must always be gentle and good, carefully avoiding the use of strong language.[57]

Here and there in these letters we note traces of Victorian hypocrisy. For example, we find Douglas informing his daughter that:

When the mind is assailed with evil or revengeful thoughts, I always have recourse to prayer . . . I feel strengthened, refreshed and relieved from every embittered thought.

He appears not to have noticed that only a few lines farther on in the same letter he declares that:

The Grits, as the opposition faction is termed, are a low set, and nothing good is to be expected from them.[58]

Douglas' almost excessive solicitude for his daughter's welfare perhaps had its roots in the sad fate of her sister Alice, whose marriage to Charles Good had collapsed. There are several references to this in these letters, as for example:

The Bishop called yesterday, and we had a long conversation about Alice. We both heartily desire she should be reconciled to her husband, but I fear the wish is vain. What a painful subject for me to dwell upon. I trust God will change her heart in his own good time, and produce in her a better state of mind.[59]

Douglas drew a moral from this melancholy affair for Martha's benefit:

How carefully young people should eschew mystery and secrecy in the all-important step in life, doing nothing that may compromise their future happiness, without the full knowledge and consent of their parents.[60]

This also perhaps explains why Douglas was unwilling to accede to Martha's request that she attend school for a time in the romantic and dazzling city of Paris:

It might improve your manners, by associating with kind, easy, engaging French girls. There is one strong objection, however, which I cannot overcome: that is the dread of French morals and sentiment —which I believe to be so different from our own. It may be bigotry on my part, their moral sentiments may be as pure as our own, but still the impression remains unchanged in my mind.[61]

So the months and years passed, and with them some of the old ways:

"May day" passed away without any public notice, the old English observance of the day once in vogue here has fallen into disuse, and its pleasant associations are gone with the day. We are fast lapsing from English and adopting Canadian customs. The 1st of July—"Dominion Day"—is now the great celebration of the year.[62]

Douglas seems to have been in generally good spirits as he passed into the evening of his days. He endeavored to keep his weight down, one method he employed giving us a vivid and amusing picture of the man whose unbending dignity had once been thought by some excessive:

> Had a good jumping on the verandah, with the skipping rope for exercise.[63]

We also have a glimpse of the old man in his seventieth year:

> What glorious weather; up this morning a little after 6 o'clock, bath and morning devotions detained me till 8, when I rode out; the air was deliciously cool, the birds singing gaily . . . The sky and the earth were redolent of beauty, all nature proclaiming the love and mercy of a benevolent Creator. The enjoyment was perfect, pure unalloyed happiness.[64]

Then, while Martha was still in England, her father decided that he would visit the old land once more. Leaving Victoria on the 25th of June 1874, he went first to San Francisco and then — the American railroad builders having wrought their own miracle of building through the mountains—crossed the continent by train. He stopped briefly at Chicago, was much impressed by Niagara Falls, reached New York, and crossed the Atlantic on the German steamer *Rhein*.

Arrived in Southampton, he journeyed to London and was soon visiting English relatives. He once again visited the British Museum and the Royal Academy, went shopping for presents for those dear to him, and later went to Edinburgh and saw Holyrood Palace. Late in August, accompanied by Martha, he sailed from Liverpool on the *Peruvian* and arrived at Quebec ("Hotels all full. Desperate hunt for quarters"). From Toronto he went to Chicago (there was of course no transcontinental railway as yet in Canada), crossed the wide Missouri, stopped briefly at Omaha, reached San Francisco, and eventually arrived at Victoria on September 26 in the *Angelos* and "found all well".

It is evident, though, from reading his diary for this period, that he was no longer the man he had been ten years before. His reactions were less lively, the trip itself much less ambitious; he was tired.

He was still occasionally in the public eye. When the great "doctrinal controversy" shook Victoria to its very foundations between 1872 and 1875, many wondered what Douglas would do. He had always supported respectability and authority, but in this case he did not hesitate to break old ties. Having decided that the Anglican church, at least in Victoria, was encouraging practices which he felt were imported from Roman Catholicism,[65] he left that body and with numerous friends set up the "Reformed Episcopal Church" at what is now the corner of Blanshard and Humboldt streets. Douglas himself donated the land (and later the organ) for the new building, and his old friend, the Rev. Mr. Cridge, assumed direction of the new church's affairs.

On August 15, 1876 (which may have been his 73rd birthday) he welcomed Lord Dufferin, the Governor General, at Esquimalt. It was one of his last public acts; he was an old man now; the world was passing him by.

On the first of March, 1876 he began a diary in which he recorded the early morning weather conditions of each day. Occasionally there are other details: 21st April (1876). Asparagus: had the first dish yesterday; 19th May (1876) Lilac coming into blossom, also apple and pear trees; 17th May (1877): The early sown potatoes about Hillside were nipped by frost last night. No damage was done about James Bay. In his firm clear handwriting the entries—usually no more than three lines each—go down the pages, until one comes to:

Thursday August 2nd. Few showers of rain in the night. 8 a.m. Clouds and sunshine.

The rest of the page, and all the remaining pages, are blank. That afternoon, he went out for a drive in his carriage. About ten o'clock that evening, he began to complain of pains near his heart. Dr. Helmcken was summoned, and he and his father-in-law sat and "conversed cheerfully";[66] suddenly, the old man's head fell back, and all was over.

For a few days the body lay in state at home, and many came there to pay their last respects. The *Colonist* reported some details:

On the breast of the deceased lay a large and beautiful cross and a wreath formed of flowers. The expression of the face was serene. The features were unchanged—Sir James appearing as if he had just fallen into a beautiful slumber—as, indeed, he really has.[67]

The funeral on August 7, 1877 was the most elaborate ever held in Victoria, before or since. It seemed as if the entire city took part, and a steamboat was chartered by the residents of New Westminster to enable them to attend en masse.[68] The procession from Douglas' home to the Reformed Episcopal Church contained 63 vehicles, and was over a mile long. All the bells of the city's numerous churches tolled solemnly, and H.M.S. *Rocket* fired its guns continuously. All schools and nearly all businesses were closed, and many private houses and public buildings were hung with black crepe. In the way of the times, many wore bands of crepe on their left arms. The navy, led by Rear Admiral De Horsey, added to the dignity of the scene. Among the pallbearers were Judge Begbie, Premier A. C. Elliott, Dr. Trimble, Roderick Finlayson, Dr. Tolmie, and J. D. Pemberton. Victorians knew they had lost the greatest of their citizens, and they had come to say good-bye.

For his text, Bishop Cridge took a verse from the Proverbs:

The hoary head is a crown of glory, if it be found in the way of righteousness. (XVI. 31).

Paying his last tribute to Victoria's founder, the Bishop dwelt on Douglas' religious faith, declaring "its simplicity uncorrupt and undisputed by scientific theories"; his regular attendance at church was also praised. His many private virtues were detailed, and his services to the public eulogized, the bishop declaring that Douglas

... had no idea that affairs could be left to take care of themselves; but was of opinion that if we would accomplish anything, good or great, we must put our shoulder to the wheel.[69]

The great days of Douglas' career were for some, at least, now only stories told by the "old-timers", and the Bishop recalled them for the congregation. Wisely deciding not to dwell on any matters of detail, he summed them up in a single sentence that said everything: "The right man was in the right place".

The *Colonist* had already paid its own tribute:

The career of Sir James Douglas is another exemplification of the saying that every person who would rise in the world must depend upon himself. He was essentially a self-made man.

No history of the province can be written without Sir James Douglas forming the central figure around which will cluster the stirring events that have marked the advance of the Province from a fur-hunting preserve for nomadic tribes to a progressive country of civilized beings, under the protection of the British flag and enjoying a stable and settled form of Government .[70]

He is buried in Ross Bay Cemetery, beneath a dignified but modest monument; an iron railing surrounds the grave. Here, too, were eventually to be gathered his wife Amelia[71] and his son James.[72]

It is a peaceful spot. Though not far from the bustling city, its sounds do not penetrate here; only the cries of the seagulls as they dip and soar. Close by is the beach where he came ashore in 1843, while across the blue waters, outlasting all man's restless striving, the Olympics look serenely down. Reflecting in this quiet place, one thinks of Shakespeare's line:

After life's fitful fever, he sleeps well.

NOTES

[1] The account in the *Colonist* for March 11, 1864, in summarizing Douglas' speech, says that he "would beg to thank the company most cordially for this sincere expression of their good-will. It was highly gratifying to him to see so hearty a demonstration of approval of the policy of his government, and to know that the community approved of his course during the long term of his protracted administration . . . He felt that the community were disposed to place a higher value on his services than they deserved (loud cries of "no, no"). The progress was due rather to the effects of their highly patriotic legislature (applause). In closing his relations with the colony, he would ever retain a grateful recollection of this day's proceedings, and of the high honor conferred upon him, and in whatever part of the world he should spend the remainder of his days, he would ever rejoice to hear of the welfare and progress and prosperity of this colony." (Tremendous cheering).
It is evident that Judge Begbie's remarks on this occasion were not well received. The *Colonist* of March 11 says that Begbie admitted he had differed from Douglas in many matters, and "went on for some time in a very rambling manner, amid considerable impatience exhibited by the audience".

The *British Columbian* of New Westminster for March 12, 1864 says that the judge's remarks "were probably more truthful than well-timed, and were received with hisses". The same newspaper on March 16 said that Begbie had been hissed down for what it termed his "manly frankness", of which the paper's editors approved, contrasting it with the "contemptible toadyism" of some of the other speakers. There is a satire in verse in the *British Columbian* for March 26, 1864 on the banquet, in which Douglas is referred to as "Fitzjames" (a possible reference to his illegitimacy) and mention is also made of "C. J. Bugbie, with whisky jug by".

An interesting sidelight on social customs of the day is that only the men sat down to the banquet "while about 50 ladies looked on". (*British Columbian*, March 12, 1864.

2 *British Columbian*, March 23, 1964.

3 *Colonist*, April 11, 1864.
British Columbia 6 percent bonds were quoted at this time at 102-104 (*British Columbian*, March 12, 1864). In effect, this was the "bloodless verdict of the market-place" on what Douglas had accomplished.

4 *Colonist*, April 11, 1864.

5 Dallas married Jane in 1858, and they had a large family. In 1861 he succeeded Sir George Simpson as Governor of Rupert's Land (i.e. the Hudson's Bay territories in North America). He left Victoria with his family in the spring of 1861 to take up his duties at Fort Garry. He died on Jan. 2, 1882, and the *Colonist* declared: "The late Mr. Dallas was a remarkable man. He possessed great ability as a financier, was a shrewd, bold operator, and had his health held good, would have long ago stood at the head of the Hudson's Bay Company affairs. About 40 years ago, when a young man, Mr. Dallas went to China. There he amassed a large fortune, but at the expense of his health, which was greatly shattered by the trying climate."
Dr. Helmcken's views of Dallas are worth recording: "Dallas . . . was a pretty penurious man and looked after comparatively small things — he was a business man — shrewd, sharp, sensible and active, fond of dogs and horses." (*Reminiscences*, IV. p. 76).
Dallas Mountain on San Juan Island is named after him, but there is some dispute as to whether Dallas Road, Victoria is named after him or after his son, Major-General Alister Grant Dallas, C.B., C.M.G.
There is an interesting article on Dallas by J. K. Nesbitt in the *Colonist* for Nov. 26, 1950.

6 Readers may estimate for themselves the likelihood of any contemporary director of British Columbia's affairs making such a pilgrimage.

7 Writing to his daughter Martha on July 17, 1873, about this trip, Douglas admitted "I should have felt happier had I not been alone".

8 "The colony continues depressed, and property next thing to valueless. People dissatisfied and losing courage". (Douglas to Dallas, April 29, 1867; Sir James Douglas, Correspondence Outward, PABC).
"It is in fact a most melancholy thing to see the general and fatal depression that exists among all classes. Confidence has vanished, capital is locked up,

278 / JAMES DOUGLAS: SERVANT OF TWO EMPIRES

and employment is not to be had. People are going away by every opportunity, merely because they are forced to leave, by having nothing to do,
and being unable to make a living". (Letter to Mr. Warner, Feb. 24, 1870.
Sir James Douglas Correspondence Outward, PABC).

9 Letter to Cecile, Sept. 7, 1869. I have not been able to identify this
correspondent.

10 Letter to Crease, April 4, 1867.

11 *Colonist*, April 24, 1866.

12 Letter to "my dear Henry" (possibly Crease), Sir James Douglas, Correspondence Outward, PABC, Victoria.

13 Douglas to Mrs. A. G. Dallas, Dec. 15, 1866.

14 Tod to Ermatinger, Nov. 12, 1868. Ermatinger Papers, PABC.

15 Tod to Ermatinger, March 15, 1869. Ermatinger Papers.

16 See, for example, Douglas' letter of Nov. 2, 1869 to his Montreal attorneys:
"Lady Douglas as you may suppose, is delighted with the decision of the
Court of Appeal". Also his letter to Jane Dallas of Nov. 13, 1869: "We
are now all full of the great Connolly case". Both letters are in Sir James
Douglas, Correspondence Outward, Provincial Archives, Victoria.

17 Douglas to Dallas, Nov. 8, 1867.
As late as 1869, when it seemed possible that Governor Seymour might be
forced to resign by reason of ill health, a petition was circulated requesting
that in that case Douglas should be appointed as Administrator. (Ormsby,
British Columbia, p. 227).

18 Tod to Edward Ermatinger, March 22, 1870. Ermatinger Papers.

19 Douglas to Jane Douglas, July 13, 1868.

20 Douglas to Dallas, July 23, 1867. Sir James Douglas, Correspondence Outward, PABC.

21 Douglas to James Douglas, May 17, 1867. Sir James Douglas Correspondence Outward, PABC.

22 Douglas to James Douglas, April 8, 1868.

23 Douglas to James Douglas, June 16, 1868.
Douglas did however write to James' sister Jane two days later, telling her
about the matter.

24 Douglas to James Douglas, July 3, 1868.

25 Douglas to James Douglas, Sept. 16, 1868.

26 Douglas to James Douglas, Feb. 16, 1870.

27 In an undated letter to the Rev. Longmore, one of his son's English tutors,
Douglas said:
"He is the child of many cares, the only one out of a family of 13 who is
not in the enjoyment of robust health.
The attack from which he never fully recovered and the marks of which he
will carry to the grave came on when he was three days old. We never
expected he would live and had it not been for a naturally good constitution he
must have sunk under the days and nights of suffering that have been
crowded into the brief span of his existence." (Sir James Douglas, Correspondence Outward, Miscellaneous Letters, 1859-1863).

28 Douglas to Jane Dallas, Jan. 22, 1870.

29 Letter to "Jeanie" (probably Jane Dallas), June 11, 1869.
30 Douglas to Martha Douglas, June 11, 1873.
   An interesting article by W. K. Lamb on the "Letters to Martha" is to be found in the *BCHQ*, Vol. I, 1937.
31 Douglas to Martha Douglas, August 13, 1872.
32 *Ibid.*
33 Douglas to Martha Douglas, August 14, 1872.
34 Douglas to Martha Douglas, August 18, 1872; May 6, 1873; Jan. 27, 1873; Sept. 15, 1872.
35 Douglas to Martha Douglas, Dec. 5, 1872.
36 For a full account of this controversy, see "Edward Cridge and George Hills: doctrinal conflict 1872-1874, and the founding of Church of our Lord, in Victoria, British Columbia, 1875." (M.A. Thesis, U. of Victoria, by Susan Dickinson).
37 Entries of Oct. 8, 1872; June 15, 1873; April 28, 1874.
38 Entry for Sept. 18, 1873.
39 Entries for March 18, 1873 and Feb. 20, 1874.
40 Entry for April 26, 1873.
41 Entries for Feb. 9, 1873; March 6, 1873; Nov. 19, 1872; Oct. 10, 1873.
42 Entry for March 3, 1874.
43 Entry for Sept. 23, 1872.
44 Entry for Feb. 24, 1873.
45 Entry for March 18, 1873.
46 Entry for Nov. 10, 1873.
   Douglas was by this time wealthy. A letter to his London brokers dated May 23, 1870 suggests that he had £33,000 in British Government Securities alone. This would be equivalent to more than $300,000 in modern purchasing power. In a letter to Dallas, dated June 3, 1869, he had stated that his income from property and investments was $27,300 a year, whereas it was costing him less than $5000 a year to live. (Sir James Douglas, Correspondence Outward, Provincial Archives, Victoria).
47 Douglas to Martha Douglas, Oct. 8, 1873.
48 Douglas to Martha Douglas, Sept. 19, 1872. The previous structure had been destroyed by fire in 1869. Douglas referred to it in one of his letters as "the first and mother church of the colony, about which clustered so many dear and cherished memories".
49 Douglas to Martha Douglas, Oct. 24, 1873.
50 Douglas to Martha Douglas, Dec. 4, 1873.
   Both these buildings are still in use.
51 Douglas to Martha Douglas, April 11 and 15, 1874.
52 Douglas to Martha Douglas, October 26 and Dec. 12, 1872.
53 Writing to a friend as early as April 4, 1867, Douglas had declared regarding a coast-to-coast highway: "The work demands the attention of Government & should be taken in hand by Canada on the one side and British Columbia on the other, each starting from their own limits, and working toward the central point of the continent, as proposed in a report

which I transmitted, some years ago, to Her Majesty's Government, I think in the month of April '62 or '63, accompanied by a map of the route". (Douglas to Crease, Sir James Douglas, Correspondence Outward, PABC).

[54] Douglas to Martha Douglas, July 17, 1873. The actual building of the C.P.R. was held up by the "Pacific Scandal", which resulted in the fall of Sir John A. Macdonald's government.

[55] Douglas to Martha Douglas, August 22, 1873.

[56] Douglas to Martha Douglas, Feb. 10, 1874. De Cosmos was premier of B.C. from 1872 to 1874.

[57] Douglas to Martha Douglas, May 5, 1874.

[58] Douglas to Martha Douglas, Nov. 4, 1873. We might note also his remarks, quoted above, regarding De Cosmos.

[59] Douglas to Martha Douglas, Jan. 30, 1874.

[60] Douglas to Martha Douglas, May 1, 1873.

[61] Douglas to Martha Douglas, March 19, 1874. Douglas also felt a "reluctance to my lamb being committed to the care of wolves".

[62] Douglas to Martha Douglas, May 4, 1874.

[63] Douglas to Martha Douglas, Oct. 2, 1872. On May 5, 1870, Douglas had written to his daughter Jane: "Outdoor work and exercise I get on with very well—it is delightful to plan and direct, to see things growing up, as it were, under your hand."

[64] Douglas to Martha Douglas, Sept. 23, 1873.

[65] In his sermon at Douglas' funeral, Bishop Cridge said that Douglas "highly disapproved of anything that would come between the sinner and the Saviour, or impede liberty of access to the fountain of life". (Colonist, Aug. 15, 1877).

[66] Colonist, August 4, 1877.

[67] Colonist, August 5, 1877.

[68] Colonist, August 5, 1877. A detailed account of the funeral is given in the Colonist for August 8, 1877.

[69] The text of Bishop Cridge's sermon takes up two columns of the Colonist for August 15, 1877.

[70] Colonist, August 4, 1877. It should be noted that this issue of the Colonist contains an account of Douglas' life which is highly inaccurate. It says, for example, that he was born at Demerara of Scottish parents on the 14th of August 1803; that his parents died while he was still young; that he came to the "northwest territory" in 1815 at the age of 12; that while in New Caledonia "he was seized by one of the tribes and held captive for some weeks, eventually escaping and reaching the company's fort after enduring great hardships"; that in 1832 he was placed in charge of Fort Vancouver; that he founded Fort Victoria in 1842; that he succeeded Governor Blanshard in 1852; that during the San Juan crisis of 1859 "the calm judgment and great tact of the Governor were invaluable"; and that the colonies of Vancouver Island and British Columbia were separated in 1865.

[71] Amelia died on January 8, 1890. There are still a few Victorians who remember her, yet when she was born (January 1, 1812) Napoleon had not yet set out for Moscow.

An interesting picture of Lady Douglas in old age may be found in an article "A few items of the west" by Angus McDonald in the *Washington Historical Quarterly* for July 1917: "Lady Douglas still lives in her husband's house, built in the middle of a splendid garden, whose every tree and bush were planted by his care. She often expresses a desire to see the Indian country before she dies . . . she is very fond of bitter root and kamas and of a buffalo tongue when she can have them . . . she is much bored by the compound dishes which the rank and wealth of civilization offer her table every day. She is about 75. Her youngest daughter, a kind girl, Martha, has lately married."

72 James was born June 1, 1851 and died November 7, 1883, aged 32. He was married in 1878 to Mary Rachel Elliott, daughter of A. C. Elliott, premier of B.C. from 1876 to 1878. His widow lived on till 1937. (The last of Douglas' grandchildren, we might note, died in 1966, aged 87. See *Colonist* for November 10, 1966, p. 7).

CHAPTER TWELVE | *Reflections*
and
Conclusions

*History with its flickering lamp stumbles along the trail of the past,
trying to reconstruct its scenes, to revive its echoes, and kindle
with pale gleams the passion of former days. What is the worth of
all this? The only guide to a man is his conscience; the only shield
to his memory is the rectitude and sincerity of his actions. It is
very imprudent to walk through life without this shield, because we
are so often mocked by the failure of our hopes and the unsettling
of our calculations; but with this shield, however the fates may
play, we march always in the ranks of honour.*
WINSTON CHURCHILL
House of Commons
Nov. 12, 1940

WHAT MANNER of man was James Douglas? With this question we
began, and all that followed was intended to suggest an answer. Now it
is time to reduce, if we can, a long narrative to a smaller compass,
wherein its central figure may be seen more clearly. We may begin
by forming some picture of the outward man; then sketch at least the
outlines of his complex character; finally we may try to fix his place in
the history of British Columbia and of Canada.

As to his physical presence, all who knew him agreed it was exceptional. Dr. Helmcken recalled him as

> . . . muscular, broad-shouldered — with powerful legs a little
> bowed—common to strong men; in fact he was a splendid specimen
> of a man.[1]

Admiral Moresby, who in 1852 when a young lieutenant had been stationed at Esquimalt, half a century later also recalled him vividly:

> It was easy to see that here indeed was a man, middle-aged, tall and well-knit, with keen features, alert and kindly. I recognized the type that has broken out of our island home in all centuries to colonise and civilise—the born pioneer.[2]

This impressive physical equipment no doubt did much to bring him from humble beginnings to the forefront of affairs. It must sometimes also have helped to save the day when its outcome hung doubtful in the balance—for example, when he boldly faced down the assembled warriors of the Cowichans and demanded the surrender of the murderer of the Company shepherd Peter Brown.

This aspect of Douglas was remarked by many, though some were to wish it mingled with more geniality. Even John Tod, for example, though he was one of Douglas' oldest friends and associates, found it hard, even after the old Governor had retired into private life, to reach the man behind the mask:

> I had a long chat the other day with our friend Douglas (now Sir James), ever stiff and formal as in times past, qualities which from long habit he could not now lay aside if he would, and probably ought not, if he could.[3]

On another occasion, Tod gave, even if somewhat unwillingly, an even harsher judgment:

> You may probably think me unjustly severe on our old friend, but it is with sorrow I say it, that to all those who have known him for years, he has ever appeared cold, crafty and selfish; and justly merits the reward he now reaps of isolation and desertion of all who have known him from the early times.[4]

Dr. Helmcken confirmed this verdict, declaring that although "there was something grand and majestic about Douglas", he "had a wooden hard face when necessary".[5] There was, in fact, Dr. Helmcken was forced to concede, a certain lack of common humanity in what he termed this "cold brave man"[6] whom it was natural to respect but almost impossible to love:

Mr. Douglas was not humorous—never joked—always staid and decorous and often had some subject to talk about which often he had picked up in a review or newspaper.[7]

Helmcken admitted, however, that Douglas' outward dignity perhaps concealed a warmer interior:

Mr. Douglas was coldly affable, but he improved vastly on acquaintance afterward.[8]

Yet even Dr. Helmcken had to confess that it was difficult to form a close relationship with his "cold and unimpassioned"[9] father-in-law:

He was a very self-contained man—rarely giving his confidence to anyone, and to me, scarcely ever, he considering me to be a "radical"—his abhorrence.[10]

That Douglas should consider his conventional son-in-law a "radical" is a measure of his own ingrained conservatism. The old ways of government were good enough for him, and though he saw that they were yielding irrevocably to the new, he saw no occasion either to rejoice in the fact or to hasten it. One recalls how even the efforts of John Robson and the merchants of New Westminster to secure a more popular form of government in the mainland colony suggested to him—at least at first—"revolution", and certainly he would not have asserted, as did John McLoughlin, that he approved of Papineau.[11]

Douglas was indeed a man of strong prejudices. Although Bishop Cridge at his funeral declared that

If he had occasion to speak of people's faults, it was with gentleness and moderation,[12]

this is not borne out by the record. He did not hesitate, for example, to tell one of his daughters that "it is suspected De Cosmos is betraying the country",[13] and when writing to another daughter to say:

I have no patience either with those who planned or those who are carrying out the new system of government. It makes one savage even to think of the ruin and oppression this measure will lead to. Garrotting is far too good for the stupid Assembly that passed the fatal unconditional union resolutions—this poor colony now lies prostrate and bleeding at every pore.[14]

Not only in politics but also in small matters of dress and behavior, Douglas was a scrupulous adherent of propriety. A typical expression of his outlook is a sentence in a letter to his daughter Martha:

I have given orders for the new croquet lawn, to be executed by Mitchell and Johnson; it will therefore be the correct thing.[15]

In a letter to his London outfitters, we find a similar attitude evinced, though this time a wintry gleam of humor can also, with some effort, be detected:

Let the material and finish be of the very best description and suitable in style to a staid elderly gentleman of three score and five, who is yet, however, very particular about the fit and appearance of his clothes.[16]

One suspects, however, that in these matters Douglas lacked something of the zeal of the true believer, and was merely anxious to make no false steps. He was, one sometimes feels, the courtier of convention; even its lovers hold a higher place in heaven.

There was also perhaps a tendency for his natural dignity to merge into a sense of his own importance. Even when Fort Victoria held only 300 souls, he felt the necessity of being accompanied in public by a uniformed bodyguard. To some, indeed,

. . . his efforts to appear grand, and even august, were ludicrously out of proportion to the insignificant population he governed, numbering less than the inhabitants of many a country town in England. When he spoke to anyone within the precincts of the Government House, his quixotic notions of his office, which he evidently thought splendid, prompted him to make use of the sesquipedalian diction he employed in his despatches . . . His attitude toward the officials serving under his government was austere and distant . . . I have heard magistrates addressed by him in a pompous manner that no English gentleman would assume toward his porter.[17]

The historian Bancroft, who admired many of his qualities, was inclined to agree with this estimate:

Douglas venerated the institutions under which he was born, the conventionalities under which he lived, and thence proceeding, soon learned to venerate himself, which important figure he never for a moment lost sight of.[18]

There is, of course, another, more favorable interpretation of Douglas' austere public manner. He may have felt that as the representative of the world's largest empire, then in the flood tide of its glory, and holding dominion not only "over palm and pine" but also the "lesser breeds without the law", he was the modern successor and counterpart of the consuls and proconsuls of the greatest empire of antiquity, and as such entitled to full public recognition of his status.

Yet, despite his conservatism, when occasion demanded it, he could launch out boldly into waters yet uncharted. Often, especially in the upheaval that followed the great "invasion" of 1858, he devised expedients and deliberately gambled with the fates. Moreover, when his greatest and most cherished project—the Cariboo Road—was at stake, he did not hesitate, though with expressions of the profoundest regret, to evade, as far as possible, the instructions of his superiors. Obedience, he never ceased to inform his subordinates, was among the highest virtues; yet he also knew there was a time when the telescope must be resolutely held to a blind eye.

His courage, certainly, was measureless. He had shown it at Fort St. James; again, when in his Fort Vancouver days he had plunged into an icy stream to rescue a fellow-traveller. Later, at Cowichan in 1853, he had sat calmly amid two hundred armed and angry warriors, the table in front of him holding both presents and his cutlass "the use of either to depend on circumstances".[19]

On a later expedition to the same region in 1856, he personally led his forces in what might well have proved a dangerous venture; yet his only apparent reaction to the perils he passed through was to send to his London outfitters on his return for "a good serviceable sword". He apparently acquired one, we might note, for when a modest riot broke out in Victoria in the turbulent summer of 1858, his "first impulse was to fix on his sword".[20]

He was also highly industrious. One has only to work one's way through the hundreds of large pages that make up his despatches to see this. His capacity for work was no doubt aided by his rugged constitution and moderate personal habits. He himself declared, in a letter written in old age to his daughter Martha (Nov. 4, 1873):

As a rule, alcoholic liquors impair health. I have given up their use entirely, and my health was never better. Tipplers are my aversion.

Dr. Helmcken, his personal physician, confirmed this feature of his father-in-law:

He was a man of temperate, almost abstemious habits—smoked in moderation, but always on the verandah, never in his own house. Early to bed—early to rise—a very indefatigable worker, in fact the great fault he had was attending too much to details, a property probably inherited, arising from his H.B. Co's education.[21]

Douglas himself had evidently formed an estimate as to what qualities had enabled him to rise in the world. Though conceding that "the works of men are moulded by the hands of Providence",[22] he had little doubt that Providence required assistance:

Self-reliance is a lesson that all must learn. Look at the man who is continually waiting to be pushed on by his friends, who is afraid to take a step that is not directed or steadied by another. Few men of that stamp ever make their mark in the world. It is the bold, resolute, strong, self-reliant man, who fights his own way through every obstacle and wins the confidence and respect of his fellows. As with men so it is with nations.[23]

His will was tireless and inflexible. Once he had decided that Vancouver Island and later British Columbia should remain British, he pursued this aim unrestingly until success had crowned his efforts; later, when he resolved that a network of roads must link the interior with the coast so that all the trade of the vast hinterland should be channeled through the mouth of the Fraser, he advanced, despite every obstacle that nature or his superiors could interpose, toward his chosen goal until he reached it.

Nor was he content to direct operations from somewhere safely in the rear. In his younger days, his duties had carried him as far afield as Alaska and California; in 1853 at Cowichan he had boldly advanced into the very jaws of death. Of his later expedition to the same area, he wrote:

> I took the field in person with the expeditionary force, directed all their movements, and adopted every other precaution, dictated by experience, to avert disaster and ensure success . . .
> I may further assure Her Majesty's Government that I was not influenced by the love of military display in assuming the great responsibility involved in directing the Cowegin expedition; but solely by a profound sense of public duty, and by a conviction, founded on experience, that it is only by resorting to prompt and decisive measures of punishment, in all cases of aggression, that life and property can be protected, and the native tribes of this colony kept in a proper state of subordination.[24]

In more peaceful settings, too, wherever the frontier of civilization was being pushed back, there Douglas was to be found in the front line. At Nanaimo, he trod the sunless galleries of the coal mines; in the gold fields, he chatted with the miners. The Cariboo, the Okanagan, the Similkameen: to many British Columbians, even in an age of rapid and convenient transport, these are still only names. Douglas over a century ago had admired their scenery and estimated their resources.

Indeed, though a sturdy Briton (or Scot), he was also in some ways cosmopolitan. Though distrustful of what he fancied were French morals,[25] he spoke French as fluently as any Frenchman, as well as several Indian dialects. He sympathized with the long struggle of the black man for his fair measure of dignity and equality, and gave public support to it by appointing them to be the guardians of the law in the gold rush days in Victoria. For the Indians he had a special regard: his wife had Indian blood, and although he saw the native tribes without blinkers, having no nice scruples about calling them savages, yet he dwelt in their affections and they in his. As Dr. Helmcken recorded,

> " The Indians loved him—looked on him as a father or friend and felt certain of favor and justice at his hands; so much so that his name and character extended from one end of the coast to the other and to the interior likewise.[26] "

Douglas had also an uncommonly wide-ranging mind; his record of his European tour of 1864-65 makes this abundantly clear. Museums, art galleries, musical events, scenery, the history and geography of other lands, various kinds of statistics — all were scrutinized closely and described or recorded in some detail.

Moreover, he was capable of seeing his own era not as the climax of all the ages but as merely an episode in the continuing larger processes of history:

The pioneer is soon overtaken by advancing civilization, the log shanty is replaced by the comfortable farm house, villages spring up, the mud road is drained and gravelled, every settler along the line doing his share, schools are established and in process of time the whistle of the locomotive is heard awakening the echoes of the province.[27]

On occasion, his keen eye was able to penetrate a little way into the mists of time:

The territories of the H.B. Company are now annexed to Canada. This will make a wide opening for the adventurous and discontented, throwing open to them a territory, part of the dominion, which can accommodate millions of people. On this continent, there is an unconquerable inclination to move about. The constant cry is for more room.[28]

Indeed, in a remarkable flash of prescience, he even discerned the identity of the two "super-powers" of the subsequent century:

While our old European centre resembles a volcano, which consumes itself in the centre, I see at the present day only two governments which fulfil well their providential mission. These are the two colossuses which exist—one at the extremity of the new, the other at the extremity of the old world. These two nations of the east and west march without hesitation on the road of improvement, one of them through the will of one man, the other through liberty.[29]

Despite this high estimate of the destiny of their country, he was not unduly enthusiastic about Americans, but his grounds were not likely personal. He recognized the rising republic as the rival of Great Britain for the sovereignty of North America, and having taken his stand in the struggle, he followed out its implications. Yet he recognized the energy and inventiveness of the newcomers to the two colonies he guided, and believed that when they had shed their earlier loyalties they would add a valuable element to these still unshaped societies.

In some respects he was stern; he saw no objections to floggings or executions, provided that on balance society was the gainer. His reasoning, though out of fashion today, at least was based on argument rather than sentimentality:

> In free states the laws must be rigidly enforced. It is by law that liberty is founded. Freedom cannot exist in contempt of the law without degenerating into license, and this last always ends by bringing on convulsions fatal to all free institutions.[30]

Yet despite his belief that the defence of civilization occasionally required harsh measures, he was much enamored of the beauties and intricate workings of nature. During the most hectic period of his career, for example, when beset with countless problems and dangers on all sides, he yet found time to write to an English friend:

> The weather is at present fine, and the opposite hills still retain their hue of green; a single Castle rose, somewhat faded, was picked yesterday, and the humble daisy, heart's ease, and wall-flower, growing exposed in my garden, have not yet entirely lost their bloom. Those few facts will perhaps give a clearer idea of the climate than any description.[31]

Even in old age, some of his earliest experiences of Canadian scenery were still vividly before him:

> I can recall nothing more delightful than our bivouac on a clear moonlight May night, near the Punch Bowls—the highest point of the Jasper Pass. The atmosphere was bright, sharp and bracing, the sun set in gorgeous splendour, bringing out the towering peaks and fantastic pinnacles dressed in purest white into bold relief. Our camp was laid and our fire built on the firm hard snow which was about 20 feet deep. As the daylight faded away, and the shades of night gathered over the Pass, a milder light shot up from behind the nearest peak, with gradually increasing brilliancy, until at last the full orbed moon rose in silent majesty from the mass of mountains, shedding a mild radiance over the whole valley beneath. It was a scene of unrivalled beauty, and tired as we all were at the close of a fatiguing day's march, it was long before we could turn our eyes from this assemblage of glorious objects.[32]

In his relations with those nearest to him, there are signs that the public mask was on occasion laid aside. His wife he treated at all times with the greatest possible respect. In his letters to his children, he was certainly a typical Victorian father, full of weighty moral maxims, but he was also at heart an affectionate parent, according them small kindnesses and solicitous for their welfare. Those who saw him as unyieldingly severe had not been permitted to glimpse this softer side of his nature, as revealed in the privacy of family life.

Even the young of others could call forth at times the gleam of humanity. When two children were born at the Fort on the same day, he had wine served at the mess table, and publicly toasted the new additions to the colony;[33] while in a letter to a friend, he wrote:

> I especially deprecate any undue severity with children. Obedience should proceed more from a sense of duty than from slavish fear which destroys the generous impulses of our nature.[34]

Some faults undoubtedly he had. He was uncommonly anxious to do well financially for himself. He tried for years to secure "back pay" for the period (May 1849 to March 1850) when in his own estimation he had been the first governor of Vancouver Island; he exerted himself to acquire an additional payment for his services as Lieutenant-Governor of the Queen Charlotte Islands, even though this had involved him in no duties. When ordered to sever all ties with the HBC, as the condition of becoming Governor of British Columbia, he strove mightily to retrieve some financial stake in its profits, and the evidence suggests that he evaded the instructions of his superiors to dispose of his holdings in its subsidiary.[35]

Even pettier examples could easily be cited. At a time when he was almost certainly the richest man in British Columbia, he thought it worth while when writing to his London outfitters to ask them to pack his clothes "in as small a compass as possible, as the express company charges by the measurement & not by weight";[36] he also asked that the 5 percent rebate he received for prompt cash payments should be subtracted in advance, as the local authorities charged a 20 percent ad valorem duty; he would thus effect a saving of 1 percent.[37] He seems to have considered the raising of the allowance of his son James, then almost a grown man in a country where there was so much to see and do, to two shillings a week as a great concession, and made it dependent upon the strictest good conduct.[38]

There is, indeed, no reason to dispute the verdict of John Tod, as the two old men approached the end of the trail:

> Notwithstanding his ample means, he is as eager and grasping after money as ever, and, I am told, at times seized with gloomy apprehensions of dying a beggar at last . . .[39]

He was also disinclined to waste sympathy on lost causes. His affection for John McLoughlin, to whom he largely owed his climb up the ladder of success, would seem to have diminished as soon as McLoughlin could be of no further use to him, and he recorded his death in terms which in the circumstances seem callous. Although he had been the faithful servant of the HBC for thirty years, defending its interests tenaciously, once the ties of employment and remuneration were severed, the ties of affection seem also to have snapped.

Yet these shortcomings and others like them were in the long run lost amid his countless virtues. In his own dour way, he was an idealist. From the time when he first was entrusted with a modicum of responsibility, he strove to employ it not merely for the amassing of wealth for himself or his employers, but also for the moral renovation of society, both white and Indian. Slavery, barbarism and ignorance were among the foes he challenged, and wherever he was stationed he used his talents and energies to push back the wavering line that divided them from civilization. In whatever place he stood, it might be said of it,

> Here Nature first begins
> Her farthest verge, and Chaos to retire
> As from her outmost works, a broken foe.[40]

In religious matters, he was not inclined to be venturesome. He seems to have been unaware of the rival claims of science and theology to be the ultimate source of knowledge, a conflict which rumbled and reverberated, at least in educated circles, throughout the nineteenth century. The skeptical attitude of his old associate John Tod toward all formal creeds and other manifestations of religion would have shocked him, had he known of it.[41] Yet when he became convinced that the Anglican church of Victoria was moving steadily in the direction of Roman Catholicism, he did not hesitate, though after much soul-searching, to leave what was sometimes termed the "state church" or "the unofficial established church", even though he knew that it would lead to many an awkward social situation.

Despite his rejection of Roman Catholicism, however, he would hear no slander about it, and was at all times on the best and most respectful terms with its leading representatives in Victoria. When it came to his attention that his daughter Jane, then the wife of A. G. Dallas, chief HBC officer in North America, was suspected of spreading calumnies about the Catholics of the Red River Settlement, he wrote her what can only be described, even though addressed to "my dearest child", as a blistering letter:

> I have lately received a communication from your aunt Soeur Connolly which has excited the most painful emotions in my mind. Her feelings have been deeply wounded and I fear the entire Roman Catholic community of Red River share in those feelings, by calumnies alleged to have originated with you. I can hardly believe it possible that my dear child Jane has been guilty of the cruelty of accusing the truly pious and Christian ladies of the Convent of disgusting crimes of designating their abode as a house of prostitution and even implicating the Venerable Bishop Tache as an accomplice in these revolting practices.
>
> Surely my dear Jane you never gave utterance to such calumnies or so cruelly injured ladies who are so eminently distinguished for benevolence and Christian charity. I hope you do not believe the false and foul tales of Maria Monk which were published some years ago in Canada. No one who knows anything about the Roman Catholic Sisters of Canada could be so unjust to them; and I hope dear Jane that you will always treat and speak of them with the greatest respect.
>
> Someone may possibly have been imposing upon your credulity and filling your mind with those absurd tales, I have heard the same myself, but know them to be as false as their wicked and heartless inventors. If you have injured these good ladies by giving countenance to such fabrications pray make every reparation in your

power—prove that you are above the prejudice of ignorant narrow-minded bigots, and as you value the blessing of God on you and yours, let no false pride restrain you from doing what is honorable and right.

On the other hand if you are unjustly charged with being the author of these absurd tales, let Aunt Connolly know the truth at once that you may be relieved from the odium which never fails to visit the slanderer. I will write to the good sister without delay and say everything in my power to soothe her wounded feelings."[42]

The rarer exaltations of religion, however, were not apparently for him; he treated its representatives with respect—except when he felt they had forfeited it—but saw them as he saw himself: as the servants of the public weal. The inner conflicts between the heights and depths of human nature, the almost unbearable tensions they produce, and to which religion, art and love each struggles to supply an answer: all this (to judge from what we know of him) was a world of experience to which he had no entry, and perhaps would have wished for none. Sufficient unto the day for James Douglas were the many duties thereof.

All this, however,—these lights and shadows—are now no longer with us, but before whatever tribunal there may be beyond the grave. What has he left behind "for us the living"?

Here we can tread more firmly, for his mark is writ large across the great area from the Rockies to the Pacific, which he was the first to govern. In its hour of crisis, when the ship of state was struck by a tidal wave, his was the hand that seized the wheel and steered it safely through many perils into calmer waters. Because of him, the foundations of British government and justice were established, schools and churches erected in the wilderness, an important naval base created. He it was who united the vast areas entrusted to his charge by a network of roads which has since expanded into the highway system of today.[43] Rightly, then, is he called, rightly will he be known to our descendants, as "the father of British Columbia".

One question yet remains: can an even higher claim than this be made for Douglas? Does Canada itself owe him more than is generally recognized?

In the history books, when the era of Confederation is approached, the spotlight is invariably turned on John A. Macdonald and his associates, and remains there until July 1, 1867 sets the seal of success upon their efforts. The Charlottetown Conference of 1864, the negotiations in London, the British North America Act, the celebration of the first Dominion Day: these hold the stage, and their principal participants are given the glory.

Yet is it not time to examine this view of things, this "conventional wisdom", more closely? Macdonald and the other fathers of confederation may indeed have placed the keystone in the arch, but it was an arch whose pillars had first been firmly anchored at the shores of the two great oceans.

What would have been the result, we should ask, if one of these two pillars had been but a crumbled ruin? If in the years before 1867 not the flag of Britain but of the United States had been raised along the whole coast from Alaska to California, could there ever have been a dominion "from sea to sea"?

It is surely obvious that there could not. Moreover, if the vast region between the Rockies and the Pacific had become American, it seems likely that the area between the Rockies and the Great Lakes would soon have gone the same way. The prairies were as yet almost untenanted, and immigration from the south was far easier than from the east, especially as with no British colonies on the Pacific coast, there would have been no Canadian Pacific Railway. It is easy to picture the tide of "manifest destiny" sweeping almost unconsciously across the 49th parallel, and the "struggle for the border" being lost forever, virtually by default of the energy and will to pursue it.[44]

In that case, would Canada exist today? A union of the British colonies in North America might still have come into being, either in 1867 or some other year, but would it long have survived? The triumphant republic, its rulers flushed with their victory in the Civil War, its industrial expansion assured, its ranks being daily swollen by a tidal wave of immigrants, would surround the infant confederation on all sides. It is hard to believe that in such circumstances the Stars and Stripes would not before too long have flown across all of North America from the Rio Grande to the Pole.

Why, then, does it not? Is it not because the two British colonies on the Pacific coast were saved from incorporation into the American Union, were preserved to form part of the western arch of the future Confederation of Canada?

It seems clear that this is the case, and we may thus ask how it was that the present Far West of the Dominion (its population for several years after 1858 overwhelmingly American by origin) is not American today. There can surely be but one answer. It is that in the hour of crisis, when all but the bravest would have abandoned the unequal struggle, one man stood up and was counted. That man was James Douglas.

Almost alone, with the odds seeming hopeless, he bore the heat and burden of the day till others could rally to his side, and because he did so, British Columbia and Canada still exist. Regardless of whether this conclusion is widely held today, it is the one to which all who examine the record without prejudice are destined eventually to come.

Out of the indistinct shadows long ago he came, into the silence of the grave he has long since gone; but while he lived and breathed, and made his force and wisdom a power in local and Imperial policy, he made possible a modern nation. This, then, is the claim to be made for James Douglas, the answer to the question with which this account began: that the Canada of today could not have been formed without him, and that he is thus one, and perhaps the greatest, of the Fathers of Confederation.

NOTES

[1] Helmcken, Reminiscences (unpublished MS in Provincial Archives, Victoria, 1892), II. 84.
[2] Moresby, Two Admirals, London, John Murray, 1909, p. 122.
[3] Tod to Edward Ermatinger, May 20, 1868. Ermatinger Papers, PABC.
[4] Tod to Edward Ermatinger, March 22, 1870. Ermatinger Papers, PABC.
[5] Helmcken, Reminiscences, III. 63.
[6] Loc. cit.
[7] Helmcken, Reminiscences, III. 84.

[8] *Ibid.*, II. 85.

[9] *Ibid.*, II 84.

[10] *Ibid.*, IV 92. It is also apparent from Douglas' letters to his son James that he never established any real rapport with him.

[11] In his private journal written during his trip to Europe in 1864-65, Douglas wrote: "The best form of government if attainable (is) that of a wise and good despotism". (Entry for May 2, 1865).

[12] *Colonist*, August 15, 1877.

[13] Douglas to Martha Douglas, Feb. 10, 1874. De Cosmos was then premier of B.C.

[14] Letter to Mrs. A. G. Dallas, Dec. 20, 1866.

[15] Douglas to Martha Douglas, Dec. 4, 1873.

[16] Douglas to Ollivier and Brown, June 2, 1869.

[17] Matthew Macfie, *Vancouver Island and British Columbia*, London, 1865, pp. 394-5.

[18] Bancroft, *History of British Columbia, 1792-1887*, San Francisco, 1887 p. 302.

[19] Moresby, *Op. Cit.*, p. 126.

[20] Bishop Cridge, writing in the *Colonist* for Dec. 22, 1907.

[21] Helmcken, Reminiscences, IV. 93.

[22] Memorandum of April 22, 1869.

[23] Memorandum of July 22, 1869.

[24] Douglas to Labouchère, Feb. 24, 1857.

[25] Douglas to Martha Douglas, March 19, 1874.

[26] Helmcken, Reminiscences, IV. 93.

[27] Memorandum of July 6, 1869. Sir James Douglas, Correspondence Outward, Miscellaneous Papers.

[28] *Ibid.*

[29] Memorandum of Oct. 4, 1869. Sir James Douglas, Correspondence Outward, Miscellaneous letters.

[30] Memorandum of July 22, 1869.

[31] Douglas to Blackwood, Dec. 27, 1858.

[32] Memorandum of March 19, 1869. (Sir James Douglas, Correspondence Outward, Miscellaneous Letters).

[33] Helmcken, Reminiscences, III. 27.

[34] Letter to H. M. Doughty, April 30, 1862. (Sir James Douglas, Correspondence Outward, Miscellaneous Letters).

[35] See Chapter IX.

[36] Letter to Ollivier and Brown, June 2, 1869. Sir James Douglas, Correspondence Outward, PABC.

[37] Letter to Ollivier and Brown, Sept. 17, 1869.

[38] Douglas to James Douglas, April 8, 1868.

[39] Tod to Edward Ermatinger, March 22, 1870. Ermatinger Papers, PABC.

[40] Milton, *Paradise Lost*, II. 1037-1039.

[41] For example, on May 20, 1868, Tod wrote to his friend Edward Ermatinger: "My Lord Bishop Hills, I trust, will soon find that his food for babes is no longer palatable to any intelligent community in this 19th

century". (Ermatinger Papers, PABC. Numerous other examples of Tod's views are to be found in these letters; See, for example, his letter of March 15, 1869).

42 Sir James Douglas, Correspondence Outward, Miscellaneous Letters, March 2, 1863.

43 Dr. Helmcken in his "Reminiscences" (IV. 92-93) declared: "The waggon road to Cariboo was the greatest of his works—a wonder at the time—as well in projection as the determination to carry it out to its completion". The *Colonist* of August 4, 1877 had earlier given the same verdict: "This magnificent road will remain for ages a monument to the genius of the great mind that conceived and executed it, as the Roman roads are to this day a monument to the genius of the greatest of the Roman rulers."

44 Bruce Hutchison's admirable *The Struggle for the Border* (Toronto, Longmans Green, 1955) gives numerous illustrations of this recurrent theme in Canadian history.

Bibliography

A very full collection of Douglas' public correspondence and his private letters and diaries is to be found in the Provincial Archives, Victoria. Unfortunately it is scattered throughout a large number of items, some printed, some in typewritten transcript and some in his own handwriting or that of his secretaries. It is to be hoped that eventually the Government of British Columbia will see its way to producing a properly organized printed collection of all this material, so essential to the full understanding of the formative years of our province. Until this is done, there is, I feel, little to be gained by giving a list of formal catalogue titles here.

Newspapers:

> Gazette
> Colonist
> British Columbian

Periodicals:

> American Historical Review
> Beaver
> British Columbia Historical Quarterly
> Oregon Historical Society Quarterly
> Washington Historical Quarterly

Unpublished manuscripts in Provincial Archives, Victoria:

ANDERSON, A. C., History of the North West Coast, Victoria, 1878.

ANDERSON, J. R., Notes and comments on early days and events in British Columbia, Washington and Oregon, 1925.

DICKINSON, Susan, Edward Cridge and George Hills; doctrinal conflict 1872-1874 and the founding of Church of our Lord in Victoria, British Columbia, 1875. M. A. Thesis, U. of Victoria.

ERMATINGER Papers.

HELMCKEN, J. S., Reminiscences, Victoria, 1892.

MACLAURIN, D., The history of education in the crown colonies of Vancouver Island and British Columbia and in the province of British Columbia, PhD thesis, U. of Washington, 1936.

PALMER, P., A fiscal history of British Columbia in the colonial period, PhD thesis, Stanford, 1932.

PILTON, J. W., Negro settlement in British Columbia 1858-1871, M.A. Thesis, U.B.C., 1951.

REID, J. H., The Road to Cariboo, M.A. Thesis, U.B.C., April 1942.

ROSS, Margaret, Amor de Cosmos: a British Columbia reformer, M.A. Thesis, U.B.C., April 1931.

TOD, John, History of New Caledonia and the North West Coast, 1878.

WILSON, C. W., Journal of Service, 1858-1862.

Official Publications:
B.C. Archives Reports for 1913 and 1914.
Minutes of the House of Assembly of Vancouver Island, King's Printer, Victoria, 1918.
Miscellaneous papers relating to Vancouver Island, 1848-1863, Great Britain, Colonial Office.
Papers relative to the affairs of British Columbia, 4 parts, 1859-1862, Great Britain, Queen's Printer.
Transactions of the Royal Society of Canada.
Vancouver Island Miscellaneous Letter-book No. 2.

Books:
BANCROFT, H. H., *History of British Columbia*, San Francisco, 1890.
BANCROFT, H. H., *History of Oregon*, San Francisco, 1890.
BARKER, B. B., (ed.), *Letters of Dr. John McLoughlin, 1829-1832*, Bintfords and Mort, Portland, Oregon, 1948.
CORNWALLIS, K., *The New El Dorado*, London, 1858.
DOWN, Mary Margaret, *A Century of Service 1858-1958*, Morriss Printers, Victoria, 1966.
FINLAYSON, R., *Biography*, Victoria, 1891.
GALBRAITH, J. S., *The Hudson's Bay Company as an Imperial Factor 1821-1869*, U. of Toronto Press, 1957.
HAIG-BROWN, R., *Fur and Gold*, Longmans, Toronto, 1962.
HOLMAN, F. V., *Dr. John McLoughlin, the Father of Oregon*, A. H. Clark Co., Cleveland, Ohio, 1907.
HOWAY AND SCHOLEFIELD, *British Columbia from the earliest times to the present*, 4 vols., Vancouver, 1914.
HOWAY, F. W., *The early history of the Fraser River Mines*, B.C. Archives Memoir No. 6, King's Printer, Victoria, 1926.
HUTCHISON, B., *The Fraser*, Clarke Irwin, Toronto, 1950.
JOHNSON, R. B., *Very Far West Indeed*, London, 1872.
JOHNSON, R. C., *John Mcloughlin: Father of Oregon*, Metropolitan Press, Portland, Oregon, 1935.
KANE, Paul, *Wanderings of an Artist among the Indians of North America*, The Radisson Society, Toronto, 1925.
LAMB, W. K. (ed.), *The letters and journals of Simon Fraser 1806-1808*, Macmillan, Toronto, 1960.
LONGSTAFF, F. V., *Esquimalt Naval Base*, Clarke and Stuart, Vancouver, 1942.
MACDONALD, D. G., *British Columbia and Vancouver's Island*, Longmans Green, London, 1862.
MACFIE, Matthew, *Vancouver Island and British Columbia*, London, 1865.
MACKAY, Douglas, *The Honourable Company*, McClelland and Stewart, Toronto, 1937.

McLEAN, John, *Notes of a twenty-five years' service in the Hudson's Bay Territory*, London, 1849. Reprinted by the Champlain Society, Toronto, 1932.

MACLEOD, M. A. (ed.), *The letters of Letitia Hargrave*, The Champlain Society, Toronto, 1947.

MAYNE, R. C., *Four Years in British Columbia and Vancouver Island*, London, 1862.

MONTGOMERY, R. G., *The White-headed Eagle*, Macmillan, New York, 1934.

MORESBY, John, *Two Admirals*, John Murray, London, 1909.

MORICE, A. G., *History of the northern interior of British Columbia, formerly New Caledonia, 1660-1880*, William Briggs, Toronto, 1904.

ORMSBY, M., *British Columbia: A History*, Macmillan, 1958.

PEMBERTON, J. D., *Facts and figures relating to Vancouver Island and British Columbia*, London, 1860.

PETHICK, D., *Victoria: The Fort*, Mitchell Press, Vancouver, 1968.

RICH, E. E. (ed.), *The letters of John McLoughlin, First series, 1825-1838*, The Champlain Society, Toronto, 1941.

ROBINSON, L. B., *Esquimalt: place of shoaling waters*, Quality Press, Victoria, 1947.

SAGE, W., *Sir James Douglas and British Columbia*, U. of Toronto Press, 1930.

SHELTON, W. G. (ed.), *British Columbia and Confederation*, Morriss Printers, Victoria, 1967.

SMITH, D. B., *James Douglas in California 1841*, The Library's Press, Vancouver, 1965.

TOLMIE, W. F., *William Fraser Tolmie, Physician and Fur Trader*, Mitchell Press, Vancouver, 1963.

WALBRAN, J. T., *British Columbia Coast Names*, Ottawa, 1909.

WALKEM, W. W., *Stories of early British Columbia*, Vancouver, 1914.

WILD, Roland, *Amor De Cosmos*, Ryerson Press, 1958.

Index

Moody, Col. Richard, 160, 166, 174·178, 222, 235, 242
Moresby, Admiral (father), 101
Moresby, Lt. (son), 17, 284
Mormons, 69, 144
Muir family, 84, 99, 128

Nanaimo, 106·108, 120, 123, 127, 133
Needham, Judge Joseph, 135
Negroes, 158, 289
New Westminster, 175, 178, 199, 200
Nisqually, 55, 120
Nootka Sound, 4
North West Company, 6, 14

Ogden, Peter Skene, 26, 61, 103
Okanagan, 16, 60, 139
Oregon Territory, 6, 51, 59, 61, 153
Oregon Treaty of 1846, 61, 111
O'Reilly, Peter, 185, 211, 238
Otter, (ship), 107, 117, 149
Overlanders, 204, 214

Parliamentary Inquiry of 1857, 92
Pearse, B. W., 133
Pelly, Sir John, 46, 50, 67, 77
Pemberton, J. D., 103, 201, 224, 234
Perrier, George, 150
Plumper, H.M.S., 171, 209
Princess Royal (ship), 122
Puget Sound Agricultural Company, 119, 162, 210

Quadra, Captain, 4
Quah, Chief, 17, 19
Queen Charlotte Islands, 98, 125, 183
Quesnel, 197, 199, 213

Racoon, H.M.S., 6
Recovery (ship), 99, 105, 107
Roads:
On Vancouver Island, 94, 104, 121
Harrison-Lillooet, 153·155, 167, 196
Bute Inlet, 155
Cariboo, 155, 207, 215·241

To eastern Canada, 198, 222, 279
Robson, John, 216, 225·227, 245
Ross, Charles, 49, 57
Royal Engineers, 159, 164, 174, 178, 199, 220, 225, 235, 237
Royal Grant of 1849, 66, 114
Rupert (Fort), 77, 96
Russian American Fur Company, 5, 37, 38, 118

Salt Spring Island, 202, 214
San Juan Islands, 7, 112, 125, 186· 195, 271
Santiago (ship), 4
Satellite (ship), 142, 148, 149
Schools, 32, 81, 95, 101, 107·109, 115, 122, 127
Simpson, Sir George, 18, 27, 45, 46, 59, 61
Sitka, 35, 37
Skinner, Thomas, 108
Sonora (ship), 4
Sooke, 52, 94, 103, 121
Spence, Thomas, 222
Spuzzum, 63, 223, 233
Staines, Rev. R. J., 73, 114, 115, 122, 183

Thetis, H.M.S., 105
Thompson, David, 6
Tod, John, 15, 18, 47, 87, 263, 284, 298
Tolmie, Dr. W. F., 32, 48, 136, 275
Tory (ship), 84, 85
Travaillot, O. J., 152
Tribune, H.M.S., 188
Trimble, Dr., 237
Trutch, Joseph, 222, 233, 241

Vancouver, Captain George, 5
Victoria (Fort):
Founding of, 55·58
Effect of gold rush on, 145, 158, 163, 181, 203
Becomes a city, 1862, 232
Victoria Voltigeurs, 124, 126, 130

Waddington, Alfred, 155
Warre, Lt., 71

Bibliothèques Université d'Ottawa Echéance	Libraries University of Ottawa Date Due

APR 03 1991

23 FEV. 1998

MAR 24 1998

25 MARS 1991

01 DEC. 1993

17 MARS 1998

26 NOV. 1993

NOV 1 4 2004

01 OCT. 1994

19 SEP. 1994

UO NOV 05 2004

MAR 13 1996

UO29 OCT 2005

NOV 1 4 2005

27 MARS 1996

UO05 NOV 2005

FEV 13 2006

APR 10 1996

10 AVR. 1996

UO19 MAR 2006